全国电子信息类优秀教材

高等院校电子信息类专业"互联网+"创新规划教材

信息与通信工程专业英语

（第3版）

主　编　韩定定　包依红　李明明

参　编　赵菊敏　胡亚琴　史健婷

　　　　董自健　王　锦　陈　趣

内 容 简 介

本书旨在进一步提高读者英语阅读及翻译的水平，锻炼科技论文写作能力。本书所选的资料大多从国外书刊和科学文献中精选而来，在选材上注重科学性、知识性、趣味性和文体语言的规范化及时间性，并配套二维码数字资源，以顺应"互联网+"创新规划教材的特征。本书不仅从理论上概述了英语翻译的主要技巧和写作的基本技巧，而且辅以大量的例句及实践性练习，通过不断训练，培养学生对这类技巧和方法灵活运用的能力。

全书共分为3章：第1章介绍翻译理论与方法，包括科技专业词汇的翻译方法和疑难句子、科技文体的翻译技巧及翻译要求；第2章介绍科技英语文献的阅读及翻译，所选文章的编排和选材根据电路与系统、信息处理技术、人工智能、现代通信技术及网络应用等分成相应的10个部分，并配套疑难句和专业词汇的注释，课后练习用以巩固相关知识点，课文中的二维码数字资源科普解释相关学科内容；第3章介绍科技论文写作的基础知识。

本书可作为本科电子信息工程专业和通信工程专业三、四年级的专业英语教材，也可供研究生及广大工程技术人员使用。

图书在版编目（CIP）数据

信息与通信工程专业英语/韩定定，包依红，李明明主编. —3版. —北京：北京大学出版社，2022.3

ISBN 978-7-301-32868-2

Ⅰ.①信… Ⅱ.①韩…②包…③李… Ⅲ.①信息技术—英语—高等学校—教材②通信工程—英语—高等学校—教材 Ⅳ.①G202②TN91

中国版本图书馆 CIP 数据核字（2022）第 029467 号

书　　　名	信息与通信工程专业英语（第3版） XINXI YU TONGXIN GONGCHENG ZHUANYE YINGYU (DI-SAN BAN)
著作责任者	韩定定　包依红　李明明　主编
策划编辑	郑　双
责任编辑	郑　双
数字编辑	蒙俞材
标准书号	ISBN 978-7-301-32868-2
出版发行	北京大学出版社
地　　　址	北京市海淀区成府路 205 号　100871
网　　　址	http://www.pup.cn　新浪微博：@北京大学出版社
电子邮箱	编辑部 pup6@pup.cn　总编室 zpup@pup.cn
电　　　话	邮购部 010-62752015　发行部 010-62750672　编辑部 010-62750667
印　刷　者	河北文福旺印刷有限公司
经　销　者	新华书店
	787 毫米×1092 毫米　16 开本　15.5 印张　458 千字 2006 年 8 月第 1 版　2012 年 8 月第 2 版 2022 年 3 月第 3 版　2023 年 10 月第 2 次印刷
定　　　价	45.00 元

未经许可，不得以任何方式复制或抄袭本书之部分或全部内容。
版权所有，侵权必究
举报电话：010-62752024　电子信箱：fd@pup.cn
图书如有印装质量问题，请与出版部联系，电话：010-62756370

第 3 版前言

本书第 1 版自 2006 年出版以来,在各兄弟院校师生和广大读者的关注下,至今已成为信息与通信领域中深受喜爱的教材和参考资料。同时,第 2 版的修订出版也在 2012 年完成。

随着通信与信息技术的飞速发展,大量优秀的科技成果喷涌而出,结合党的二十大报告中提到的"教育强国""科技强国",本次修订的第 3 版重点结合了当代信息领域发展的最新成果,补充了新的应用型科技文章,涉及射频及无线电路系统、网络信息安全、人工智能、现代通信技术及标准、光电技术等多个创新型研究方向,既涵盖了信息与通信工程领域的基础理论,又反映了近年来该领域出现的热点与新技术的进展。一方面,为了激发学生的学习兴趣,教材融入科技新元素,增设视频资源的二维码,进行文章内容的实景展现,以便学生沉浸式地理解专业文献的科普内容。另一方面,语言学的发展也直接影响了构词法及科技文体的变革,为此,教材对最新的科技术语翻译方法、处理词汇现象的技巧、科技文体翻译方法等进行修订,旨在为广大师生提供更好的学习资源。

本次教材的修订融入了课程思政元素,以立德树人为根本,实现专业知识与思政内容的有机融合,将德育渗透、贯穿课堂教学的全过程,助力学生全面发展。

复旦大学韩定定和西安科技大学李明明完成修订和整理本书第 3 版中的 1.3 节、1.4 节、1.6 节;复旦大学韩定定完成第 2 章中第 2 课、第 3 课、第 5 课~第 8 课的修订,课文二维码资源的补充,课程思政方案的设计,参考文献、参考译文和习题答案的修订补充,附录 A 和附录 B 的修订。包依红和胡亚琴等人参与编写和讨论。韩定定负责教材修订的校对和审核,并作为第一主编,负责组织各章节的内容及定稿。

本书第 2 版于 2012 年被中国电子教育学会评选为"全国电子信息类优秀教材"。

信息与通信技术不断地发展,专业英语教学改革任重道远,编者的能力与这两方面的发展所提出的要求相比还存在很大差距,因此恳请读者一如既往地对书中的不足之处多加指正,以使编者不断改进。

编　者

资源索引

目　　录

第 1 章　翻译理论与方法 1

1.1　翻译的概念 1
1.2　中西方文化、思维差异与英汉语对比 2
1.3　科技术语的主要翻译方法 7
1.3.1　概述 7
1.3.2　科技英语的翻译 8
1.3.3　合成科技术语的语义分析 9
1.3.4　科技术语构词中的前缀和后缀 10
1.3.5　类比构词及其翻译 13
1.3.6　音译及形译 15
1.4　处理词汇现象的技巧 16
1.4.1　选择和确定词义 16
1.4.2　词量的改变：增词和减词 18
1.4.3　词义的引申 20
1.4.4　词类的转换 21
1.4.5　词汇的重复 21
1.4.6　动词时态的翻译 22
1.4.7　名词化结构的翻译 23
1.5　句子的主要翻译方法 25
1.5.1　英汉句式比较及常见的翻译方法 25
1.5.2　一些英语特别句式的翻译 28
1.6　科技文体的翻译 34
1.6.1　文体浅说 34
1.6.2　科技文体的特点及翻译要求 35

第 2 章　Application and Appreciation 39

Lesson One　Digital Signal Processing & Modern Digital Design 39
　　Text A　Introduction to Digital Signal Processing 39
　　Text B　Modern Digital Design 46
Lesson Two　AI and Its Applications 54
　　Text A　What Is Artificial Intelligence? 54
　　Text B　Smart City Artificial Intelligence Applications and Trends 59
Lesson Three　Optoelectronic Technology and Its Circuit 66
　　Text A　Introduction to Optoelectronics 66
　　Text B　Optoelectronic Devices &Their Applications 71
Lesson Four　Design Patterns 80

  Text A Intro to Design Patterns（Ⅰ）..80
  Text B Intro to Design Patterns（Ⅱ）...88
 Lesson Five RF Technology and Its Circuits 97
  Text A What Is RF? 97
  Text B Active Components in RF Circuits 102
 Lesson Six 5G Communication and Standards 107
  Text A 5G Wireless Communication Systems 107
  Text B 5G Key Technologies: Identifying Innovation Opportunity 111
 Lesson Seven Industrial Internet 120
  Text A Introduction to Industrial Internet 120
  Text B Industrial Internet of Things 123
 Lesson Eight Intelligent Transportation Systems 127
  Text A Introduction to Intelligent Transportation Systems 127
  Text B Applications of Intelligent Transportation Systems 130
 Lesson Nine Complex Networks and Its Applications 135
  Text A Exploring Complex Networks（Ⅰ）..135
  Text B Exploring Complex Networks（Ⅱ）...139
 Lesson Ten Cloud Computing 145
  Text A An Introduction to Cloud Computing（Ⅰ）..................................145
  Text B An Introduction to Cloud Computing（Ⅱ）.................................150

第 3 章 科技论文写作的基础知识 156
 3.1 概述 156
  3.1.1 科技论文的定义及分类 156
  3.1.2 科技论文的突出特点 158
  3.1.3 科技论文的结构及编写格式 160
 3.2 科技论文写作 161
  3.2.1 科技论文写作步骤 161
  3.2.2 风格 168
  3.2.3 几个问题 169
  3.2.4 学位论文 178
  3.2.5 科技期刊文章 184
 3.3 科技写作实例 189
  3.3.1 摘要 189
  3.3.2 实验报告 192
  3.3.3 技术指南 194
  3.3.4 科技广告 203

附录 A 常用通信与电子信息词汇及注解 205

附录 B 科技论文写作常用句型 227

参考文献 237

第1章 翻译理论与方法

1.1 翻译的概念

人类社会的发展和进步是从古至今不同文化的民族之间沟通和交流的结果，而不同文化之间的交流离不开翻译。翻译是人类社会发展和进步的需要，正如张培基曾说："翻译是沟通各族人民的思想，促进政治、经济、文化、科学、技术交流的重要手段，也是进行国际斗争的必要武器。翻译是学习好外语的重要手段之一，也是探讨两种语言对应关系的一门学科。"

"翻译是一项对语言进行操作的工作，即用一种语言文本来替代另一种语言文本的过程。"(J.C.卡特福德，1991)；"翻译是把一种语言的言语产物在保持内容方面，也就是意义不变的情况下，改变为另一种语言的言语产物的过程。"(巴尔胡达罗夫，1985)；"翻译乃是与语言行为抉择密切相关的一种语际信息传递的特殊方式。"(沃尔弗拉姆·威尔斯，1989)；"翻译是一种跨文化的信息交流与交换的活动，其本质是传播。" (吕俊，1997)；Translating consists in reproducing in the receptor language the closest natural equivalent of the source language message, first in terms of meaning and secondly in terms of style. (Nida，2004)；"翻译是一种创造性的工作，好的翻译等于创作，甚至还可能超过创作。" (郭沫若，1959)；"…translation is first a science, which entails the knowledge and verification of the facts and the language that describes them here, what is wrong, mistakes of truth, can be identified; secondly, it is a skill, which calls for appropriate language and acceptable usage; thirdly, an art, which distinguishes good from undistinguished writing and is the creative, the intuitive, sometimes the inspired, level of the translation; lastly, a matter of taste, where argument ceases, preferences are expressed, and the variety of meritorious translation is the reflection of individual differences."(彼得·纽马克，2001)

翻译是一门综合性的学科，因为它集语言学、文学、社会学、教育学、心理学、人类学、信息理论等学科之特点于一身，在长期的社会实践中已经拥有了它自己的一套抽象的理论、原则和具体方法，形成了它自己独立的体系，而且在相当一部分的语言材料中这些方法正在逐渐模式化。由此可见，视角的不同可以导致对翻译性质认识的差异。

在以上众多定义中，哪种更准确、更贴切？要回答这个问题，先来看看翻译活动本身。

翻译的具体形式很多，有口译、笔译、机器翻译等，从翻译的物质形态来说，它表现为各类符号系统的选择和组合，具体可分为4类。

(1) 有声语言符号，即自然语言的口头语言，其表现形式为电话通信、内外谈判和接待外宾等。

(2) 无声语言符号，包括了文字符号和图像符号，其表现形式为谈判决议、社交书信、电文、通信及各种文学作品等印刷品。

(3) 有声非语言符号，即传播过程中所谓的有声而不分音节的"类语言"符号，其常见方式为：说话时的特殊重读、语调变化、笑声和掌声，这类符号无具体的音节可分，语义也不是固定不变的，其信息是在一定的语言环境中得以传播的。例如，笑声可能是负载着正信息，也可能负载着负信息，又如掌声可以传播欢迎、赞成、高兴等信息，也可以是传递一种礼貌的否定等。

(4) 无声非语言符号，即各种人体语言符号，表现为人的动作、表情和服饰等无声伴随语言符号，这类符号具有鲜明的民族文化性，例如，人的有些动作，在不同的民族文化中所表示的语义信息完全不同，不仅如此，它还能强化有声语言的传播效果。例如，在交谈时，如果伴有适当的人体语言，会明显增强口头语言的表达效果。

这四大类符号既可以表达翻译的原码，也可以表达翻译出的译码，它们既可以单独作为原码或译码的物质载体，也可以由两种、三种、四种共同组成译码或原码的载体。

从翻译的运作程序上看，实际包括了理解、转换、表达3个环节。理解是分析原码，准确地掌握原码所表达的信息；转换是运用多种方法，如口译或笔译的形式，各类符号系统的选择、组合、引申、浓缩等翻译技巧的运用等，将原码所表达的信息转换成译码中的等值信息；表达是用一种新的语言系统进行准确的表达。

翻译的形式和内容如此纷繁复杂，从中抽象出一个具有哲学高度的翻译的定义也是一项非常艰难的重任，国内外的众多学者对此做出了许多努力，仁者见仁，智者见智，从不同的角度对翻译活动做出了概括和总结。

在众多的定义中，有些学者将翻译纳入传播学的研究范围，将翻译学视为传播学的一个分支，这给人们以有益的启迪：它更明确了翻译学是一个开放的动态系统，它充分注意了在信息传递过程中有影响作用的其他诸多因素，如传播方式、传播渠道、传播目的、传播的不同对象等，它可以更广泛地借鉴其他学科的研究成果或对其他学科的研究起到影响和指导的作用。

在上文的诸多翻译形式中可以归纳为一点，翻译实际上是一种特殊形式的信息传播。整个翻译活动实际上表现为一种社会信息的传递，表现为传播者、传播渠道、受者之间的一系列互动关系。与普通传播过程不同的是，翻译是在两种文化之间进行的，操纵者所选择的符号不再是原来的符号系统，而是产生了文化换码，但其原理却是与普通传播相同的。

要做好翻译工作，一是要具备良好的政治素质，二是要具备良好的业务素质。政治素质包括译者对党和国家方针政策（如党的二十大报告）的正确了解和贯彻执行、严肃认真的工作态度以及一丝不苟的工作作风；良好的业务素质指的是扎实的语言功底、出色的写作技能、丰富的文化知识以及过硬的翻译理论知识和熟练应用翻译技巧的能力。

1.2　中西方文化、思维差异与英汉语对比

既然翻译涉及两种语言的相互转换，而语言是与文化和民族思维息息相关的，所以，要掌握有效的翻译方法，必须先了解语言之间的差异，了解引起语言差异的中西方在文化、思维等方面的差异。本节通过对比词汇在中、英两种语言文化背景下，反映在含义、日常

生活、称呼、社交礼节、性别、感情色彩等方面的差异来探讨在英语翻译中如何融文化知识于语言中，以导入文化的适度性。

词是语句的基本单位，通常所说的话都是由一个个词构成的。如果只是把单词按字面意义串起来，而丝毫不懂有关文化背景知识，在实际运用中是行不通的。例如下述两句。

(1) 英语 green with envy 是什么意思？人们忌妒或羡慕时脸色真的变绿或发青吗？

(2) 英语 Paul was in blue mood 中 Paul(保罗)是什么情绪？高兴、激动、悲哀，还是什么？

在上述两句中，green(绿)和 blue(蓝)都不是指颜色，两个词都有其他意思——某种文化方面的联想，从字面上看这种意思不明显。在词典中，green 这个词有"(脸色)变绿"的意思，但 green with envy 是个固定词组，不过表示"十分妒忌"而已。blue 这个词与 mood 之类的词连用表现某种情绪时，表示"沮丧的""忧郁的"，例(2)之意为"保罗情绪低落"。以上两个例子都涉及词的字面意义和联想内涵意义，这就是语言文化差异问题，在翻译过程中许多在理解目的语(target language)时，遇到的障碍并非语言知识造成的，而是由文化差异导致的。由此可见，加强语言文化因素的对比显得尤为重要。

1. 语言与文化

学语言的目的是交流。人类的交际不单是一种语言现象，也是一种跨文化现象。要对两种交际文化进行对比，首先要从文化谈起。

文化(culture)一词是一个含义极其广泛的词语。它狭义上是指文学、音乐、美术等，而广义上讲是一个社会学术语。按照社会学家和人类学家对"文化"所下的定义，人们所说的"文化"是指一个社会所具有的独特的信仰、习惯、制度、目标和技术的总模式。语言是文化的一部分，又是文化的载体和折射镜。通过一个民族的语言，可以窥见该民族绚丽多姿的文化形态。英语词汇作为英语中最活跃、最具生命力的组成部分，最能反映英美文化独特的魅力和内涵。学习英语，实际上也是学习西方文化。一方面，对于在母语环境下学英语的中国人来说，应该了解在中西方不同文化背景影响下，英汉词语之间所存在的差异；从另一方面来看，语言又受文化的影响，反映文化。可以说语言反映一个民族的特征，它不仅包含着该民族的历史和文化背景，而且蕴藏着该民族对人生的看法、生活方式和思维方式。

汉语的文化氛围中，"东风"即"春天的风"；夏天常与酷暑炎热联系在一起，"赤日炎炎似火烧""骄阳似火"是常被用来描述夏天的词语。而英国地处西半球，北温带、海洋性气候，报告春天消息的却是西风，英国著名诗人雪莱的《西风颂》正是对春的讴歌。英国的夏季正是温馨宜人的季节，常与"可爱""温和""美好"相连。莎士比亚在他的一首十四行诗中把爱人比作夏天，Shall I compare thee to a summer's day?/Thou art more lovely and more temperate，能体会到莎翁的"爱"吗？

关于英汉习俗差异，最典型的莫过于在对狗这种动物的态度上。狗在汉语中通常是一种卑微的动物。汉语中与狗有关的习语大多含有贬义："狐朋狗党""狗急跳墙""狼心狗肺""狗腿子"等，尽管近些年来养宠物狗的人数大大增加，狗的"地位"似乎有所改变，但狗的贬义形象却深深地留在了汉语言文化中。而在西方英语国家，狗被认为是人类最忠诚的朋友。英语中有关狗的习语除了一部分因受其他语言的影响而含有贬义，大部分都没有贬义。例如，You are a lucky dog(你是一个幸运儿)；Every dog has his day(凡人皆有得意日)；

You can't teach an old dog new tricks(你不能使守旧的人接受新事物)等。又如，形容人"病得厉害"用 as sick as a dog；"累极了"是 dog-tired。与此相反，中国人十分喜爱猫，用"馋猫"比喻人贪嘴，常有亲昵的成分，而在西方文化中，"猫"被用来比喻"包藏祸心的女人"。

与宗教信仰有关的习语也大量出现在英汉语言中。佛教传入中国已有近两千年的历史，与此有关的习语很多，如"借花献佛""闲时不烧香，临时抱佛脚"等。在许多西方国家，特别是在英美，人们信奉基督教，相关的习语如 God helps those who help themselves (上帝帮助自助的人)，也有 Go to hell(下地狱去)这样的诅咒。

英语属于印欧语系(Indo-European Languages)，包含印度、西亚和欧洲的语言。目前使用的英语单词中，有不少是从非印欧语系"拿来"的，这在狭义上，就是英语中的外来语。这些白皮黄心的"鸡蛋词"，无须向"英语世界"做额外解释，就能被顺利地理解、沟通。脱胎于汉语的"鸡蛋词"，早就默默地影响全世界了。除了"孔夫子(Confucius)""中国功夫(kungfu)""麻将(mahjong)""豆腐(tofu)"之类绝无仅有的称谓，"silk"的发音，显然是汉语"丝绸"的音译，茶——tea 是英国人从拗口的闽南话里拿走的，世外桃源——Shangrila 出自西藏的传说之地——香格里拉，点心——dim sum，一听发音就知道，这个略带小资情调的词来自闽粤，走狗——running dogs，纸老虎——paper tiger，大款、巨亨——tycoon 这种称呼是近些年才流行街巷的，指有钱有势的商人或者企业家，中国传统的叫法是"大掌柜"，也是闽粤之地的音译，被英语拿走。

2. 字面意义和含义

字面意义就是基本的或明显的意义。词的含义是词的隐含或附加意义。如 peasant 一词，是"农民"之义，但英语中的 peasant 与汉语中的"农民"所体现的意义并不完全相同，可能有不同的含义，英语中的 peasant 是贬义。《美国传统词典》给 peasant 下定义：乡下人、庄稼人、乡巴佬，教养不好的人、粗鲁的人。《韦氏新大学词典》：一般指未受过教育的、社会地位低下的人。在汉语中，"农民"指直接从事农业生产劳动的人，无论在革命斗争中或是在社会主义建设中都是一支重要的力量，丝毫无贬义，所以一般应把"农民"译成 farmer。再如，politician 和 statesman 这两个英语词。politician 是"政治家"吗？反过来说，汉语中的"政治家"这个词应该怎样译成英语呢？有些略懂英语的学生译作 politician，这是不合适的。politician 这个词在美国英语中，往往有很强烈的贬义色彩，会引起别人的蔑视。它指为谋取个人私利而搞政治、耍手腕的人。这个词还有"精明圆滑的人"(smooth-operator)之义，指一个人做事和说话时，信心十足，非常老练。汉语"政治家"这个词应译为 statesman，在英国英语和美国英语中都很贴切，statesman 主要表示善于管理国家的明智之士，人们通常把有威望的高级政府官员称为 statesman。

事实上，汉英两种语言在字面意义和含义上有以下关系。

1) 字面意义与含义相同或相似

(1) Look before you leap. 三思而后行。

(2) Burn one's boat. 破釜沉舟。

(3) Strike while the iron is hot. 趁热打铁。

(4) An eye for an eye, a tooth for a tooth. 以眼还眼，以牙还牙。

(5) To lose one's face, to save one's face. 丢面子，保面子。

2) 含义相似，字面意义不同

(1) The grass is always greener on the other side of the fence. 这山望着那山高。

(2) Nothing ventured, nothing gained. 不入虎穴，焉得虎子。

(3) That's a piece of cake. 那是小菜一碟。

(4) As poor as a church mouse. 一贫如洗。

(5) Let sleeping dogs lie. 切勿打草惊蛇。

3) 含义不同，字面意义相似

(1) To fish in muddy water. (英语：形容多管闲事，自讨没趣)浑水摸鱼。

(2) To make one's hair stand on end. (英语：令人毛骨悚然)令人发指。

(3) To blow one's own horn. (英语：自我炫耀，自吹自擂)各吹各的号。

(4) To lock the stable gate after the horse has bolted. (英语：太迟了)亡羊补牢。

4) 含义与字面意义都不同

(1) Modest dogs miss much meat. (英语：谦虚的狗没肉吃)满招损，谦受益。

(2) Where there is fear there is modesty. (原为拉丁语格言：谦虚源于胆怯)老王卖瓜，自卖自夸(反讽)。

(3) An excess of modesty obstructs the tongue. (英语：谦虚过分束缚舌头)自知之明(赞誉)。

3. 日常谈话中的文化区别

中国人在吃饭前后打招呼时常用："吃(饭)了吗？"而美国人则用"Hello"或"Hi"等。如果不理解其含义，美国人会认为这种打招呼是说："没有吃的话，我正要请你到我家去呢。"总之，这样打招呼在西方有时意味着邀请对方去吃饭。

再如，汉语中的"上哪儿去啊？"以及"到哪儿去啊？"这样打招呼的话直译成英语就是 Where are you going? 和 Where have you been? 而大部分讲英语的人听了会不高兴，他们对此的反应很可能是：It's none of your business！(你管得着吗？)

所以，英语国家人打招呼通常以天气、健康状况、交通、体育以及兴趣爱好为话题。

4. 其他社交礼节上的不同

以 please "请"为例，在某些场所却不宜用英语 please。让别人先进门或先上车时，不说 please，一般说：After you。但是初学英语的人常用 You go first，这是不对的。在餐桌上请人吃饭、喝酒或者请人抽烟时，一般用 Help yourself (to something)，而不用 please。

一般来说，中国人在家庭成员之间很少用"谢谢"。如果用了，听起来会很怪，或相互关系上有了距离。而在英语国家"Thank you"几乎用于一切场合，所有人之间，即使父母与子女，兄弟姐妹之间也不例外。送上一瓶饮料，准备一桌美餐，对方都会说一声"Thank you"。公共场合，不管别人帮你什么忙，你都要道一声"Thank you"，这是最起码的礼节。当别人问是否要吃点或喝点什么时(Would you like something to eat/drink?)，中国人通常习惯于客气一番，回答："不用了""别麻烦了"等。而按照英语国家的习惯，你若想要，就不必推辞，说声"Yes, please"，若不想要，只要说"No, thanks"就行了。这也充分体现了中国人的含蓄和英语国家的人直率的两种不同风格。

在英语国家，赞美也常用来作为交谈的引子。赞美的内容主要有个人的外貌、外表、新买的东西、个人财物、个人在某方面出色的工作等。通常称赞别人的外表时只称赞她努力(打扮)的结果，而不是她的天生丽质。因此赞美别人发型的很多，赞美别人漂亮头发的很少。对别人的赞美，最普通的回答是："Thank you"如下所述。

A: Your skirt looks nice.

B: Thank you.

中国人初次见面问及年龄、婚姻、收入(表示关心)，而英语国家的人却对此比较反感，认为这些都涉及个人隐私。例如，在 JEFC Book 1 Lesson 16 中有这样的对话："How old are you, Mrs. Read?" "Ah, it's a secret！"为什么 Mrs. Read 不肯说出自己的年龄呢？因为英语国家的人希望自己在对方眼中显得精力充沛、青春永驻，对自己实际年龄秘而不宣，女人更是如此。再如，中国人表示关心的"你去哪儿？"(Where are you going?)和"你在干什么？"(What are you doing?)，在英语中就成为刺探别人隐私的审问或监视别人的话语而不受欢迎。

中国和英语国家的文化差异还显著地表现在节日方面。在节日里，对于别人送来的礼物，中国人和英语国家的人也表现出不同的态度。中国人往往要推辞一番，表现得无可奈何地接受，接受后一般也不当面打开。如果当面打开并喜形于色，可能招致"贪财"的嫌疑。而在英语文化中，人们对别人送的礼物，一般要当面打开称赞一番，并且欣然道谢。

总之，文化差异现象的根源主要由于概念意义的差异和联想意义的差异。概念意义即基本意义。它是客观事物在人们意识中的反映和概括。在中西方不同文化背景下，客观事物本身存在差异，人们对客观事物的反应和概括便会留下深刻的文化烙印，因此，英汉词汇在概念意义上常具有不同的内涵，如西方饮食中的 sandwich, hamburger, salad, 中国人既未看过，也未吃过，只好音译为"三明治""汉堡包""色拉"，美国人生活中特有的 drugstore, 汉语中还没有一个词语能贴切地表达其内涵，也只能以注释性的文字说明它是"出售药物、糖果、饮料及其他日用杂品的店铺"。同样，汉语里的一些词，如"天干""地支""楷书""普通话""太极拳"等，在英语中也找不到对应词。

联想意义是人们在概括自己对客观世界的感性认识和情感体验之后，通过联系、类比等手段赋予词汇一定的象征意义。联想意义是词汇内涵的重要组成部分，同样植根于文化的土壤之中。正如上文所述，英汉颜色词，从物理学角度讲是没有区别的，但在语言交流中，它们却各具不同的联想意义，此时的颜色不再是自然色彩，而是象征色彩。例如，黄色(yellow)在中国文化中象征至高无上的权力或色情淫秽，人们常说"黄袍加身""黄色书刊""黄色录像"等，但在美国，yellow 没有这种特定的内涵，人们常用蓝色(blue)来指代色情(如 a blue movie)。再如，绿色(green)在汉语中象征春天、新生的希望，但一提到它，英美人却会由此想到嫉妒(green eyed)与缺乏经验(green hand)。

要使译文在功能上与原文对等，翻译时译者除了在语言层面(音韵、词法、句法、修辞等)有效再现原文特征，还要充分考虑双语间的文化及民族心理差异等因素。美国的 Coca-Cola 之所以在中国如此畅销，恐怕与"可口可乐"这一完美的译名不无关系；而美国杂志 *play boy* 在国内几乎难觅其踪影，这与其译名"花花公子"具有"衣着华丽、只会吃喝玩乐、不务正业的富家子弟"之意是有一定关系的。由此可见，广告翻译中充分考虑文化差异及民族心理差异的重要性。

1.3 科技术语的主要翻译方法

1.3.1 概述

翻译标准或原则的共同特点是：翻译既要"忠实"又要"通顺"，即译文必须既要考虑原作者又要考虑译文的读者。用张培基等人的话说就是：

"所谓忠实，首先指忠实于原作的内容。译者必须把原作的内容完整而准确地表达出来，不得有任何篡改、歪曲、遗漏阉割或任意增删的现象。……忠实还指保持原作的风格——原作的民族风格、时代风格、语体风格、作者个人的语言风格等译者对原作的风格不能任意破坏和改变，不能以译者的风格代替原作的风格。……所谓通顺，指译文语言必须通顺易懂，符合规范。译文必须是明白晓畅的现代语言，没有逐词死译、硬译的现象，没有语言晦涩难懂、佶屈聱牙的现象，没有文理不通、结构混乱、逻辑不清的现象……"（《英汉翻译教程》）

翻译过程主要包括理解、表达和校核3个方面。下面重点对"理解"进行说明。

理解可分为广义理解和狭义理解。广义理解指对原文作者的个人、原文产生的时代背景、作品的内容以及原文读者对该作品的反映。狭义的理解仅指对原作文本的理解。这种理解主要包括语法分析、语义分析、语体分析和语篇分析(grammatical analysis, semantic analysis, stylistic analysis and text analysis)。理解是翻译成功与否的先决条件和重要步骤，务必正确可靠，杜绝谬误。

表达是理解后能否保证译文成功的又一个关键步骤，是理解的深化和体现。在此过程中，译者要注意恰到好处地再现原文的思想内容和语体色彩，使译文既忠实于原作又符合译入语的语法和表达习惯。要做到这一点，译者就必须在选词用字、组词成句、组句成篇上下功夫，在技巧运用上下功夫。能直译时尽可能地直译，不能直译时则可考虑意译，灵活运用翻译技巧。例如下述例子。

The winds of November were like summer breezes to him, and his face glowed with the pleasant cold. His cheeks were flushed and his eyes glistened; his vitality was intense, shining out upon others with almost a material warmth. 十一月的寒风，对他就像夏天吹拂的凉风一样。令他舒适的冷空气使其容光焕发、两颊通红、两眼闪光。他生气勃勃，让别人感到是一团炙手的火。(英语 material warmth 的字面意思是"物质的温暖"，这里译作"一团炙手的火"，言明意清，让人一看就懂。)

My dear girls, I am ambitious for you, but not to have you make a dash in the world—marry rich men merely because they are rich, or have splendid houses, which are not homes because love is wanting…亲爱的姑娘们，我对你们期望很高，可并不是叫你们在世上出人头地——要你们去嫁给富人，仅仅因为他们有钱，有奢华的住房，缺少爱情的话，就算是豪华的住房也算不上家。(英语 ambitious 既可表示"雄心壮志的"的意思，也可表示"野心勃勃的"的意思，这里选用褒义词"期望很高"比较妥当。)

It was morning, and the new sun sparkled gold across the ripples of gentle sea. 清晨，初升的太阳照着平静的海面，微波荡漾，闪耀着金色的光芒。(英语 the ripples of gentle sea 译成汉

语时在结构上做了调整，这样，译文念起来意思清楚，行文漂亮。)

　　The sea was wonderfully calm and now it was rich with all the colors of the setting sun. In the sky already a solitary star twinkled.大海平静得出奇，晚霞映照得绚丽多彩，天空已有孤星闪烁。(英语原文两句译成汉语合为一句。)

　　表达时还应注意避免翻译腔、过分表达和欠表达。所谓翻译腔，是指译文不符合汉语语法和表达习惯，佶屈聱牙，晦涩难懂。例如下面的表达。

　　To appease their thirst, its readers drank deeper than before, until they were seized with a kind of delirium. 为了解渴，读者比以前越饮越深，直到陷入了昏迷状态。

　　这个句子的译文死抠原文形式，死抠字典释义，翻译腔严重，让人难以明白其意思，可改译为：读者为了满足自己的渴望，越读越想读，直到进入了如痴如醉的状态。

　　所谓过分表达，是指译文画蛇添足，增加了原文没有的东西；而欠表达则是省略或删节原文的内容。翻译时均应避免这类错误。

　　校核是对理解和表达质量的全面检查，是纠正错误、改进译文的极好时机，切不可认为是多余之举。优秀的译者总是十分重视校核的作用，总是利用这一良机来克服自己可能犯下的错误，初学翻译的人就更应该如此了。

1.3.2　科技英语的翻译

　　科技英语(English for Science and Technology)诞生于 20 世纪 50 年代，是第二次世界大战后科学技术迅猛发展的产物。20 世纪 70 年代以来，科技英语在国际上引起了广泛的关注和研究，目前已经发展成为一种重要的英语文体。科技英语泛指一切论及或谈及科学技术的书面语和口语，其中包括：科技著述、科技论文和报告、实验报告和方案；各类科技情报和文字资料；科技实用手册的结构描述和操作规程；有关科技问题的会谈、会议、交谈用语；有关科技的影片、录像、光盘等有声资料的解说词等。

　　术语是表示某一专门概念的词语，科技术语就是在科技方面表示某一专门概念的词语。因此翻译时要十分注意，不能疏忽。英语科技术语的特点是词义繁多，专业性强，翻译时必须根据专业内容谨慎处理，稍不注意就会造成很大的错误。如有的人把"the newly developed picture tube"错译为"新近被发展了画面管"，正确的翻译应该是："最新研制成功的显像管"。因为这里的 picture tube 应该意译为"显像管"。又有人把"a unique instant-picture system"错译为"独特的图像系统"，正确的翻译应该是："独特的瞬时显像装置"。再以"cassette"这个术语为例，它除了其他方面的意思之外，在录音磁带方面还有两个意思：一个是"装填式磁带盒"，另一个是"盒式磁带"。究竟应译为哪个意思，要从上下文的具体意思去分析判断。如进口的收录两用机的使用说明书上有"checking the cassette"和"to insert cassette"两个小标题，究竟应当怎么译呢？分别将其译为"检查盒式磁带"和"装上盒式磁带"，要比分别译为"检查磁带盒"和"装上磁带盒"更好一些。

　　随着当今世界科学技术的迅速发展，新的科技术语不断涌现。因此，统一科技术语对科学知识的跨国传播、新学科的开拓、新理论的建立等方面都是不可缺少的，更是当前信息时代的紧迫要求。然而科技术语的准确翻译不仅是个学术问题，同样也是伴随科技进步后需要经常研讨的永恒课题。本书基于一些典型科技术语翻译实例的各种疑难表现，结合有关翻译原则和特点，针对性地提出了一些问题的解决办法。

1.3.3 合成科技术语的语义分析

科技翻译不仅仅是词汇、语法、修辞等语言问题，还涉及许多非语言方面的因素。逻辑便是其中最活跃、最重要的因素。巴尔胡达罗夫曾举过这样一个例子："John is in the pen"，任何人也不会把句中的"pen"译为笔，而只能译为"牲口圈"，因为"人在钢笔里"是不合逻辑的。这说明在翻译中常常会碰到需要运用逻辑来判断和解决一些似乎不合逻辑的语言现象，这里说的逻辑判断，主要是指对原文语言思维逻辑的判断和译文的技术逻辑的判断。

就科技英语而言，理解原文的过程，在多数情况下，是一个语义辨认、语法分析和逻辑分析3方面交互作用的过程。

无论是理解原文的过程，还是寻求适当的汉语表达形式的过程，都是跟判断分析打交道的过程。科技英语因其专业特点及其相关背景知识，逻辑判断、语义分析在进行译文处理时，显得尤其重要。语言具有民族的特点，而判断则具有全人类的性质。

逻辑判断、语义分析中常见的错误有以下几种。

1. 判断中的相关概念搭配不当

判断可以看成是表达概念间的关系的。判断所表达的概念之间的关系必须符合客观事物之间的真实关系，否则就会导致判断错误或判断不当。如下所述。

The subject of computers, which also began its development at that time, began to grow and become a separate subject itself.

原译：计算机这一项目也是在那时开始研制、发展并成为一个独立的学科的。

分析：如果"计算机这一项目"是指作为机械的计算机本身，则可以说"研制"，但不能说"成为一个学科"；如果"计算机这一项目"是指作为科学分支的"学科"，则可以说"成为一个学科"，但不能说"研制"，众所周知，"学科"是不能研制的。

译文：计算机这一学科也是在那个时候开始兴起，并逐渐发展成为一门独立的学科的。

2. 判断反映的思想自相矛盾

True eccentrics never deliberately set out to draw attention to themselves. They disregard social conventions without being conscious that they are doing anything extraordinary. This invariably wins them love and respect of others…

原译：真正的怪人从不有意做些什么怪事来引人注目。他们玩世不恭，却并未意识到他们自己的所作所为与众不同。他们因此总是赢得尊敬和爱慕……

分析：他们"玩世不恭"，居然还能"赢得尊敬和爱慕"，这不是有点矛盾吗？把 disregard social conventions 译为"蔑视社会习俗"，便可避免这一逻辑错误。

译文：真正的怪人从不有意做些什么怪事来引人注目。他们蔑视社会习俗，却并未意识到他们自己的所作所为与众不同。因此他们总是赢得尊敬和爱慕……

3. 判断不严密

如果一个判断有明显的不严密之处，那么这往往是由于译者误解原文所致，请看下面的句子及其译文。

Some other factors which may influence reasoning are (a) faulty analogizing; (b) the inhibiting effect on further research of concepts which have been widely accepted as satisfactory…

原译：其他会影响推理的一些因素是：(a)错误的类比；(b)对一些概念进一步研究的抑制性影响，而这些概念是被广泛认为满意的……

分析：什么是"抑制性影响"，是什么东西的抑制性影响？"抑制性影响"怎么会成为影响推理的因素？所有这些都是不明确的，因而，这个判断很不严密。一查原文，发现译文果然有误。从译文看，译者把介词短语 of concepts 看成 research 这个动作名词的逻辑上的宾语了。实际上，介词短语 of concepts 在语法上是 the effect 的定语，而在逻辑上则表示施动性的主语。句中的关键结构是 the effect A (up) on B of A，它的意义是：A 对 B 的作用，或者 A 对 B 的影响。由此可见，the inhibiting effect on further research of concepts…并不是"对一些概念进一步研究的抑制性影响"，而是"某些被公认正确的概念对进一步研究的阻碍作用"。

译文：影响推理的一些其他因素：(a)错误的类比；(b)某些被公认为正确的概念对进一步研究的阻碍作用……

4. 判断之间缺乏逻辑联系

前面用实例探讨了某些成分由于句子本身的内容而不允许分译的情形，下面再用实例探讨一下它们由于上下文的逻辑联系而不允许分译的情形。

Before these metals in their natural state can be converted into useful forms to be of service to man, they must be separated from the other elements or substances with which they are combined. Chemists, who are well acquainted with the properties of metals, have been able to develop processes for separating metals from substances with which they are combined in nature…

原译：处于天然状态的金属在转换成为人类服务有用形式之前，必须从和它结合在一起的其他元素或物质中分离出来。化学家十分熟悉金属的性能。他们已能创造出一些方法，把金属从和它在自然界中结合在一起的物质中分离出来……

分析：这里引用的两个句子，虽然很长，但从上下文的联系来看，是一气呵成、前后连贯的。译文将定语从句"who…metals"拆译成独立的句子，插在两个句子中间，显得很突兀，不仅破坏了前后两个句子之间的紧密的逻辑联系，而且也使语气无法连贯下去。再者，从概念上说，并不是任何化学家都十分熟悉金属的性能。

译文：……分离出来。熟悉金属性能的化学家们已经研究出来一些方法，能够……

1.3.4　科技术语构词中的前缀和后缀

让我们了解一下英语缀合词的构词要素，即前缀、后缀、词根。

1. 前缀

前缀(prefix)是加在词根或单词前面的部分，具有一定的意义。相同词根前加以不同前缀会有不同的意义，构成新词。在许多单词中，只有一个前缀，但也有一些单词有两个前缀，甚至有多个前缀。例如，incompatible(不兼容的)，其中前缀 in 表示"不"。前缀 com

表示"共同，一起"，词根 pat 表示"忍受，忍耐"，后缀-ible 表示"可……的"。前缀一般不改变词性，只改变原来单词的意思。例如，load 与 unload 的词意不同，词性相同，如下所列。

(1) milli-，表示毫，千分之一：
volt 伏——millivolt (毫伏)　　　　　　liter 升——milliliter (毫升)
gram 克——milligram (毫克)

(2) mis-，表示误，错，坏：
fortune 运气——misfortune (不幸)　　　lead 引导——mislead (误导)
understand 理解——misunderstand (误解)

(3) mono-，表示单，一：
tone 音调——monotone (单音，单调)　　chrome 铬，铬合金——monochrome (单色)

(4) multi-，表示多：
color 颜色——multicolor (多色的)　　　program 程序——multiprogram (多程序)
form 形式——multiform (多形的，多样的)

(5) non-，表示非，不，无：
stop 停——nonstop (直达，中途不停)　　metal 金属——nonmetal (非金属)
conductor 导体——nonconductor (绝缘体)

(6) over-，表示过分，在……上面，超过，压倒，额外：
load 负载——overload (过载)　　　　　current 电流——overcurrent (过电流)
exposure 曝光——overexposure (曝光过度)

有的前缀含义狭窄，有的含义广泛。前者大多意义明显，后者则较为隐晦。

2. 后缀

后缀(suffix)是加在词根或单词后面的部分。后缀不仅可以改变原来单词的意思，而且可以改变单词的词性，实现词类转变。因此，给单词加后缀是构成新词，尤其是不同类型词类的常用方法。例如：work 是动词，表示"工作"的意思，加-er 构成名词 worker，表示"工人"的意思；加-able 构成动词 workable，表示"可加工的"的意思，可见加不同后缀构成的单词，其词性不同。根据后缀构成单词的词性，通常把后缀分为名词后缀、动词后缀、形容词后缀及副词后缀等。

每一后缀都有一定的含义。有的后缀只有单一的意思，有的后缀有多种意思。同时，同一个意思又可以由不同的后缀表示。使用后缀的单词可以只有一个后缀，也可以有两个后缀，甚至有多个后缀。例如，geosynchronous 表示"与地球同步的"；interchangeably 表示"可交换地"。

(1) 名词后缀有许多种，使一个非名词成为名词的后缀，如下所列。

表示人	-er: worker (工人)	-ist: artist (艺术家)
表示物	-or: tractor (拖拉机)	-ant: disinfectant (消毒剂)
抽象名词	-hood: childhood (童年)	-ship: friendship (友谊)
集合名词	-ry: peasantry (农民总称)	-age: mileage (英里数)
场所地点	-ery: piggery (养猪场)	-arium: planetarium (天文馆)
表示小	-let: streamlet (小溪)	-ock: hillock (小丘)
	-et: floweret (小花)	

表示阴性	-ine: heroine (女英雄)	-ess: lioness (母狮)
	-enne: comedienne (女喜剧演员)	
表示疾病	-oma: trachoma (沙眼)	-itis: bronchitis (支气管炎)
	-ism: rheumatism (风湿)	
表示行为	-ade: blockade (封锁)	-ation: visitation (访问)
	-ism: criticism (批评)	
化学名词	-ane: methane (甲烷)	-ide: oxide (氧化物)
	-one: acetone (丙酮)	
身份地位	-age: pupilage (学生身份)	-cy: captaincy (船长职位)
	-dom: serfdom (农奴地位)	
……学	-logy: zoology (动物学)	-ics: electronics (电子学)
	-ry: forestry (林学)	

(2) 形容词后缀，表示一种事物具有或属于某种性质或状态。表示"是……的""似……的""具有……的""多……的""关于……的""有……性质的"，等等，如下所列。

-ic: atomic (原子的)　　　　　　　　　　-al: digital (数字的)
-ful: powerful (有力的)　　　　　　　　 -y: hilly (多山的)

(3) 动词后缀，表示使成为……、致使、做……化、变成……，等等，如下所列。

-fy: glorify (使光荣)　　　　　　　　　 -ize: modernize (现代化)
-en: lengthen (加长)　　　　　　　　　 ate: hyphenate (加连字符)

(4) 副词后缀，表示状态、方式、方向等，如下所列。

-wise: clockwise (顺时针地)　　　　　　 -ways: crossways (交叉地)
-wards: southwards (向南)　　　　　　　 -ly: hourly (每小时地)
-s: outdoors (户外地)

3. 词根

词根 (root)是一个单词的根本部分，表示单词的根本意义，是同根词可以辨认出来的部分。词根是组成单词的最主要元素。一个单词可以没有前缀，也可以没有后缀，但不能没有词根。由相同词根构成的一系列单词叫作"同根词"。

大部分词根都是单音节的，只包含一个元音，如 part。但是，还有一些词根是双音节的，包含两个元音，如 laser。还有少量的词根由多音节构成，包含两个以上的元音，如 algebra。随着技术的发展，原来一些单词变成了词根。例如，atom 表示"原子"，它是由前缀 a (表示"不")，与词根 tom (表示"切割")组成的单词，现在已经成为词根了。同时，由于计算机技术的发展，也出现了一些新的词根，如 cyber 表示"与计算机有关的"。例如：

eulogize (称赞)　　　　　　　　　　　　prologue (序言)
monologue (独白)　　　　　　　　　　　 dialogue (对话)
epilogue (结束语)　　　　　　　　　　　apologize (道歉)
logogram (语标)　　　　　　　　　　　　neologism (新语)

以上例子都有一个共同的部分"log"，它们表示一个共同的意思——言，"log"就是这些单词的词根。一个词根可以派生出许多新词。

词根大部分是单音节的，小部分是多音节的。有的词根可以单独成词，如 act，man，work 等。

前缀和后缀原来也是独立的词或词根，由于经常缀在别的词上辅助中心意义，就逐渐失去其独立性，成为附加成分。

1.3.5 类比构词及其翻译

类比构词 (Word-Formation by Analogy) 是英语中一种有趣而又实用的构词方式。其构词特点是：以某个同类词为模式，在语义上进行联想类比，替换其中某个词素，构造出与之对应或类似的新词来。例如，workaholic (工作迷) 是仿 alcoholic (嗜酒者) 而造的，而 seajack (海上劫持) 和 skyjack (空中劫持) 则是类比 hijack (拦路抢劫) 而成的，故都属类比构词。

从原形词与类比构词的联系来看，英语类比构词大致可分以下 3 类。

1. 数字、色彩类比

先看数字类比，例如，"美国总统夫人"，在英语中称 First Lady (第一夫人)，通过该词又联想类比出 Fist Family (第一家庭)，First Mother (第一母亲) 等词。就连总统的爱犬也身价倍增，获得了 First Dog (第一狗) 的殊荣，可谓一人得道，鸡犬升天。

再看色彩类比，例如，Black Power (黑人权力) 最初是美国黑人在争取自身权力斗争中提出的政治口号，后为美国其他少数族裔所借用，为了反歧视、争平等。印第安人提出 Red Power，美籍墨西哥人也提出了 Brown Power。另外，老年人为维护自身权益则提出 Gray Power。美国英语中还因美元为绿色钞票而类比出 green power 一词，借指"金钱的力量"。green power 虽与上述种种 power 风马牛不相及，但同属色彩类比，甚是有趣，亦含幽默。再看一例，较早出现的 blue-collar (蓝领阶层的) 和 white-collar (白领阶层的) 分别指"体力工作者的"和"脑力工作者的"，稍后产生的 pink-collar (粉领阶层的) 和 gray-collar (灰领阶层的)，则分别指"典型女性职业工作者的"和"维修保养行业工作者的"。近年来，又有两个新的英语类比词问世，即 gold-collar (金领阶层的) 和 bright-collar (亮领阶层的)，分别表示"高级专业人士的"和"计算机及通信专业人士的"。

2. 反义、对义类比

这方面英语类比词数目不少，俯拾可得，如下所列。

brain-gain (人才流入)　　　　　　　　brain-drain (人才流失)
flash-forward (超前叙述)　　　　　　flashback (倒叙)
low-tech (低技术的)　　　　　　　　　high-tech (高技术的)

在这方面，有些类比词来得有趣，仿造奇特。例如，man Friday 源于小说《鲁滨孙漂流记》，指主人公于星期五救出的一个土人，后成其忠仆，故名。该词进入英语词汇后泛指"忠实的仆人"或"得力的助手"。后来出现的 girl Friday 一词系彷此而造，专指"忠实的女仆"或"得力的女助手"。又如，boycott (联合抵制) 一词的来历可追溯到 19 世纪末。当年在爱尔兰的梅奥郡有个地主名叫 Charles Cunnigham Boycott，他压榨佃农，灾年拒不减租，结果激起公愤。全郡居民联合行动，拒绝与他往来，迫使他逃离本地。此事成了报刊上的头号新闻，Boycott 姓氏不胫而走，成为"联合抵制"的代用语，并为法语、德语、西班牙语等欧洲语言所借用。最为有趣的是，人们将本为姓氏的 boycott 中的"boy"视为与 girl 相对应的 boy(男子)一词，故意加以错误类比，仿造出 girlcott 一词，作为"妇女界联合抵制"之意。

3. 近似情形类比

在英语类比词中，这部分词为数最多。

Olympiad (奥运会)　　　　　　　　Asiad (亚运会)
baby-sit (临时代人照看孩子)　　　house-sit (临时代人照看房子)
escalator (自动扶手电梯)　　　　　ravolator (设在机场等处的自动人行道)
chain-smoke (一支接一支地抽烟)　chain-drink (一杯接一杯地喝酒或饮料)
human rights (人权)　　　　　　　animal rights (动物权)
hunger strike (绝食罢工或抗议)　　sleep strike (绝眠罢工或抗议)
boat people (乘船出逃的难民)　　land people (陆路出逃的难民)

有时英语里还发生连锁类比现象，以某原形词为模式仿造出一系列类比词来，令人叹为观止。例如，从 marathon (马拉松赛跑)一词中类比出的新词就有以下几个。

walkathon (步行马拉松)　　　　　talkathon (马拉松式冗长演说)
telethon (马拉松式电视节目)　　　sellathon (马拉松式推销)

又如，以 racism (种族歧视)为模式类比出的新词为数也不少。

sexism (性别歧视)　　　　　　　　ageism (对老年人的歧视)
ableism (对残疾人的歧视)　　　　fattism (对胖子的歧视)
alphabetism (对姓氏按首字母顺序排列在后面的人的歧视)。-ism 实际已成为表示歧视之义的后缀。再如，hamburger(汉堡包)这个词的类比也很有趣，它用作食物名本源于地名，但人们有意进行错误类比，将该词中的"ham"理解为"火腿"，并据此仿造出一系列新词，用以指称类似汉堡包，夹有各种馅子的食品，如 fishburger，cheeseburger，nutburger，beefburger，soyburger 等。

在现代英语中，类比构词一直很活跃。由于它合乎人们的思维习惯，操作简便，故在百姓口语、报刊文章里均有运用，加之构词范围广，因而新词语不断涌现，层出不穷。

科技的发展常产生新的英语类比构词。例如，EQ(情商)是当前颇流行的心理学新概念，该词系仿 IQ(智商)而造，指一个人控制自己情绪、承受外来压力、保持心理平衡的能力。航天技术的发展也为英语增添了一些类比词，如下所列。

sunrise (日出)　　　　　　　　　　earthrise (地出)
earthquake (地震)　　　　　　　　moonquake (月震)
starquake (星震)　　　　　　　　youthquake (青年动乱)

有趣的是，在后一组词的类比过程中，人们从地球联想到太空，然后思路一转，又回到地球上的美国社会。

政治运动及社会生活也是英语类比构词的另一重要来源。20 世纪 60 年代，美国黑人曾掀起大规模的反种族隔离运动。当时黑人举行的室内静坐示威叫 sit-in。随着运动的深入与扩大，黑人纷纷进入原先严禁他们入内的各种公共场所表示抗议，以 verb+in 为模式仿造的新词随之大量出现。黑人与白人同乘一车叫 ride-in，到白人游泳池游泳叫 swim-in，进白人图书馆阅读叫 read-in，入白人教堂做礼拜叫 pray-in。后来，-in 的含义又扩展到其他内容或方式的抗议示威活动上。如下所列。

camp-in (露营示威)　　　　　　sign-in (签名示威)
talk-in (演讲示威)　　　　　　mail-in (邮寄示威)
lie-in (卧街示威)　　　　　　　lock-in (占驻示威)
laugh-in (哄笑示威)　　　　　　stall-in (阻塞交通示威)
turn-in (退还征兵令示威)

凡此种种，不一而足，英语类比构词的活跃性和创造性，由此可见一斑。

直译加注指直译原文，并附加解释性注释。注释可长可短，既可采用文中注释，也可采用脚注，还可二者合用。如下所列。

big apple　大苹果 (纽约的别称)
mad-cow disease　疯牛病 (牛海绵状脑病)
oval office　椭圆形办公室 (美国白宫总统办公室)
desert storm　沙漠风暴行动 (1991 年以美国为首的盟国部队对伊拉克军队进行的一场大规模军事打击行动)

1.3.6　音译及形译

由于英汉文化存在着许多差异，因此英语中某些文化词语在汉语中根本就没有对等词，形成了词义上的空缺。在这种情况下，英译汉时常常要采用加注法来弥补空缺。加注通常可以用来补充诸如背景材料、词语起源等相关信息，便于读者理解。加注法可分为音译加注和直译加注两种。

1. 音译

音译是翻译英语专业名词的一种常用方法，就是根据英语单词的发音译成读音与原词大致相同的汉字。科技英语中某些由专有名词构成的术语、单位名称、新型材料的名称等，在翻译时都可采用音译法。考虑到译名的规范化和通用性，用词要大众化，读音应以普通话的语音为标准。举例如下。

(1) 新发现的自然现象或物质名称。例如：gene 基因，quark 夸克。
(2) 计量单位名称一般用音译。例如：hertz (Hz) 赫兹 (频率单位)，bit 比特 (度量信息的单位，二进制位)，calorie 卡路里(热量单位)，var 乏 (无功功率单位)。
(3) 新型材料的名称一般采用音译。例如：celluloid 赛璐珞，nylon 尼龙。
(4) 专有名词：cartoon 卡通片，hamburger 汉堡包，Benz 奔驰车。

音译加注指音译后附加解释性注释。注释可长可短，可采用文中注释，也可采用脚注，还可二者合用。如下所列。

clone 克隆 (一种无性繁殖方法)
sauna 桑拿浴 (源于芬兰的一种蒸汽浴)
hacker 黑客 (在信息空间中主动出击，对他人的计算机或网络系统进行诸如窥探、篡改或盗窃保密数据及程序的过程，并可能由此造成混乱和破坏的计算机迷)

El Niño 厄尔尼诺(现象)(指严重影响全球气候的太平洋热带海域的大风及海水的大规模移动)

Bunsen 本生灯 (一种煤气灯)

AIDS 艾滋病 (获得性免疫缺陷综合征)

一般来说，音译比意译容易，但不如意译能够明确地表达新术语的含义。因此，有些音译词经过一段时间后又被意译词所取代，或者同时使用。如下所列。

valve 凡尔→阀门　　　　　　　　motor 马达→电动机
washer 华司→垫圈　　　　　　　engine 引擎→发动机
laser 莱塞→激光　　　　　　　　vitamin 维他命→维生素
penicillin 盘尼西林→青霉素　　　telephone 德律风→电话

2. 形译

用英语常用字母的形象来为形状相似的物体定名。翻译这类术语时，一般采用形译法。常用的形译法又分为下列 3 种情况。

(1) 选用能够表达原字母形象的汉语词来译。

T-square 丁字尺　　　　　　　　I-column 工字柱
U-bend 马蹄弯头　　　　　　　　V-slot 三角形槽

(2) 保留原字母不译，在该字母后加"形"字，这种译法更为普遍。

A-bedplate A 形底座　　　　　　D-valve D 形阀
C-network C 形网络　　　　　　　M-wing M 形机翼

(3) 保留原字母不译，以字母代表一种概念。

X-ray X 光　　　　　　　　　　　α-iron α 铁
Y-ray Y 射线　　　　　　　　　　p-n-p junction p-n-p 结

1.4　处理词汇现象的技巧

1.4.1　选择和确定词义

英汉两种语言都有一词多类、一词多义的现象。一词多类指的是一个词属于不同的词类，具有几个不同的意义。一词多义就是说同一个词在同一个词类中又有几个不同的词义。

在翻译的过程中，在弄清原句的结构后，要善于选择和确定原句中关键词的词义。选择和确定词义通常可以从以下两个方面入手。

1. 根据词在句中的词类来选择和确定词义

选择某个词的词义，首先要判明这个词在原句中应属于哪一种词类，然后进一步确定其含义。

e.g. 1　Like charges repel; unlike charges attract.

译文：同性电荷相斥，异性电荷相吸。

这句话中的 like 是 charges 的定语，用作形容词，它与汉语相对应的含义应当是"同性的"。同样，unlike 也是形容词性，含义为"异性的"。

但在以下各句中，like 又分别属于其他几个不同词类。

e.g. 2　Servers are computers exactly <u>like</u> the W.S.

译文：服务器是与 W.S.(工作站)非常<u>相似</u>的计算机。

这里的 like 是介词，可译为"相似，像"。

e.g. 3　Never do <u>the like</u> again.

译文：不要再做<u>这样</u>的事了。

这句话中的 like 与定冠词 the 组合成名词性词组，相当于汉语中的"形似的人或事物"。

e.g. 4　Some theorems <u>like</u> regarding noise as Gaussian white noise.

译文：许多理论<u>倾向于</u>将噪声看作高斯白噪声。

这里的 like 用作动词，表示"喜欢"。

e.g. 5　The <u>sampling</u> theorem shows that all values of a signal can be determined by sampling the signal at a rate equal to at least twice the bandwidth.

译文：抽样定理表明信号的<u>抽样</u>频率至少为信号频率的两倍时，信号才能全部恢复。

这里的 sampling 显然是动词的现在分词，作 theorem 的定语，它与汉语相对应的词义应当是"抽样"。

e.g. 6　Air oxidation is accelerated by <u>light</u> (*n.*) and catalysis.

译文：<u>光</u>和催化剂加速空气氧化。

e.g. 7　This instrument is <u>light</u> (*adj.*) in weight and simple to operate.

译文：这台机器<u>轻</u>而且操作简单。

例 6 和例 7 中的 light，也反映出不同的词类有不同的含义。

2. 根据上下文的联系以及在句中的搭配关系，来选择和确定词义

英语中的同一个词、同一类词，在不同的场合往往也有不同的含义，必须根据上下文的联系以及词的搭配关系或句型来判断和确定某个词在特定场合下的具体词义。

e.g. 1　Most DSPs are based on the so-called Harvard <u>architecture</u>, where the data path (including the <u>bus</u> and memory units) is made distinct from the program path, allowing an instruction search to be performed simultaneously with another instruction execution and other tasks.

译文：大部分的 DSP 采用的是所谓的 Harvard <u>结构</u>，这种结构的数据线(包括<u>总线</u>和存储单元)与程序线相互独立，这样就能在执行某个指令或任务的同时接受其他指令的执行请求。

这里的 architecture 的含义应该是"结构"，bus 的含义应该是"总线"。也就是说，在专业英语中一些词汇会有特殊的含义。

e.g. 2　Chips require much less space and power and are cheaper to manufacture than an equivalent circuit built by employing <u>individual</u> transistors.

译文：与使用<u>分立</u>的三极管构造的等效电路相比，芯片需要的空间更小，功率更低，更便宜。

将 individual 译作"分立"比译作"独立""个人"更合适。

e.g. 3　An electric charge will flow for a short time and accumulate on <u>the plate</u>.

译文：一个电荷在很短的时间内移动并到达负极。

the plate 在该句中应指"负极",故可以将该词的所指范围确定为"负极"。

e.g. 4　When a current passes through the coil, a magnetic field is set up around it.

译文：当电流流过线圈时,就会在线圈周围产生磁场。

由于原文是介绍电磁场产生的原理,句中的 coil 的含义很明确,指的是"线圈"。

e.g. 5　In practice, a relationship is used in which the received power is related to the transmitted power by a factor which depends on the fourth power of the inverse of the distance.

译文：实际上,在接收功率和发送功率之间有一个关系是由距离的倒数的 4 次幂这个因素所决定的。

句中前两个 power 都是功率的含义,第三个 power 是幂,即乘方的含义。

e.g. 6　Few of these charge carriers combine with the charge (positive in NPN, negative in PNP) in the base.

译文：载流子中很少一部分与基区中(NPN 结的正电荷,PNP 结的负电荷)的电荷结合。

第一个 charge 指的是"载流子";第二个 charge 是电荷的含义。

e.g. 7　The motor can feed several machines.

译文：这部电动机可以给几部机器供应动力。

e.g. 8　The roller press feeds the existing grinding plant depending on the circulating load of the mill.

译文：辊压机按照现有破碎系统的循环破碎能力供料。

1.4.2　词量的改变：增词和减词

由于表达习惯的不同,在专业英语的翻译过程中,有时需要将英语原文中省略的词语在译文中添加进来,即增词；有时又需要原文中多次重复的词在翻译时省略,即减词。这样使得译文更加符合汉语表达的习惯。

1. 增词

增词法就是在翻译时按意义上和句法上的需要增加一些词来更忠实、自然、通顺地表达原文的内容。一般而言,增词法的情况有两种。一种是根据意义上或修辞的需要,如增加表示时态意义的词,增加英语不及物动词隐含的宾语意义的词。另一种是根据句法上的需要,把原文中省略的句子成分补充进去,使译文的句子具有完整的意思。

e.g. 1　Three symbols are used to represent the three types of bus, the symbols for data bus is D.B., for address bus A.B., for control bus C.B..

译文：我们用 3 种符号来表示 3 种总线,用符号 D.B.表示数据总线,用符号 A.B.表示地址总线,用符号 C.B.表示控制总线。

这个句子的原文中两处省略了 the symbols,尽管英语表达含义非常清楚,但是汉语的表达习惯却不做这样的省略,故需要增词。

e.g. 2　When being negative, grid repels electrons, and only a fraction of the electrons emitted by the cathode can reach the anode.

译文：当栅极为负时,就会排斥电子,此时只有一小部分由阴极发射的电子可以到达阳极。

这个句子省略了一个 grid。因为当从句的逻辑主语与主句一致时，从句的主语可以省去，但在中文翻译时需将省略的词翻译出来。

e.g. 3　The classical Greek civilization knew of seven metals: gold, silver, copper, iron, tin, lead and mercury.

译文：古希腊文明时期，人们已经知道使用金、银、铜、铁、锡、铅和汞 7 种金属。

很明显，为了使译文更加符合汉语的语法习惯，译文的最后增加了"使用"，并对句子的顺序进行了调整，即把 seven metals 的翻译由句中放到句末的位置。

e.g. 4　The leakage current of a capacitor is an important measure of its quality.

译文：电容器漏电流的大小，是衡量电容器质量好坏的重要尺度。

此句在增加了或补充了"大小""好坏""衡量"几个词之后，译文质量就大为改善了。

2. 减词

减词法指的是原文中的有些词在译文中不翻译，原因是译文中尽管没有译出这个词但已经包含了其含义，或者这个词所表达的含义是不言而喻的。也就是说，减词就是将英语表达方式中习惯使用的一些词而汉语表达方式中却不必使用的词在翻译时不予翻译。

e.g. 1　If you know the frequency, you can find the wave length.

译文：如果知道频率，就可求出波长。

这里省略了两个 you，译文简洁明了。

e.g. 2　If we should select some sample function $n(t)$, we could not predict the value attained by that same sample function at the time $t+\tau$ with the help of $n(t)$.

译文：如果我们选定某样本函数 $n(t)$，则它在 t 时刻的值不能有助于预测相同样本函数在 $t+\tau$ 时刻的值。

这里主从句中都有 we，在翻译时若将二者都译出，则显重复。故在翻译时只译 if 从句中的 we。

e.g. 3　Throughout this text we shall assume that the random processes with which we shall have occasion to deal are ergodic.

译文：在整篇文章中，我们假定要研究的随机过程均为各态历经过程。

本句中介词 with 引导的宾语从句中重复使用了 we，为了表述逻辑清晰，译文中省略了第二个 we 的翻译。

e.g. 4　The jammer covers an operating frequency range from 20～500MHz.

译文：干扰机的工作频段为 20～500MHz。

此句省略了"覆盖"一词，但意思一样完整。

e.g. 5　Stainless steels possess good hardness and high strength.

译文：不锈钢硬度大、强度高。

"possess"是"占有""拥有"的意思，如将该词直译放在译文中，则其表达不符合汉语的习惯，故省略。

e.g. 6　The mechanical energy can be changed back into electrical energy by means of a generator or dynamo.

译文：用发电机能把机械能转变成电能。

译文省略了 by means of，原因是 <u>generator or dynamo</u> 就是实现机械能与电能转换具体的工具。如果将 by means of 翻译出来，表达就会有些啰唆。

总之，为了能够更加清楚地表达原文的含义，在进行翻译的过程中，要先弄清原文，再根据汉语的语法习惯进行适当的"增词""减词"，但增词、减词不能影响对原文含义的理解。

1.4.3 词义的引申

在阅读的过程中，人们会遇到这样一些词语，辞典上给出的这些词语的词义放在句子中都不能够清楚地表达原文的含义，而如果硬要把辞典中的意思直接套进译文中，就会使得译文生硬晦涩，不能确切表达原意，甚至让读者误解原文。在这种情况下，就要根据上下文以及逻辑关系，进而从这个词的基本含义出发做一定的引申，选择比较恰当的汉语词汇来表达。

e.g. 1 To achieve its function, a video amplifier must operate over a wide band and amplify all frequencies equally and with low distortion.

译文：为了实现这一功能，视频放大器就必须在宽频带且能够对所有频率进行同样放大并且失真很小的环境下运行。

achieve 的原意是"达到"，在这里引申为"实现"，是为了和后面的"功能"相搭配。

e.g. 2 Oscillators are used to produce audio and radio signals <u>for a wide variety of purposes</u>.

译文：振荡器用于产生音频和视频信号，<u>用途广泛</u>。

purposes 是"目的"的意思，这里引申为"用途"更为贴切。

e.g. 3 This CD-ROM feature over 100 applets for you to learn from the <u>master</u>.

译文：此光盘提供了 100 多个程序，供你向<u>专家</u>学习。

master 的原意是"主人"，这里指为版权所有者，译为"专家"。

e.g. 4 The instrument is used to <u>determine</u> how fully the batteries are charged.

译文：这种仪表用来<u>测定</u>电瓶充电的程度。

本句中的 determine 一词译作"确定"不符合专业规范，而应译为"测定"。

e.g. 5 Then hundreds of years from now, billions and billions of miles away, the embryos will be thawed and their hearts will start beating. These <u>space-farers</u> of the future will not grow inside a mother's body but will be incubated in a machine.

译文：几百年后，在距离地球数十亿英里处，冷冻的胚胎将会解冻，胎儿的心脏便开始跳动。这些未来的<u>太空旅人</u>，并非在母体内孕育，而是在机器中孵育。

本句中的 space-farers 一词在《英汉大词典》中的释义是"宇航员，宇宙飞行员"，但将其直接译为"宇航员"，似值得商榷。而"宇宙旅行者"又略显生硬。farer 一词是由 fare 派生而来的，而 fare 用作动词时，表示"行走，旅行"，《英汉大词典》特别注明【诗】。这个【诗】提醒译者：fare 是一个语体高雅之词。这样，人们可以把其译得文绉绉些, 令驰骋想象的行文顿显庄重：太空旅人。

e.g. 6 The <u>pure scientists</u> study phenomena in the universe.

译文：<u>从事理论研究的科学家</u>研究宇宙中的各种现象。

不可将 pure scientists 译为"纯的科学家"。

e.g. 7 The major contributors in component technology have been in the semi-conductors.
译文：电子元件中起主要作用的是半导体元件。

查阅词典，contributors 的意思是"贡献者"，表示具体的人，但逐字翻译不符合汉语的语言习惯，只能根据实际含义，将"主要贡献者"作抽象化引申，译为"起主要作用"。

1.4.4　词类的转换

在专业英语的翻译过程中，有些句子可以逐词翻译，有些句子则由于英汉两种语言表达方式的不同，不能一个词接一个词地简单罗列。实际上，在翻译的过程中有些词需要进行转换才能使译文通顺自然。

e.g. 1 The process of quantization leads to unavoidable error.
译文：量化过程不可避免地产生误差。(形容词转化为副词)

e.g. 2 Taking the former view gives a good insight into the behavior of the quantization error .
译文：经过前面的讲解使我们更好地理解量化误差的特性。(名词转化为动词)

e.g. 3 Most satellites are designed to burn up themselves after completing mission.
译文：按照设计大部分卫星在完成任务后自行燃烧。(动词转化为名词)

e.g. 4 He has no knowledge of how electricity is generated.
译文：他不知道电是如何产生的。(名词转化为动词)

e.g. 5 The salts of some organic acid are capable of fluorescing while the free acid are not.
译文：有些有机酸盐能发荧光，而其游离酸则不能。(形容词转化为动词)

e.g. 6 The electron weighs about 1/1850 as much as atom of hydrogen.
译文：电子的重量约为氢原子的 1/1850。(动词转化为名词)

e.g. 7 Alloy steel is stronger and harder than carbon steel.
译文：合金钢的强度和硬度比碳钢大。(形容词转化为名词)

e.g. 8 It's well - known that neutrons act differently from protons.
译文：大家知道，中子的作用与质子不同。(动词转化为名词)

e.g. 9 In certain cases frictions is an absolute necessity.
译文：在一定场合下摩擦是绝对必要的。(名词转化为形容词)

e.g. 10 The acquaintance of science means mastering the law of nature.
译文：认识科学意味着掌握自然规律。(名词转化为动词)

1.4.5　词汇的重复

重复法实际上也是一种增词法，所增加的词是上文刚刚出现过的词。尽管翻译和写作的要求相同，应当力求精练，尽量省略一些可有可无的词，但有时为了明确强调某个事件或表达生动，就需要将一些关键词加以重复。在专业英语的阅读中，往往会对某些关键性的词进行重复，这样才能给读者留下较为深刻的印象，在翻译过程中也需要采用相同的重复手段。

e.g. 1 Both CW and pulse modulation may be classed as analog modulation.
译文：连续波调制和脉冲调制都归类于模拟调制。

这里，modulation 被重复多次。

e.g. 2　I had experienced oxygen and /or engine trouble.

译文：我曾碰到过，不是氧气设备出故障，就是引擎出故障，或两者都出故障(这些情况)。

英文原文的表述中，能够清楚地由 trouble 这一个词将"麻烦"表达清楚，而在翻译过程中，为了能够将译文含义描述清晰，就多次重复了"故障"，但不觉得译文拖沓、烦琐。

e.g. 3　Under ordinary conditions of pressure, water becomes ice at 0℃ and steam at 100°C.

译文：在常压下，水在 0℃时变成冰，在 100℃时变成水蒸气。

增加了动词"变成"，使句子的含义更加明确。

e.g. 4　While stars and nebulae look like specks or small patches of light, they are really enormous bodies.

译文：星星和星云看起来只是斑斑点点，或者是小片的光，但它们确实是巨大的天体。

用"斑斑点点"来描述"天体"的小，更符合汉语的思维。

1.4.6　动词时态的翻译

由于科技英语文体本身的特点和专业性，动词时态的翻译不仅要注意动词时态的语法结构，还要考虑所含有的专业含义，才能在某一特定的专业领域达到译文的准确无误。

1. 动词时态的翻译

在科技文章中，英汉两种语言在很多情况下的时态从字面看并不一致。这是由于英汉两种语言的不同特点决定的，但两者表达的概念、条理、逻辑的要求是一致的，例如，Since the middle of the century oil has been in the fore of energy resources 可译为"本世纪石油一直是最重要的能源之一"。这样英译汉时，为了符合汉语的表达习惯，就要进行时态转换。科技英语翻译中常见的时态转换有以下几种。

(1) 英语的一般现在时译为汉语的将来时、进行时或过去时。

e.g. 1　Many diseases reverses completely thanks to early treatment.

译文：治疗及时的话，很多疾病是可以完全治愈的(将来时)。

e.g. 2　The electronic computer plays an important part in science and technology.

译文：电子计算机在科学和技术方面起着重要的作用(进行时)。

e.g. 3　These substances further speed up the decay process.

译文：这些物质进一步加速了衰变过程(过去时)。

(2) 英语动词的进行时可译成汉语的将来时。

e.g. 4　Knowing severe winter is coming would enable squirrel to store plenty of food.

译文：严冬将至，松鼠会储藏大量的食物。

(3) 英语动词的完成时翻译成汉语的过去时。

e.g. 5　The sales of industrial electronic products have multiplied six times.

译文：工业电子产品销售值增长了 5 倍。

2. 非限定性动词的翻译

作为科技英语中广泛使用的非限定性动词(分词、不定式和动名词)在句子中充当着各种成分，英译汉时也要根据它所具有的语法意义和在科技英语中暗含的科技含义转换为适当的汉语词汇意义，必要时还要进行词的增补。

(1) 汉语中没有限定动词和非限定动词的分类，非限定性动词相当于汉语中的动词，而且英语语言主要依据形态表意。汉语主要依据词汇表意，英译汉时，为了准确表达出它的科技含义，最为常见的是对词的增补和意译。如下所述。

① 增补英语中省略的词。

e.g. 1　radio telescope to be used.
译文：<u>将要交付使用的</u>射电望远镜。

e.g. 2　modulated voltage.
译文：<u>已</u>调制电压。

e.g. 3　a canning tomato.
译文：一种<u>供做罐头的</u>西红柿。

② 增加关联词语。

e.g. 4　Heated, water will change to vapour.
译文：如水受热，<u>就</u>会气化。

③ 修饰加词，语气连贯。

e.g. 5　Heat from the sun stirs up the atmosphere, generating winds.
译文：太阳发出的热能搅动大气，<u>于是</u>产生了风。

按照事件发生的逻辑顺序，译文中自然增加了"于是"使句子结构更完整。

(2) 在翻译的过程中，当非限定性动词的概念难以用汉语的动词表达时，也可转换成汉语的其他词类。

e.g. 6　Momentum is <u>defined</u> as the product of the velocity and a quantity called the mass of the body.
译文：动量的<u>定义</u>是速度和物体质量的乘积(转换成名词)。

e.g. 7　There are ten factories of varying sizes in this district.
译文：这个地区有<u>大小</u> 10 家工厂(译成形容词)。

1.4.7　名词化结构的翻译

名词化结构用词简洁、结构紧凑、表意具体、表达客观，而且整个句子的结构便于写作修辞，词句负载信息的容量得到了增加，有利于达到交际的目的。经常使用的名词化结构有以下几种。

1. 名词/(行为名词)+介词+名词

在此结构中，若"介词+名词"构成的介词短语在逻辑上是行为名词的动作对象或动作的发出者，行为名词的含义在深层中转换或变异，使原来的名词变为动词，构成了动宾或主谓的关系，那么在翻译时可以译成汉语的动宾结构或主谓结构。

e.g. 1　The flow of electrons is from the negative zinc plate to the positive copper plate.
译文：电子从负的锌板流向正的铜板。

e.g. 2　Again in the case of all motor vehicles, friction is essential in the operation of the brake.
译文：还有，所有机动车辆的制动器工作时都需要摩擦。

e.g. 3　They are the employers of managers, as much as they are the employers of work people.
译文：他们不仅雇用工人也雇用经理。

e.g. 4　Television is the transmission and reception of moving objects image by radio waves.
译文：电视通过无线电波发射和接收活动物体的图像。

e.g. 5　Farm tractors are big users of diesel power.
译文：农用拖拉机也大多以柴油机为动力。

2. 介词+名词(行为名词)

在此结构中，往往因行为名词的动作意义相对完整，与它同句中的其他部分之间存在着一定的逻辑关系，能起到时间状语、原因状语、条件状语和让步状语等作用，因此在翻译时可以用这种介词短语来代替各种状语从句。

e.g. 1　Before germination, the seed is watered.
译文：在发芽前给种子浇水。

e.g. 2　A soluble crystalline solid may be separated from a solution by evaporation.
译文：可溶性晶体可以通过蒸发从溶液中分离出来。

3. 名词+行为名词(介词短语)

此结构可以将宾语(介词宾语)转换成谓语。

e.g. 1　Rockets have found application for the exploration of the universe.
译文：火箭已经用来探索宇宙。

e.g. 2　Curved rails offer resistance to the movement of the train.
译文：弯曲的钢轨阻碍火车运行。

4. 与动词构成固定搭配

名词化结构与动词构成固定搭配的常用形式为：动词名词化结构/动词+介词名词化结构。这种搭配大量地以动词短语的形式出现，约定俗成。

e.g.　call attention to　　　　　　　注意
　　　draw a distinction between　　区分
　　　lay emphasis on　　　　　　　强调
　　　take possession of　　　　　　拥有

5. 行为名词+短语/从句

在此结构中，行为名词可以译成动词，与后面的成分一起构成汉语的动宾结构。

e.g.　　I have a doubt whether the news is true.
译文：我怀疑这消息的真实性。

6. 名词+名词(行为名词)

在此结构中，名词在表层结构上是前置定语，但在翻译过程中，其深层结构的内在含义可以译成动宾词组，行为名词转换成谓语。

e.g.　　power generation　　　　发电
　　　　hail prevention　　　　　防冰雹

1.5　句子的主要翻译方法

1.5.1　英汉句式比较及常见的翻译方法

翻译英语句子时，有时可以把原文的句子结构整个保存下来或只稍加改变即可，也就是通常所说的直译。

e.g. 1　Thus for a fixed signal power and in the presence of white Gaussian noise the channel capacity approaches an upper limit.
译文：因此，对于一定的信号功率，且存在白高斯噪声时，信道容量将趋近于上限值。

e.g. 2　The pulses are of the same form but have random amplitudes.
译文：这些脉冲形状相同，但幅度随机。

e.g. 3　Only by studying such cases of human intelligence with all the details and by comparing the results of exact investigation with the solutions of AI (Artificial Intelligence) usually given in the elementary books on computer science can a computer engineer acquire a thorough understanding of theory and method in AI, develop intelligent computer programs that work in a human-like way, and apply them to solving more complex and difficult problems that present computer can't.
译文：只有很详细地研究这些人类智能情况，并将实际研究得出的结果与基础计算机科学书上给出的人工智能结论相比较，计算机工程师才能彻底地了解人工智能的理论和方法，开发出具有人类智能的计算机程序，并将其用于解决目前计算机不能解决的更复杂和更难的问题。

e.g. 4　Moving around the nucleus are extremely tiny particles, called electrons, which revolve around the nucleus in much the same way as the nine planets do around the sun.
译文：围绕着原子核运动的是一些极其微小的粒子，称为电子，这些电子围绕着原子核旋转，正像九大行星围绕着太阳旋转一样。

e.g. 5　The development of industrial technology largely strengthens human physical capabilities, enabling people to harness more energy, process and shape materials more easily, travel faster, and so on, while the development of microelectronics extends mental capabilities, enabling electronic "intelligence" to be closely related to a wide range of products and processes.

译文：工业技术的发展大大增强了人的能力，使人们能更广泛地利用能源，更方便地对材料进行加工和成形，更快地旅行，等等；而微电子学的发展则增强了人的智力，使电子"智能"用于各种各样的产品和过程。

然而，由于英语和汉语的语法习惯不同，在多数情况下需要对原文中的句子进行调整。这里从以下几个方面进行说明。

1. 句子顺序的调整

e.g. 1　The presence or absence(or, alternatively, the sign) of pulses in a group of pulses is made to depend, in a some what arbitrary manner, on message samples.

译文：从属性的角度来说，每组脉冲中脉冲信号的存在或消失都取决于消息样本。

e.g. 2　Electronic amplifiers are used mainly to increase the voltage、current or power of a signal.

译文：电子放大器主要用于对信号的电压、电流及功率进行放大。

e.g. 3　A linear amplifier provides signal amplification with little or no distortion, so that the output is proportional to the input.

译文：线性放大器可以在失真很小或没有失真的情况下放大信号，这样输出信号就与输入信号成正比例变化。

e.g. 4　DPCM works well with data that is reasonably continuous and exhibits small gradual changes such as photographs with smooth tone transitions.

译文：DPCM 适用于比较连续且变化缓慢的数据，如经过平滑处理后的图片。

e.g. 5　This university has 6 newly-established faculties, namely Electronic Computer, High Energy Physics, Laser, Geo-physics, Remote Sensing and Genetic Engineering.

译文：这所大学现在有电子计算机、高能物理、激光、地球物理、遥感技术、基因工程 6 个新建的专业。

e.g. 6　The structure of an atom can be accurately described though we cannot see it.

译文：虽然我们看不见原子结构，但能准确地描述它。(被动句倒译成主动句)

e.g. 7　These data will be of some value in our research work.

译文：这些资料对于我们的研究工作有些价值。

e.g. 8　This wavelength division multiplexed operation, particularly with dense packing of the optical wavelengths (or, essentially, fine frequency spacing), offers the potential for a fiber information-carrying capacity which is many orders of magnitude in excess of that obtained using copper cables or a wideband radio system.

译文：应用波分复用(技术)，尤其是密集波分复用(或者说，实质上的精细频分复用)，使光纤的信息载容量能超过电缆或宽带无线系统好多个数量级。

e.g. 9　In particular, it has to be possible to provide extension telephone service on the same channel as it exists in homes today, to communicate between an ISDN telephone and a PSTN telephone, and to send data between an ISDN terminal, with its direct digital connection to the ISDN, and a terminal - modem combination communicating data through a PSTN voice channel.

译文：特别的是，目前家庭使用的同一个信道上提供扩展的电话业务，在 ISDN 电话和 PSTN 电话之间进行通信，在直接用数字连接的 ISDN 终端与通过 PSTN 语音信道进行数据通信的终端——调制解调器组合之间传达数据应该是可能的。

e.g. 10　On the other hand, the detained decomposition gas might become the cause of reducing the purity of the metal oxide coating adhered to the ribbon glass in the case the aforementioned decomposition gas is not thoroughly removed from the spraying locale.

译文：从另一方面来说，如果上面提到的分解气体在喷射处没有被彻底地清除掉，那么，留下来的分解气体就会使黏附在带状玻璃表面上的金属氧化膜的纯度降低。

e.g. 11　It may be economically sound, in the long run, to subsidize their initial production, even at prices above the projected marked for natural hydrocarbon fluids, in order to accelerate the deduction of dependence on oil imports.

译文：从长远的观点来看，资助开发气体等燃料，即使价格高于天然碳氢化合液的市场价格，但为了加快减少对进口石油的依赖，这在经济上可能还是合算的。

由以上的例句可以看到，英语的语法习惯与汉语有着明显的差别。在英语的表达中能够较为灵活地将原因放到结果之后进行表述，并且将做状语的介词短语放在句子中间，突出了句子的主题。而在译文中，可以看到汉语的语法表述，尤其在科技文章中是很讲究逻辑关系的。

2. 简单句译成复合句

e.g. 1　Operational amplifiers (op-amps), built with integrated circuits and consisting of DC-coupled, multistage, linear amplifiers are popular for audio amplifiers.

译文：运算放大器的内部结构是直流耦合的多级线性放大器组成的集成电路，该元件在音频放大器中经常用到。

e.g. 2　An integrated circuit consists of many circuit elements such as transistors and resistors fabricated on a single piece of silicon or other semi-conducting material.

译文：集成电路包含大量的电子元件，如晶体管和电阻，它们是被加工在一个硅晶体上或其他半导体材料上的。

e.g. 3　The signal handled by the amplifier becomes the visual information presented on the television screen, with the signal amplitude regulating the brightness of the spot forming the image on the screen.

译文：经过放大器处理后的信号就成为可视信息在电视屏幕上显示出来，图像每个像素的亮度由信号的幅度进行调整。

3. 复合句译成简单句

e.g. 1　For example, the largest early computers occupied a volume of hundreds of cubic meters and required many tens of kilowatts of electrical power and a sizable air conditioning installation to allow this amount of energy to be dissipated without raising the room temperature to unbearable values.

译文：例如，早期最大的计算机要占据数百立方米的空间，需要几十千瓦的电源和一个相当大的空调设备来消除大量的热,从而避免室温超过允许值。

e.g. 2　The resulting coded wideband speech not only sounds better than telephone bandwidth speech, but is also more intelligible for humans and works well with modern speech recognition system.

译文：得到的宽带编码语音不仅听起来比电话带宽的语音好,而且更清晰,适用于现代语音识别系统。

e.g. 3　The porous wall acts as a kind of seine for separating molecules.

译文：多孔壁的作用就像一把筛子,它把不同质量的分子分开。

e.g. 4　This body of knowledge is customarily divided for convenience of study into the classifications: mechanics, heat, light, electricity and sound.

译文：为便于研究起见,通常将这门学科分为力学、热学、光学、电学和声学。

e.g. 5　Crossbar switching was carried out by a special circuit called a marker, which provide common control of number entry and line selection for calls.

译文：纵横制交换由一个称为标志器的特定电路控制,标志器提供整个号码的公共控制并选择所有呼叫的路由。

e.g. 6　It will mediate human - machine interactions that are inseparable parts of many customer applications, and pull to get her the scattered resources, some belonging to the network and some not, to create communications sessions that might invoke a multiplicity of connections and computer applications.

译文：它将协调与客户应用密切相关的人机交互作用,并将分散的资源集中在一起。这些资源有些属于网络,有些则不是,这就可以建立进行多种连接和计算机应用的通信业务了。

e.g. 7　Computer simulation results show that, with an antenna spacing as low as 1m, a DF error of less than 1° can be obtained on a signal with a bandwidth of 100MHz at a received power level lower than -100dBm, using an integration time of a few milliseconds.

译文：计算机模拟结果表明,当天线间距短到 1m 时,可以在接收功率电平低于-100dBm 时,仅用几毫秒的积分时间,对带宽为 100MHz 的信号进行测量,其测量误差小于 1°。

1.5.2　一些英语特别句式的翻译

1. 被动语态的译法

由于专业英语的客观性,决定了其所用非人称的表达方式和常用句型为一般现在时时态及被动语态,这主要是因为不需要明确动作的执行者是谁,或者不必关心谁是动作的执行者。例如：Two problems are considered…一般不写成 We consider two problems…在阅读和翻译的过程中要将这类句子进行适当的转化。

e.g. 1　MATLAB is originally written to provide easy access to matrix software developed by the LINPACK and EISPACK projects.

译文：MATLAB 是为了方便使用由 LINPACK 和 EISPACK 项目组开发的矩阵软件而编写的。

e.g. 2　The signals which fall outside the channel bandwidth are attenuated by filters so that they will not interfere with other signals.

译文：滤波器将削弱信道带宽以外的信号，因此这些信号就不会干扰其他信号。

这里将原句的主语译为宾语。

e.g. 3　Computers may be classified as analog and digital.

译文：计算机可分为模拟计算机和数字计算机两种。

e.g. 4　The switching time of the new-type transistor is shortened three times.

译文：新型晶体管的开关时间(比原来)缩短了三分之二。(或缩短为原来的三分之一)

e.g. 5　This steel alloy is believed to be the best available here.

译文：人们认为这种合金钢是这里能提供的最好的合金钢。

e.g. 6　Attention must be paid to the working temperature of the machine.

译文：应当注意机器的工作温度。

e.g. 7　Today different measures are taken to prevent corrosion.

译文：今天，为预防腐蚀，人们采取了各种措施。

e.g. 8　Virtual leaks should be paid attention to.

译文：应该注意假性渗漏。

2. 句式为 It…结构

专业英语中的表达常用到非人称的语气和态度，尤其常见的句式为 It…结构。对于以 it 作为形式主语的句子而言，在译文中常要改成主动形式，有时需要加主语，有时则可加不确定主语，如"有人""大家""人们""我们"等。

e.g. 1　It can be shown that a system using a three-level code must have a signal-to-noise ratio of 8.5dB, or 3.7dB greater, for equal performance in the same channel.

译文：这表明对于相同的信道特性，使用三级编码的系统信噪比为 8.5 分贝，或高于 3.7 分贝。

e.g. 2　It is evident that a well lubricated bearing turns more easily than a dry one.

译文：显然，润滑好的轴承，比无润滑的轴承容易转动。

e.g. 3　It seems that these two branches of science are mutually dependent and interacting.

译文：看来这两个科学分支是相互依存、相互作用的。

e.g. 4　It has been proved that induced voltage causes a current to flow in opposition to the force producing it.

译文：已经证明，感应电压使电流的方向与产生电流的磁场力方向相反。

e.g. 5　It is thus essential for the carbonaceous materials to be decomposed and returned to the atmosphere in order for higher organisms to continue to thrive.

译文：因此，为了使高等生物能继续茁壮成长，含碳物质就必须分解并回归到大气中去。

另外，常见的这类表达方式还有以下几种。

It is hoped that…	希望
It is reported that…	据报道
It is said that…	据说
It must be admitted that…	必须承认

It must be pointed out that…	必须指出
It will be seen from this that…	由此可见
It is asserted that…	有人主张
It is believed that…	有人认为
It is well known that…	众所周知
It was told that…	有人曾说
It is generally considered that…	大家认为
It is evident that…	显然
It can be shown that…	这表明
It has been proved that…	已经证明
It seems that…	看来

3. 祈使语气

科技文献的又一个特点是较多地使用祈使语气，即所谓的公式化表达方式，这主要见于理论分析和算法推导中。

e.g. 1　Let the forward-path transfer function be given by the linear difference equation.

译文：设前向传递函数由下列线性差分方程给出。

e.g. 2　Consider the case of a linear, single-input single-output discrete system regulated by a discrete feedback controller.

译文：假设线性、单输入单输出离散系统的情况由一个离散反馈控制器来调节。

e.g. 3　Action: tranquilize anxiety and reinforce memory, nourish vigor and invigorate strength.

译文：功能：宁神益智、养心活血、滋补强身。

4. The more…, the more…结构的句型

e.g. 1　The faster the data is transmitted, the greater the bandwidth will need to be to accommodate it.

译文：数据传输速率越快，所需要的传输带宽越宽。

e.g. 2　The resistance being higher, the current in the circuit was lower.

译文：电阻越大，电路中通过的电流就越小。

5. 否定句的翻译

英语表达否定有全部否定、部分否定、双重否定，分别以不同的否定词进行表达。

全部否定词：not, never, not…nor 等。

部分否定词：not many, not much, not all, not every, not both, not some 等。

双重否定词：not, no, never, neither, nobody, nothing 等与其他具有否定意义的词搭配。

还有一些词本身并非not, un-, dis-等，但也同样具有较强的否定意义，如few, too…to, but for, instead of, rather than 等。

e.g. 1　Without electricity, a computer can not work.

译文：没有电，计算机就不能工作。

e.g. 2　Not all of these results are right.

译文：不是所有的结果都是正确的。

e.g. 3　Teletype, telex and facsimile transmission are all methods for transmitting text rather than sounds.

译文：电传打字机、电报、传真都是用来传送文字而不是声音的技术。

e.g. 4　We can not estimate the value of modern science enough.

译文：我们对现代科学的评价，无论如何估计，都是不过分的。

e.g. 5　Both instruments are not precision ones.

译文：这两台仪器并不都是精密仪器。

e.g. 6　All these various losses, great as they are, do not in any way contradict the law of conservation of energy.

译文：所有这些各种各样的损耗，尽管它们的数量很大，但都没有违反能量守恒定律。

e.g. 7　The increase in mass is not appreciable until the velocity approaches that of light and therefore it ordinarily escapes detection.

译文：直到速度接近光速时，才能觉察到质量的增加，因此，通常很难检测出质量的变化。

e.g. 8　Aside from the fact that electrons are too small to be seen, we would find it impossible to count them as they flowed by.

译文：且不谈电子小得看不见这一事实，当电子从旁边流过，也不可能数一数它们。

6. 倍数增减(包括比较)的汉译

科技英语中倍数增减句型究竟应当如何翻译，在我国翻译界中一直存在着争论，国内出版的一些语法书和工具书中所持的看法也不尽一致，因此影响了对这种句型的正确翻译。这个问题比较重要，数据上的一倍之差往往会造成不可估量的损失。

1) 倍数增加的译法

英语中说"增加了多少倍"，都是连基数也包括在内的，是表示增加后的结果；而在汉语里所谓"增加了多少倍"，则只表示纯粹增加的数量。所以英语中凡表示倍数增加的句型，汉译时都可译成"是……的几倍"或"比……增加了(n-1)倍"。

e.g. 1　The production of various stereo recorders has been increased four times as against 1977.

译文：各种立体声录音机的产量比1977年增加了3倍。

e.g. 2　The output of color television receivers increased by a factor of 3 last year.

译文：去年彩色电视接收机的产量增加了2倍。

2) 倍数比较的译法

(1) "n times + larger than +被比较对象"，表示其大小"为……的 n 倍"或"比……大(n-1)倍"。

e.g.　This thermal power plant is four times larger than that one.

译文：这个热电站比那个热电站大3倍。

(2) "n times + as + 原级 + as + 被比较对象",表示"是……的 n 倍"。

e.g.　Iron is almost three times as heavy as aluminium.

译文：铁的重量几乎是铝的 3 倍。

3) 倍数减少的译法

英语中一切表示倍数减少的句型，汉译时都要把它换成分数，而不能按照字面意义将其译成减少了多少倍。因为汉语是不用这种表达方式的，所以应当把它译成减少了几分之几，或减少到几分之几。人们所说的增减多少，指的都是差额，差额应当是以原来的数量为标准，而不能以减少后的数量做标准。英语表示倍数减少时，表达方式为："……+减少意义的谓语 + by a factor of n 或 by n times"。这种表达法的意思是"成 n 倍地减少"，即减少前的数量为减少后数量的 n 倍。

e.g. 1　The automatic assembly line can shorten the assembling period (by) ten times.

译文：自动装配线能够将装配时间缩短为原来的十分之一。

e.g. 2　This metal is three times as light as that one.

译文：这种金属比那种金属轻三分之二。

e.g. 3　The dosage for a child is sometimes twice less than that for an adult.

译文：小孩的剂量有时为成年人剂量的 1/3，或小孩的剂量有时比成年人的剂量少 2/3。

7. 隐含因果关系句的翻译

在科技英语中，表示因果关系的词和词组很多。最常见的有从属连词 because、并列连词 for、复合连词 in that、普通介词 from、短语介词 due to 等。这些表示因果关系的词或词组的意思一目了然，非常明显。而有些因果关系句并没有也不需要明确地表达出来，而是隐含在某些句型或结构中、词语里或上下文内，间接地表现出来。如果不能很好地识别、理解这类隐含的因果关系句，译出来的句子就会层次不清、意义不明、逻辑性不强、让人费解。

1) 隐含在并列句中的因果关系

在科技英语中，人们越来越多地使用并列句来表示原因和结果。这主要是因为在这种结构中有的在逻辑上存在着因果关系。可以是前因后果，也可以是前果后因。在译这样的并列句时，要把两个简单句合译为汉语的一个复合句，必要时可加上适当的表示因果关系的关联词。如"因为，所以"等。

e.g. 1　Aluminium is used as the engineering material for planes and spaceship and it is both light and tough.

译文：铝用作制造飞机和宇宙飞船的工程材料，因为铝质轻而且韧性好。(前果后因)

e.g. 2　Silicon does not occur in the free state in nature, and very few people have seen the pure substance.

译文：自然界中没有游离状态的硅，所以很少有人见过纯硅。(前因后果)

有时 and 之前用祈使句表示条件或假设，"祈使句+and"是科技英语中常见的一种特殊结构，用祈使句表示条件，而用 and 连接的陈述句表示由此得出的结果。此结构的句子在语法上是并列复合句，但在意义上却是主从复合句，这里的祈使句相当于 if 引出的条件状语从句，后用陈述句表示结果或推论。汉译时可按条件从句处理，译成："只要……就……"

"如果……就……"等。

e.g. 3　Wave your hand in front of your face, and you can feel the air moving.
译文：只要在自己面前挥动手，你就会感到空气在流动。

e.g. 4　Heat the test tube further, and a yellow gas will be seen to escape into the air.
译文：将试管进一步加热，就可以看到有一种黄色的气体逸到空气中。

2) 隐含在某些从句中的因果关系

(1) 在定语从句中。在科技英语中，有些定语从句跟主句之间的关系很复杂。有的定语从句(包括限制性和非限制性)对先行词限制修饰作用很弱，而起着状语的作用。这类定语从句中隐含着原因、结果等意义，如按其定语性质来对待，往往对原句的意思理解不清，引起费解。要仔细分析主句与从句之间的逻辑关系，把具有原因及结果职能的定语从句转换成适当的表示因果关系的状语从句译出，往往译成"由于……，所以……""因为""之所以……，是因为……"等。

e.g. 1　Electric wires are made of copper or some other metals, which have good conductivity.
译文：电线是由铜或某种其他金属制成。这些金属有较好的导电性能。

e.g. 2　Aluminium, which possesses high conductivity of heat and electricity, finds wide application in industry.
译文：由于铝具有高度的导热性和导电性，所以在工业上得到广泛应用。

(2) 在状语从句中。在科技英语中，从字面上看是时间、条件、比较、地点状语从句，但在逻辑意义上这些从句有时隐含着因果关系。因此，对这些状语从句的翻译需转换成一个表示因果关系的偏正结构。

e.g. 1　The more intense the ionization of a region is, the more the energy will be refracted.
译文：电离越强烈的空域，对射频能量的折射也越严重。(比较状语从句表因果关系)

e.g. 2　Why use copper when you can use aluminium？
译文：既然能用铝，为什么要用铜呢？(时间状语从句表示因果关系)

3) 隐含在某些结构或者句型中的因果关系

(1) "there being + 名词"。这是由 there be 句型构成的分词复合结构。名词是逻辑主语，位于逻辑谓语 being 之后，保留原来 there be 句型的倒装语序。这种复合结构隐含因果关系，译成汉语时常译成"因为""由于"等。

e.g. 1　There being no iron, people had to use stone for making tools.
译文：因为那时没有铁，人们只得用石头制造工具。

e.g. 2　There being a lot of problems to deal with, the scientists worked till midnight.
译文：由于有许多问题要研究，科学家们一直工作到午夜。

(2) "what with…and what with"。what 在这里是副词，相当于副词 partly(部分地)。副词 what 与表示原因意义的介词 with 组成习惯用语，用来引出两个并列的原因状语。译成汉语时常译成"一方面由于……，一方面由于……"或"因为……和……的缘故"。

e.g. 1　What with lack of raw materials and what with shortage of labour, they just managed to fulfil the production quota.
译文：一方面由于原料缺乏，一方面由于劳力不足，他们好不容易才完成了生产定额。

e.g. 2　What with the weather and what with the heavy load board, this ship was late in getting to port.

译文：因为天气不好和负载过重，船抵港迟了。

(3)"in that"。in 与 that 构成短语连词隐含着因果关系，在意义上相当于 because 或 since，连接状语从句。in that 所说的原因范围比较窄，着重指某一方面的原因，属于庄重的文体，多用于正式的论述中。译成汉语时常译成"因为""既然"。

e.g. 1　All of above changes are alike, in that they do not produce new substances.

译文：上述所有的反应都相同，因为它们都没有产生新的物质。

e.g. 2　In that silver is expensive, it can not be widely used as a conductor.

译文：由于银的成本很高，所以不可能广泛地用作导体。

(4)"inasmuch as"。这是一个短语连词，用来引导状语从句，其中就隐含有因果关系。其意义与 because 和 since 相同。但比较正式，现只用于书面语，所以在科技英语中能见到。译成汉语时常译成"因为""由于""既然"。

e.g. 1　Machining is not an economical method of producing a shape, inasmuch as good raw material is converted into scrap chips.

译文：机械加工不是一种经济的成形方法，因为它把宝贵的原材料变成了废屑。

e.g. 2　Inasmuch as the pressure increases with depth, there is a great pressure at the lower surface of the submerged body than at the upper surface.

译文：由于压力随深度的增加而增加，所以浸入水中的物体的底面所受到的压力比顶面大。

1.6　科技文体的翻译

1.6.1　文体浅说

科技英语的文体与普通英语和文学英语相比，既有共性也有差异。根据英国兰开斯特大学著名语言学家杰弗里·李切教授下的定义，文体是某个人在某种环境中为了某种目的而使用某种语言的方式。所以影响文体的因素是多方面的，或是地理环境的，或是社会背景的，或是讲话内容的，或是个人特点的，或是时间场合的。根据语言运用的范围，通常将其分为两大类：口语文体和书面文体。根据语言的基本功能可分为信息文体(包括科学专著、技术论文、商业文摘等)、寄情文体(包括诗歌、小说、戏剧、电影等)和鼓动文体(包括广告、标语口号等)。在理论和实践上，还有人提出了日常会话文体、广告文体、新闻报道文体、圣经文体、法律文体、科技文体；等等。语言学家埃弗林·海切在《话语与语言教育》一书中指出，从修辞结构来看，文体可分为叙事体、描述体、程序体和议论体；从语言使用场合来看，文体可分为正式书面体和信息交流体。

因此，要确定和划分一篇话语的文体往往是很艰难的。这不仅是门户之见的障碍，而且更重要的是因为这些文体都是互相渗透的。然而从大量的科技英语文献资料分析来看，科技英语作者运用语言的目的和风格主要体现在正式书面文体和信息交流文体上。

1.6.2 科技文体的特点及翻译要求

1. 科技英语的特点

科技英语(English for Science and Technology，EST)是从事科学技术活动时所使用的英语，是英语的一种变体。科技英语自 20 世纪 70 年代以来引起了人们的广泛关注，目前已发展成为一种重要的英语文体。本节所讨论的科技英语主要指描述、探讨自然科学各专业的著作、论文、实验报告、科技实用手段(如仪器、仪表、机械、工具等)的结构描述和操作说明等。

科技英语由于其内容、使用领域和语篇功能的特殊性，加之科技工作者长期以来的语言使用习惯，形成了自身的一些特点，使其在许多方面有别于日常英语、文学英语等语体。这些特点主要表现在词汇和句法两个层面上。

1) 大量使用名词化结构

《当代英语语法》(*A Grammar of Contemporary English*)在论述科技英语时提出，大量使用名词化结构(nominalization)是科技英语的特点之一。因为科技文体要求行文简洁、表达客观、内容确切、信息量大、强调存在的事实，而非某一行为。举例如下。

(1) Turing's other contributions to the world of AI came in the area of defining what constitutes intelligence.

译文：图灵的另一个在人工智能领域方面的贡献是定义智能的组成成分。

句中, of defining what constitutes intelligence 是名词化结构，一方面简化了同位语从句，另一方面强调了 area 这一事实。

(2) A modern method of producing complete, miniature circuits in quantity is to use paper-thin sheets of semiconductor material.

译文：大批量生产整体微型电路的一项新方法，就是采用薄如纸片的半导体材料。

名词化结构 A modern method of producing complete, miniature circuits in quantity 使复合句简化成简单句，而且使表达的概念更加确切严密。

(3) Television is the transmission and reception of images of moving objects by radio waves.

译文：电视通过无线电波发射和接收活动物体的图像。

名词化结构 the transmission and reception of images of moving objects by radio waves 强调客观事实，而谓语动词则着重其发射和接收的能力。

2) 广泛使用被动语句

根据英国利兹大学 John Swales 的统计，科技英语中的谓语至少三分之一是被动语态。这是因为科技文章侧重叙事推理，强调客观准确。第一、二人称使用过多，会造成主观臆断的印象。因此尽量使用第三人称叙述，采用被动语态。例如：Fibers can be used throughout the video distribution network, including the final link into the subscriber's home. 用光纤穿过视频分布网络，包括最终连到用户的家中；而很少说：We can use fibers throughout the video distribution network, including the final link into the subscriber's home. 我们能用光纤穿过视频分布网络，包括最终连到用户的家中。

此外，科技文章将主要信息前置，放在主语部分，这也是广泛使用被动语态的主要原因。试观察并比较下列短文的主语。

Electrical energy can be stored in two metal plates separated by an insulating medium. Such a device is called a capacitor, and its ability to store electrical energy capacitance is called condenser. It is measured in farads.

译文：电能可储存在由某绝缘介质隔开的两块金属极板内。这样的装置称为电容器，其储存电能的能力称为电容。电容的测量单位是法拉。

这一段短文中各句的主语分别为：Electrical energy，Such a device，Its ability to store electrical energy，It (Capacitance)。它们都包含了较多的信息，并且处于句首的位置，非常醒目。4个主语完全不同，避免了单调重复，前后连贯，自然流畅。足见被动结构可达到简洁客观之效。

3) 非限定动词

如前所述，科技文章要求行文简练、结构紧凑，为此，往往使用分词短语代替定语从句或状语从句；使用分词独立结构代替状语从句或并列分句；使用不定式短语代替各种从句；介词加动名词短语代替定语从句或状语从句。这样可缩短句子，又比较醒目。举例如下。

(1) A capacitor is a device consisting of two conductors separated by a non-conductor.

译文：电容器是由非导体隔开的两个导体组成的一种装置。

(2) Expressed in a formula, the relationship between voltage, current and resistance can be written as $V=IR$.

译文：若用公式表示的话，电压、电流、电阻之间的关系可写成 $V=IR$。

(3) This reduction of Boolean expressions eliminates unnecessary gates, thereby saving cost, space and weight.

译文：布尔表达式经过这样的简化之后，去掉了不必要的门电路，从而节省了成本，缩小了体积，减轻了重量。

(4) Almost all metals are good conductors, silver being the best.

译文：几乎所有的金属都是良导体，而银为最好。

(5) For a transistor to function normally, it is necessary to apply proper voltages to its electrodes.

译文：为了使晶体管正常工作，必须给其电极加上合适的电压。

(一般不写成 To make a transistor function normally…)

4) with 结构

所谓"with 结构"一般是指以下形式。

With + 名词(或代词) + 分词(短语)或介词短语或形容词(短语)或副词或不定式短语或名词(短语)等。举例如下。

Both practical design techniques and theoretical problems are covered with emphasis on general concepts.

译文：(本节)既讲了实际的设计方法，同时也讲了理论问题，而重点则放在一般概念上。

The discovery of quarks with a charge smaller than an electron charge will shake the foundation of modern physics.

译文：夸克带有的电荷小于一个电子的电荷的(这一)发现将动摇现代物理学的基础。

科技文体崇尚严谨周密，概念准确，逻辑性强，行文简练，重点突出，句式严整，少有变化，常用前置性陈述，即在句中将主要信息尽量前置，通过主语传递主要信息。详细来讲，如果科技英语是作为一种正式书面文体出现的话，在使用词汇方面，多数用的是科技专门术语，而且在普通词汇和半技术词汇方面都属于正式书面语体的范畴。科技英语的语法结构主要为一般现在时、被动句、非谓语动词、逻辑性定语、名词化结构、静态结构和各种类型的复合句(表示时间、原因、条件、让步等)。一般来说，科技英语句子较长而句型变化较少，关系代词 that、which 和非人称代词 it 的使用频率较高，这是因为在严谨的科技主体中，作者为了表达缜密的思想和客观的事实，必须增加限制性和扩展性的成分，所以需要借助于它们，从而使句子的平均长度增加，结构更复杂，客观性大大增强。科技英语的著述来不得半点虚假，一定不能带有作者个人的感情色彩。它主要应集中论述科学事实、解释科学现象、归纳科学概念和进行严密的逻辑推理。所以在科技英语中很少采用夸张、比喻、拟人、反语、幽默等文学修饰手法。

科技英语作为一种信息交流文体，以准确、简明、客观、新颖为主要特征。而这些特征的实现主要依靠科技英语中使用的普通词汇、半技术词汇和专业词汇。虽然普通词汇在科技英语中占绝大部分，半技术词汇也属于普通词汇，专业词汇在科技英语中仅占很小一部分，但决定了科技英语具有很高的正式程度和很强的信息功能。大多数专业词汇来自拉丁语和希腊语，其意义单一，用法稳定，一般只在特定的学科中出现。

总而言之，科技文体的特点是清晰、准确、精练、严密。那么，科技文章的语言结构特色在翻译过程中如何处理，是进行英汉科技翻译时需要探讨的问题。

2. 科技英语的翻译要求

要做好科技英语的翻译工作，译者必须注意以下几点。

(1) 了解相关专业知识。由于科技英语涉及自然科学的各个领域，因此译者应有较宽的知识面，尤其要具备翻译材料所属学科的一些基本的专业知识，为此，一般翻译工作者应努力学习各科知识，要勤于向书本和专家求教，不可不懂装懂或是想当然地乱译一通。

(2) 准确理解词义。首先，要注意那些常用词在特定学科中的特定含义，不可以常义代特定义，但同时也不应将所有的常用词全部作为专业或准专业词理解，这一点很重要，因为科技英语只是英语的一种文体，并非完全不同的另一种语言，其中的词汇大部分仍是共核词汇。科技翻译中不仅要勤查词典，还要结合一个词的上下文及所在的专业领域来确定其真实含义。其次，科学技术发展迅速，相应的新词不断出现，而翻译最新科技成果与信息又往往是翻译实践的主要内容，所以译者应随时关注相关领域的最新动态与发展，同时要勤于动手动脑，这样才能准确理解并再现那些新词的意义。

(3) 仔细分析长句。科技英语中有大量长句，这些长句中往往又含有若干分句和许多短语及其他修饰限定成分，这给理解带来了一定的困难。翻译时，首先必须对长句进行深入细致的分析，先厘清主干，再层层明确各成分之间的语法关系和语义逻辑关系，然后根据情况，选择顺译、逆译或综合译法。表达时，一定要将意义的准确性和明晰性放在首位，该断句就断句，该增译就增译，不可死抠原文形式。

(4) 用词要得体。总的来讲，科技英语语体较为正式，因此翻译时要尽可能选择与该文体相当的较为正式的词语，行文要向严谨规范的书面语靠拢。此外，原文因语篇内容与功能的不同(如科普文章与学术论文)而在语气的正式程度上也会有所不同，阅读对象的接受能力和文化层次也各异。因此，翻译时应先对原文的正式程度和译文的潜在读者进行一番分析，以求得译文和原文在文体和功能上最大限度地对等。对于学术性和专业性较强的语篇中正式程度高的语汇，译者一般也应将之译成正式程度相当的语汇，如原文正式程度偏低，则译文的语体也应相应降低。如将 pink eye 译为"红眼病"，将 the runs 译为"拉肚子"。如果一些专业性较强的词语出现在通俗性的语篇中，翻译时出于为读者着想也可适当降低其译文的正式程度。

(5) 熟悉构词法。熟悉构词法，特别是科技词汇的常见构词法，对于准确理解词义，特别是新词词义，有着非常重要的意义。

要注意的是，一种缩略形式可能是好几个不同词或词组的共同的缩略形成，翻译时必须依据上下文加以分析。

例如：APC，它可以是 American Power Conference (美国动力会议) 的缩写，也可以是 Adjustable Pressure Conveyor (调压输送机) 的缩写，还可以是 Automatic Phase Control (自动相位调整)或是 Automatic Program Control (自动程序控制)的缩写。

而 AC 在不同的语境中，则可有多达 28 个不同的意义，如：①absorption coefficient (吸收系数)，②adapter cable (适配电缆)，③adjustment calibration (调整—校准)，④air condenser (空气冷凝器，空气电容器)，⑤air conditioner (空调器)，⑥analog computer (模拟计算机)，等等。所以，翻译缩略词一定要搞清它是哪些词或词组的缩写，手头有一本英汉科技词典和缩略语大词典是很有必要的。

(6) 熟悉数量增减表达法。科技英语中表述数量增减的方式多种多样，译者稍不留神就会出错，所以不仅要小心谨慎，还要熟悉它们常用的表达方式。

(7) 注意术语的准确表达与翻译。术语翻译常被视为科技英语翻译的难中之难，这主要和译者的专业知识欠缺以及原文中新词多有关。因此，译者一定要不断拓宽自己的知识面，增加自己对所译材料涉及的专业知识的了解，准确理解原文的含义，并用妥帖的术语将其意义表达出来。

第 2 章 Application and Appreciation

Lesson One Digital Signal Processing & Modern Digital Design

Text A Introduction to Digital Signal Processing

1. What Is Digital Signal Processing

Digital Signal Processing (DSP), as the term suggests, is the processing of signals by digital means. A signal in this context can represent a number of different things. Historically the origins of signal processing are in electrical engineering, and a signal here means an electrical signal carried by a wire or telephone line, or perhaps by a radio wave. More generally, however, a signal is a stream of information representing anything from stock prices to data from a remote-sensing satellite. The term "digital" comes from "digit", meaning a number (you count with your fingers—your digits), so "digital" literally means numerical; the French word for digital is numerique. A digital signal consists of a stream of numbers, usually (but not necessarily) in binary form. The processing of a digital signal is done by performing numerical calculations.

Digital Signal Processing is one of the most powerful technologies that will shape science and engineering in the twenty-first century. Revolutionary changes have already been made in a broad range of fields: communications, medical imaging, radar & sonar, high fidelity music reproduction, and oil prospecting, to name just a few. Each of these areas has developed a deep DSP technology, with its own algorithms, mathematics, and specialized techniques. This combination of breath and depth makes it impossible for any individual to master all of the DSP technology that has been developed.[1] DSP education involves two tasks: learning general concepts that apply to the field as a whole, and learning specialized techniques for your particular area of interest.

2. Analog and Digital Signals

In many cases, the signal of interest is initially in the form of an analog electrical voltage or current, produced for example by a microphone or some other types of transducer. In some situations, such as the output from the readout system of a CD (compact disc) player, the data is already in digital form. An analog signal must be converted into digital form before DSP techniques can be applied. An analog electrical voltage signal, for example, can be digitized using an electronic circuit called an analog-to-digital converter or ADC. This device generates a digital output as a stream of binary numbers whose values represent the input electrical voltages at each sampling instant.

3. Signal Processing

Signals commonly need to be processed in a variety of ways. For example, the output signal from a transducer may well be contaminated with unwanted electrical "noise". The electrodes attached to a patient's chest when an ECG is taken measure tiny electrical voltage changes due to the activity of the heart and other muscles. The signal is often strongly affected by "mains pickup" due to electrical interference from the mains supply. Processing the signal using a filter circuit can remove or at least reduce the unwanted part of the signal. Increasingly nowadays, the filtering of signals to improve signal quality or to extract important information is done by DSP techniques rather than by analog electronics.

4. Development and Applications of DSP

The development of DSP dates from the 1960's with the use of mainframe digital computers for number-crunching applications such as the Fast Fourier Transform (FFT), which allows the frequency spectrum of a signal to be computed rapidly.[2] These techniques were not widely used at that time, because suitable computing equipment was generally available only in universities and other scientific research institutions.

Because computers were expensive at that time, DSP was limited to only a few critical applications. Pioneering efforts were made in four key areas: radar & sonar, where national security was at risk; oil exploration, where large amounts of money could be made; space exploration, where data are irreplaceable; medical imaging, where lives could be saved.

The personal computer revolution of the 1980s and 1990s caused DSP to explode with new applications. Rather than being motivated by military and government needs, DSP was suddenly driven by the commercial marketplace. Anyone who thought they could make money in the rapidly expanding field was suddenly a DSP vendor. DSP reached the public in such products as: mobile telephones, compact disc players, and electronic voice mail.

This technological revolution occurred from the top-down. In the early 1980s, DSP was taught as a graduate level course in electrical engineering. A decade later, DSP had become a standard part of the undergraduate curriculum. Today, DSP is a basic skill needed by scientists and engineers in many fields. As an analogy, DSP can be compared to a previous technological revolution: electronics. While still the realm of electrical engineering, nearly every scientist and engineer have the background in basic circuit design. Without it, they would be lost in the technological world.[3] DSP has the same future. DSP has revolutionized many areas in science and engineering. A few of these diverse applications are shown in Fig.1.

第 2 章 Application and Appreciation

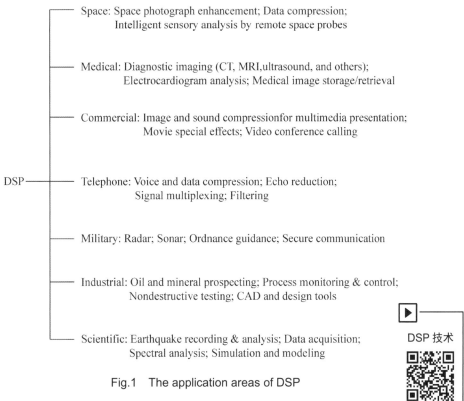

Fig.1 The application areas of DSP

5. Digital Signal Processors (DSPs)

The introduction of the microprocessor in the late 1970's and early 1980's made it possible for DSP techniques to be used in a much wider range of applications. However, general-purpose microprocessors such as the Intel x86 family are not ideally suited to the numerically-intensive requirements of DSP, and during the 1980's the increasing importance of DSP led several major electronics manufacturers (such as Texas Instruments, Analog Devices and Motorola) to develop Digital Signal Processor chips—specialized microprocessors with architectures designed specifically for the types of operations required in digital signal processing. (Note that the acronym DSP can variously mean Digital Signal Processing, the term used for a wide range of techniques for processing signals digitally, or Digital Signal Processor, a specialized type of microprocessor chip).[4] Like a general-purpose microprocessor, a DSP is a programmable device, with its own native instruction code. DSP chips are capable of carrying out millions of floating point operations per second, and like their better-known general-purpose cousins, faster and more powerful versions are continually being introduced. DSPs can also be embedded within complex "system-on-chip" devices, often containing both analog and digital circuitry.

Although some of the mathematical theory underlying DSP techniques, such as Fourier and Hilbert Transforms, digital filter design and signal compression, can be fairly complex, the numerical operations required actually to implement these techniques are very simple, consisting mainly of operations that could be done on a cheap four-function calculator. The architecture of a DSP chip is designed to carry out such operations incredibly fast, processing hundreds of millions of samples every second, to provide real-time performance: that is, the ability to process a signal "live" as it is sampled and then output the processed signal, for example to a loudspeaker or video display. All of the practical examples of DSP applications mentioned earlier, such as hard disc drives and mobile phones, demand real-time operation.

The major electronics manufacturers have invested heavily in DSP technology. Because they now find application in mass-market products, DSP chips account for a substantial proportion of the world market for electronic devices. Sales amount to billions of dollars annually, and seem likely to continue to increase rapidly.

6. The Depth of DSP

As you go through each application, note that DSP is very interdisciplinary, relying on the technical work in many adjacent fields. As Fig.2 suggests, the borders between DSP and other technical disciplines are not sharp and well defined, but rather fuzzy and overlapping. If you want to specialize in DSP, these are the allied areas you will also need to study, such as areas of science, engineering and mathematics.

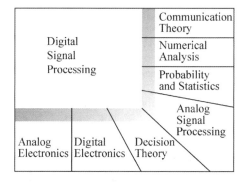

Fig.2   DSP has fuzzy and overlapping borders with other technical disciplines

7. Some Areas of DSP Affected

1) Telecommunications

DSP has revolutionized the telecommunications industry in many areas: signaling tone generation and detection, frequency band shifting, filtering to remove power line hum, etc. Three specific examples from the telephone network will be discussed here: multiplexing, compression, and echo control.

(1) Multiplexing.

There are approximately one billion telephones in the world. At the press of a few buttons, switching networks allow any one of these to be connected to any other in only a few seconds. The immensity of this task is mind boggling! Until the 1960s, a connection between two telephones required passing the analog voice signals through mechanical switches and amplifiers. One connection required one pair of wires. In comparison, DSP converts audio signals into a stream of serial digital data. Since bits can be easily intertwined and later separated, many telephone conversations can be transmitted on a single channel. This technology is called multiplexing.[5]

(2) Compression.

When a voice signal is digitized at 8000 samples/sec, most of the digital information is redundant. That is, the information carried by any one sample is largely duplicated by the neighboring samples.[6] Dozens of DSP algorithms have been developed to convert digitized voice signals into data streams that require fewer bits/sec. These are called data compression algorithms. Matching decompression algorithms are used to restore the signal to its original form. These algorithms vary in the amount of compression achieved and the resulting sound quality. In general, reducing the data rate from 64 kilobits/sec to 32 kilobits/sec results in no loss of sound quality.

(3) Echo control.

Echoes are a serious problem in long distance telephone connections. When you speak into a telephone, a signal representing your voice travels to the connecting receiver, where a portion of it returns as an echo. If the connection is within a few hundred miles, the elapsed time for receiving the echo is only a few milliseconds. The human ear is accustomed to hearing echoes with these small time delays, and the connection sounds quite normal. As the distance becomes larger, the echo becomes increasingly noticeable and irritating. The delay can be several hundred milliseconds for intercontinental communications, and is particularly objectionable. DSP attacks this type of problem by measuring the returned signal and generating an appropriate antisignal to cancel the offending echo. The same technique allows speakerphone users to hear and speak at the same time without fighting audio feedback (squealing).It can also be used to reduce environmental noise by canceling it with digitally generated anti-noise.

2) Audio Processing

The two principal human senses are vision and hearing. Correspondingly, much of DSP is related to image and audio processing. People listen to both music and speech. DSP has made evolutionary changes in both these areas.

(1) Music.

The path leading from the musician's microphone to the audiophile's speaker is remarkably long. Digital data representation is important to prevent the degradation commonly associated with analog storage and manipulation. This is very familiar to anyone who has compared the musical quality of cassette tapes with compact disks. In a typical scenario, a musical piece is recorded in a sound studio on multiple channels or tracks. In some cases, this even involves recording individual instruments and singers separately. This is done to give the sound engineer greater flexibility in creating the final product. The complex process of combining the individual tracks into a final product is called mix down. DSP can provide several important functions during mix down, including: filtering, signal addition and subtraction, signal editing, etc.

One of the most interesting DSP applications in music preparation is artificial reverberation. If the individual channels are simply added together, the resulting piece sounds frail and diluted, much as if the musicians were playing outdoors. This is because listeners are greatly influenced by the echo or reverberation content of the music, which is usually minimized in the sound studio. DSP allows artificial echoes and reverberation to be added during mix down to simulate various ideal listening environments. Echoes with delays of a few hundred milliseconds give the impression of cathedral like locations. Adding echoes with delays of 10~20 milliseconds provide the perception of more modest size listening rooms.

(2) Speech generation and recognition.

Speech generation and recognition are used to communicate between humans and machines. Rather than using your hands and eyes, you use your mouth and ears. This is very convenient when your hands and eyes are doing something else, such as: driving a car, performing surgery, or (unfortunately) firing your weapons at the enemy. Two approaches are used for computer generated speech: digital recording and vocal tract simulation.

The automated recognition of human speech is immensely more difficult than speech generation. DSP generally approaches the problem of voice recognition in two steps: feature extraction followed by feature matching. Each word in the incoming audio signal is isolated and then analyzed to identify the type of excitation and resonate frequencies. These parameters are then compared with previous examples of spoken words to identify the closest match. Often, these systems are limited to only a few hundred words; can only accept speech with distinct pauses between words; and must be retrained for each individual speaker.

8. Image Processing

Images are signals with special characteristics. First, they are a measure of a parameter over space (distance), while most signals are a measure of a parameter over time. Second, they contain a great deal of information. For example, more than 10 megabytes can be required to store one second of television video. This is more than a thousand times greater than for a similar length voice signal. Third, the final judge of quality is often a subjective human evaluation, rather than an objective criterion. These special characteristics have made image processing a distinct subgroup within DSP.

New Words and Expressions

historically	adv.	历史上，从历史的观点看
algorithm	n.	算法
sonar	n.	声呐，声波定位仪
analog	adj.	模拟的
transducer	n.	传感器，变频器，变换器
contaminate	vt.	污染
ECG=Electrocardiograph	abbr.	心电图
irreplaceable	adj.	不能代替的
acronym	n.	只取首字母的缩写词
Fourier Transform		傅里叶变换
incredibly	adv.	令人难以置信地
programmable	adj.	可编程的
interdisciplinary	adj.	各学科间的
multiplexing	n.	多路技术

amplifier	n.	放大器
decompression	n.	解压缩
digital recording		数字式录音
speech recognition		语音识别
feature extraction		特征抽取
reproduction	n.	再现，再生
prospecting	n.	采矿
digitize	vt.	数字化
electrode	n.	电极
noise	n.	噪声
mains supply		交流电源
electronic voice mail		语音邮件
Microprocessor	n.	微处理器
Hilbert Transform		希尔伯特变换
embed	vt.	使插入，使嵌入，深留，嵌入
redundant	adj.	多余的，冗余的
filtering	n.	滤波
data compression		数据压缩
artificial reverberation		人工混响
vocal tract simulation		声音模拟器
speech generation		语音产生
feature matching		特征匹配

Notes

1. Each of these areas has developed a deep DSP technology, with its own algorithms, mathematics, and specialized techniques. This combination of breath and depth makes it impossible for any one individual to master all of the DSP technology that has been developed.

译文：每个研究领域都在它自身算法、数学和特有的技术的基础上更深入地开发 DSP 技术，从而使 DSP 技术在广度和深度两个方面都得到拓展，因此，任何人都不可能单独掌握所有现存的 DSP 技术。

2. The development of digital signal processing dates from the 1960's with the use of mainframe digital computers for number-crunching applications such as the Fast Fourier Transform (FFT), which allows the frequency spectrum of a signal to be computed rapidly.

译文：数字信号处理技术源于 20 世纪 60 年代，彼时，大型计算机开始用于处理计算量较大的运算，例如，可以迅速获得信号频谱的快速傅里叶变换(FFT)等。

在本句中，The development of digital signal processing 是主语，dates from 是谓语，意思是起源于历史上的某一个年代。后面以 which 引导的定语从句用于修饰 FFT。

3. Without it, they would be lost in the technological world.

译文：没有基本的电路设计背景(经验)，他们将会被技术界淘汰。

it 是指前一句中的 the background in basic circuit design.

lost 的原意是丢失，这里意译为"淘汰"。

4. Note that the acronym DSP can variously mean Digital Signal Processing, the term used for a wide range of techniques for processing signals digitally, or Digital Signal Processor, a specialized type of microprocessor chip.

译文：需要注意的是，缩写 DSP 有多种含义，它既可以解释为"数字信号处理"，也可以解释为"数字信号处理器"，前者表示一种目前被广泛采用的数字信号处理技术，后者则表示一种专用的微处理器芯片。

5. In comparison, DSP converts audio signals into a stream of serial digital data. Since bits can be easily intertwined and later separated, many telephone conversations can be transmitted on a single channel. This technology is called multiplexing.

译文：比较而言，DSP 可以将音频信号转变为数据流。由于数字比特易于组合与分离，因此，多路电话信号可以通过一条信道实现传输。这种技术称为复用。

6. When a voice signal is digitized at 8000 samples/sec, most of the digital information is redundant. That is, the information carried by any one sample is largely duplicated by the neighboring samples.

译文：当对话音信号在 8000 次/秒的采样率基础上进行编码时，获得的数字信号大多存在冗余。也就是说，某一采样点的信息在很大程度上与其他采样点的信息重复。

Text B　Modern Digital Design

1. Overview

The speed of light is just too low. Commonplace, modern, volume-manufactured digital designs require control of timings down to the picosecond range. The amount of time that takes light from your nose to reach your eye is about 100 picoseconds (in 100 ps, light travels about 1.2 in.). This level of timing must not only be maintained at the silicon level, but also at the physically much larger level of the system board, such as a computer motherboard. These systems operate at high frequencies at which conductors no longer behave as simple wires, but instead exhibit high-frequency effects and behave as transmission lines that are used to transmit or receive electrical signals to or from neighboring components.[1] If these transmission lines are not handled properly, they can unintentionally ruin system timing. Digital design has acquired the complexity of the analog world and more. However, it has not always been this way. Digital technology is a remarkable story of technological evolution. It is a continuing story of paradigm shifts, industrial revolution, and rapid change that is unparalleled. Indeed, it is a common creed in marketing departments of technology companies that "by the time a market survey tells you the public wants something, it is already too late".

This rapid progress has created a roadblock to technological progress that this book will help solve. The problem is that modern digital designs require knowledge that has formerly not been needed. Because of this, many currently employed digital system designers do not have the knowledge required for modern high-speed designs. This fact leads to a surprisingly large amount of misinformation to propagate through engineering circles. Often, the concepts of high-speed design are perceived with a sort of mysticism. However, this problem has not come about because the required knowledge is unapproachable. In fact, many of the same concepts have been used for several decades in other disciplines of electrical engineering, such as radio-frequency design and microwave design. The problem is that most references on the necessary subjects are either too abstract to be immediately applicable to the digital designer, or they are too practical in nature to contain enough theory to fully understand the subject. This book will focus directly on the area of digital design and will explain the necessary concepts to understand and solve contemporary and future problems in a manner directly applicable by practicing engineers and/or students. It is worth noting that everything in this book has been applied to a successful modern design.

2. The Basics

As the reader undoubtedly knows, the basic idea in digital design is to communicate information with signals representing 1s or 0s. Typically this involves sending and receiving a series of trapezoidal shaped voltage signals such as shown in Fig.3 in which a high voltage is a 1 and a low voltage is a 0. The conductive paths carrying the digital signals are known as interconnects. The interconnect includes the entire electrical pathway from the chip sending a signal to the chip receiving the signal. This includes the chip packages, connectors, sockets, as well as a myriad of additional structures. A group of interconnects is referred to as a bus. The region of voltage where a digital receiver distinguishes between a high and a low voltage is known as the threshold region. Within this region, the receiver will either switch high or switch low. On the silicon, the actual switching voltages vary with temperature, supply voltage, silicon process, and other variables. From the system designers point of view, there are usually high and low voltage thresholds, known as Vih and Vil, associated with the receiving silicon, above which and below which a high or low value can be guaranteed to be received under all conditions.[2] Thus the designer must guarantee that the system can, under all conditions, deliver high voltages that do not, even briefly, fall below Vih, and low voltages that remain below Vil, in order to ensure the integrity of the data.

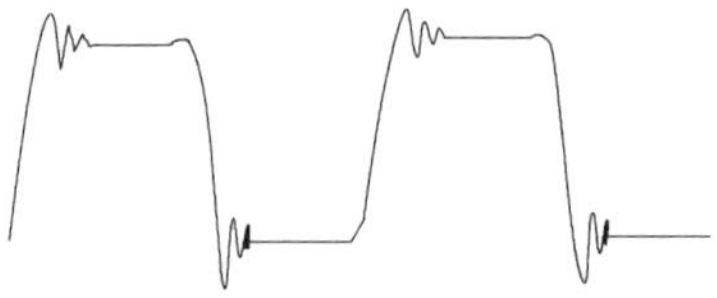

Fig.3 Digital waveform

In order to maximize the speed of operation of a digital system, the timing uncertainty of a transition through the threshold region must be minimized. This means that the rise or fall time of the digital signal must be as fast as possible. Ideally, an infinitely fast edge rate would be used, although there are many practical problems that prevent this. Realistically, edge rates of a few hundred picoseconds can be encountered. The reader can verify with Fourier analysis that the quicker the edge rate is, the higher the frequencies that will be found in the spectrum of the signal. Herein lies a clue to the difficulty. Every conductor has a capacitance, inductance, and frequency-dependent resistance. At a high enough frequency, none of these things is negligible. Thus a wire is no longer a wire but a distributed parasitic element that will have delay and a transient impedance profile that can cause distortions and glitches to manifest themselves on the waveform propagating from the driving chip to the receiving chip.[3] The wire is now an element that is coupled to everything around it, including power and ground structures and other traces. The signal is not contained entirely in the conductor itself but is a combination of all the local electric and magnetic fields around the conductor.[4] The signals on one interconnect will affect and be affected by the signals on another. Furthermore, at high frequencies, complex interactions occur between the different parts of the same interconnect, such as the packages, connectors and bends. All these high-speed effects tend to produce strange, distorted waveforms that will indeed give the designer a completely different view of high-speed logic signals. The physical and electrical attributes of every structure in the vicinity of the interconnect has a vital role in the simple task of guaranteeing proper signaling transitions through V_{ih} and V_{il} with the appropriate timings. These things also determine how much energy the system will radiate into space, which will lead to determining whether the system complies with governmental emission requirements. We will see in later chapters how to account for all these things. When a conductor must be considered as a distributed series of inductors and capacitors, it is known as a transmission line. In general, this must be done when the physical size of the circuit under consideration approaches the wavelength of the highest frequency of interest in the signal. In the digital realm, since edge rate pretty much determines the maximum frequency content, can compare rise and fall times to the size of the circuit instead, as shown in Fig.4. On a typical circuit board, a signal travels about half the speed of light (exact formulas will be in later chapters). Thus a 500 ps edge rate occupies about 3 in. in length on a circuit trace. Generally, any circuit length at least 1/10th of the edge rate must be considered as a transmission line.

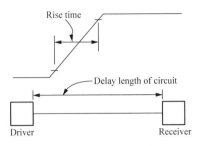

Fig.4　Rise time and circuit length

One of the most difficult aspects of high-speed design is the fact that there are a large number of codependent variables that affect the outcome of a digital design. Some of the variables are controllable and some force the designer to live with the random variation. One of the difficulties in high-speed design is how to handle the many variables, whether they are controllable or uncontrollable. Often simplifications can be made by neglecting or assuming values for variables, but this can lead to unknown failures down the road that will be impossible to "root cause" after the fact. As timing becomes more constrained, the simplifications of the past are rapidly dwindling in utility to the modern designer. This book will also show how to incorporate a large number of variables that would otherwise make the problem intractable. Without a methodology for handling the large amount of variables, a design ultimately resorts to guesswork no matter how much the designer physically understands the system. The final step of handling all the variables is often the most difficult part and the one most readily ignored by a designer. A designer crippled by an inability to handle large amounts of variables will ultimately resort to proving a few "point solutions" instead and hope that they plausibly represent all known conditions. While sometimes such methods are unavoidable, this can be a dangerous guessing game. Of course, a certain amount of guesswork is always present in a design, but the goal of the system designer should be to minimize uncertainty.

3. The Past and the Future

G.Moore, co-founder of Intel Corporation, predicted that the performance of computers will double every 18 months. History confirmed this insightful prediction. Remarkably, computer performance has doubled approximately every 1.5 years, along with substantial decreases in their price. One measure of relative processor performance is internal clock rates. Fig.5 shows several processors through history and their associated internal clock rates. By the time this is in print, even the fastest processors on this chart will likely be considered unimpressive. The point is that computer speeds are increasing exponentially. As core frequency increases, faster data rates will be demanded from the buses that feed information to the processor, as shown in Fig.6, leading to an interconnect timing budget that is decreasing exponentially. Decreased timing budgets mean that it is evermore important to properly account for any phenomenon that may increase the timing uncertainty of the digital waveform as it arrives at the receiver. This is the root cause of two inescapable obstacles that will continue to make digital system design difficult. The first obstacle is simply that the sheer amount of variables that must be accounted for in a digital design is increasing. As frequencies increase, new effects, which may have been negligible at slower speeds, start to become significant. Generally speaking, the complexity of a design increases exponentially with increasing variable count. The second obstacle is that the new effects, which could be ignored in designs of the past, must be modeled to a very high precision. Often these new models are required to be three-dimensional in nature, or require specialized analog techniques that fall outside the realms of the digital designer's discipline. The obstacles are perhaps more profound on the subsystems surrounding the processor since they evolve at a much slower rate, but still must support the increasing demands of the processor system increases.

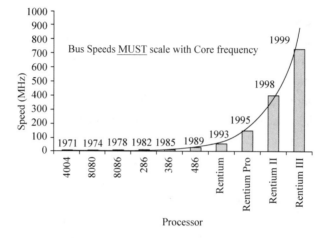

Fig.5　Moore's law in action

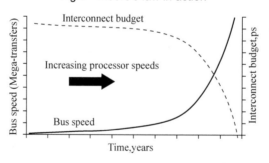

Fig.6　The interconnect budget shrinks as the performance and the frequency of the system increase

All of this leads to the present situation: There are new problems to solve. Engineers who can solve these problems will define the future. This book will equip the reader with the necessary practical understanding to contend with modern high-speed digital design and with enough theories to learn more beyond this book and solve problems that the authors have not yet encountered.

New Words and Expressions

commonplace　　　　　　　　*adj*.　　平常的，一般的

picosecond　　　　　　　　　*n*.　　皮秒，一万亿分之一秒(时间单位)

conductor	n.	导线，导体
transmission	n.	发射，发送，传输
unintentionally	adv.	无意地
roadblock	n.	障碍，障碍物
discipline	n.	纪律，学科
trapezoidal	adj.	梯形的
interconnect	vt.	互连(横向连接)
	n.	内连
socket	n.	插座(承窝，管套)
bus	n.	母线，总线
silicon process		硅过程，硅加工
realistically	adv.	实际地
herein	adv.	在这里
distributed	adj.	分布式的
transient	n.	瞬变现象，瞬态，暂态
delay	n.	延迟
glitch	n.	短时脉冲波形干扰；(俚)失灵，小故障
via	prep.	经过，经由；凭借，通过
transmission line		传输线，波导线
codependent	adj.	相互依赖的
controllable	adj.	可控制的
dwindle	v.	缩小
methodology	n.	方法学，方法论
resort	vi.	求助，诉诸，采取(某种手段等)
	n.	凭借，手段；常去之地，胜地
exponentially	adv.	指数地，幂数地
obstacle	n.	障碍，妨害物
precision	n.	精确，精密度，精度
volume-manufactured		大量制造的
motherboard	n.	母板
high-frequency effects		高频效应
ruin	n.	损坏(毁灭)
	vt.	破坏(毁灭)
mysticism	n.	神秘，神秘主义，谬论
contemporary	adj.	当代的，同时代的
conductive	adj.	传导的(导电的)
connector	n.	连接物(接线器，插头)
myriad	n.	无数，无数的人或物，<诗>一万

	adj.	无数的，一万的，各种的
threshold region		临界域
integrity	n.	完整性
encounter	v.	遇到(碰撞，遭遇)
negligible	adj.	可以忽略的，不予重视的
parasitic	adj.	寄生的
impedance	n.	阻抗
distortion	n.	失真
ground	n.	地，接地
vicinity	n.	邻近，附近，接近
realm	n.	领域
outcome	n.	结果
intractable	adj.	难处理的
guesswork	n.	臆测，猜测，凭猜测所作之工作
insightful	adj.	富有洞察力的，有深刻见解的
phenomenon	n.	现象
complexity	n.	复杂(性)，复杂的事物，复杂性

Notes

1. These systems operate at high frequencies at which conductors no longer behave as simple wires, but instead exhibit high-frequency effects and behave as transmission lines that are used to transmit or receive electrical signals to or from neighboring components.

译文：当系统工作于高频段时，导体不再是简单的导线，此时，导体将表现出高频特性，即具有传输线的功能和特性，该特性使得导体能与相邻器件之间实现信号的发送和接收。

2. From the system designer's point of view, there are usually high-and low-voltage thresholds, known as Vih and Vil, associated with the receiving silicon, above which and below which a high or low value can be guaranteed to be received under all conditions.

译文：从系统设计者的角度来说，高电压门限(Vih)和低电压门限(Vil)的取值与硅的品质有关，在任何条件下，高于 Vih 的值或低于 Vil 的值都可以保证被正确接收。

3. Every conductor has a capacitance, inductance, and frequency-dependent resistance. At a high enough frequency, none of these things is negligible. Thus a wire is no longer a wire but a distributed parasitic element that will have delay and a transient impedance profile that can cause distortions and glitches to manifest themselves on the waveform propagating from the driving chip to the receiving chip.

译文：每个导体都有电容和电感，它们的阻抗因频谱而变，当频率足够高时，必须要考虑这些因素的影响，此时，导线不再仅仅是简单的导线，而是分布参数元件，这样的元件会带来延时和瞬变阻抗，从而导致驱动芯片和接收芯片之间传输的波形发生畸变。

4. The signal is not contained entirely in the conductor itself but is a combination of all the local electric and magnetic fields around the conductor.

译文：信号不完全存在于导体本身，也在导体外产生磁场。

Exercises

Lesson Two AI and Its Applications

Text A   What Is Artificial Intelligence?

The term artificial intelligence stirs emotions. There is our fascination with intelligence, which seemingly imparts to us humans a special place among life forms. Questions arise such as "What is intelligence?" "How can one measure intelligence?" "How does the brain works?" All these questions are meaningful when trying to understand artificial intelligence. However, the central question for the engineer, especially for the computer scientist, is the question of the intelligent machine that behaves like a person, showing intelligent behavior[1].

The attribute artificial might awaken many different associations. It brings up fears of intelligent cyborgs. It recalls images from science fiction novels. It raises the question of whether our highest good, the soul, is something we should try to understand, model, or even reconstruct.

With such different offhand interpretations, it becomes difficult to define the term artificial intelligence or AI simply and robustly. Nevertheless, I would like to try, using examples and historical definitions, to characterize the field of AI. In 1955, McCarthy, one of the pioneers of AI, was the first person to define the term artificial intelligence, roughly as follows:

The goal of AI is to develop machines that behave as though they were intelligent.

To test this definition, the reader might imagine the following scenario. Fifteen or so small robotic vehicles are moving on an enclosed four by four meter surface squares. One can observe various behavior patterns. Some vehicles form small groups with relatively little movement. Others move peacefully through the space and gracefully avoid any collision. Still others appear to follow a leader. Aggressive behaviors are also observable. Is what are we seeing intelligent behavior?

According to McCarthy's definition the aforementioned robots can be described as intelligent. The psychologist Braitenberg has shown that this seemingly complex behavior can be produced by very simple electrical circuits. So called Braitenberg vehicles have two wheels, each of which is driven by an independent electric motor. The speed of each motor is influenced by a light sensor on the front of the vehicle as shown in Fig.1. The more light that hits the sensor, the faster the motor runs. Vehicle 1 in the left part of the figure, according to its configuration, moves away from a point light source. Vehicle 2 on the other part moves toward the light source. Further small modifications can create other behavior patterns, such that with these very simple vehicles we can realize the impressive behavior described above.

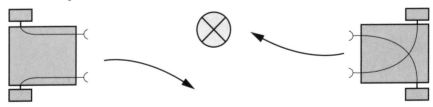

Fig.1   Two very simple Braitenberg vehicles and their reactions to a light source

Clearly the above definition is insufficient because AI has the goal of solving difficult practical problems which are surely too demanding for the Braitenberg vehicle. In the *Encyclopedia Britannica* one finds a definition that goes like:

AI is the ability of digital computers or controlled robots to solve problems that are normally associated with the higher intellectual processing capabilities of humans…

But this definition also has weaknesses. It would admit for example that a computer with large memory that can save a long text and retrieve it on demand displays intelligent capabilities, for memorization of long texts can certainly be considered as a higher intellectual processing capability of humans, as can for example the quick multiplication of two 20-digit numbers[2]. According to this definition, then, every computer is an AI system. This dilemma is solved elegantly by the following definition by Rich:

AI is the study of how to make computers do things at which, at the moment, people are better.

Rich, tersely and concisely, characterizes what AI researchers have been doing for the last 50 years. Even in the year 2050, this definition will be up to date.

Tasks such as the execution of many computations in a short amount of time are the strong points of digital computers. In this regard they outperform humans by many multiples. In many other areas, however, humans are far superior to machines. For instance, a person entering an unfamiliar room will recognize the surroundings within fractions of a second and, if necessary, just as swiftly make decisions and plan actions[3]. To date, this task is too demanding for autonomous robots. According to Rich's definition, this is therefore a task for AI. In fact, research on autonomous robots is an important, current theme in AI. Construction of chess computers, on the other hand, has lost relevance because they already play at or above the level of grand masters.

It would be dangerous, however, to conclude from Rich's definition that AI is only concerned with the pragmatic implementation of intelligent processes. Intelligent systems, in the sense of Rich's definition, cannot be built without a deep understanding of human reasoning and intelligent action in general, because of which neuroscience is of great importance to AI[4]. This also shows that the other cited definitions reflect important aspects of AI.

A particular strength of human intelligence is adaptability. We are capable of adjusting to various environmental conditions and change our behavior accordingly through learning. Precisely because our learning ability is so vastly superior to that of computers, machine learning is, according to Rich's definition, a central sub-field of AI.

1. Brain science and problem solving

Through research of intelligent system we can try to understand how the human brain works and then model or simulate it on the computer. Many ideas and principles in the field of neural networks stem from brain science with the related field of neuroscience.

A very different approach results from taking a goal-oriented line of action, starting from a problem and trying to find the most optimal solution. How humans solve the problem is treated as unimportant here. The method, in this approach, is secondary. First and foremost is the optimal intelligent solution to the problem. Rather than employing a fixed method (such as, for example, predicate logic) AI has as its constant goal the creation of intelligent agents for as many different tasks as possible. Because the tasks may be very different, it is unsurprising that the methods currently employed in AI are often also quite different. Similar to medicine, which encompasses many different, often life-saving diagnostic and therapy procedures, AI also offers a broad palette of effective solutions for widely varying applications. For mental inspiration, consider Fig.2. Just as in medicine, there is no universal method for all application areas of AI, rather a great number of possible solutions for the great number of various everyday problems, big and small.

Cognitive science is devoted to research into human thinking at a somewhat higher level. Similar to brain science, this field furnishes practical AI with many important ideas. On the other hand, algorithms and implementations lead to further important conclusions about how human reasoning functions. Thus, these three fields benefit from a fruitful interdisciplinary exchange. The subject of this book, however, is primarily problem-oriented AI as a subdiscipline of computer science.

Fig.2　A small sample of the solutions offered by AI

There are many interesting philosophical questions surrounding intelligence and artificial intelligence. We humans have consciousness, that is, we can think about ourselves and even ponder that we are able to think about ourselves. How does consciousness come to be? Many philosophers and neurologists now believe that the mind and consciousness are linked with matter, that is, with the brain. The question of whether machines could one day have a mind or consciousness could at some point in the future become relevant. The mind-body problem in particular concerns whether or not the mind is bound to the body. We will not discuss these questions here. The interested reader may consult and is invited, in the course of AI technology studies, to form a personal opinion about these questions.

2. The Turing test and chatterbots

Turing made a name for himself as an early pioneer of AI with his definition of an intelligent machine, in which the machine in question must pass the following test. The test person Alice sits in a locked room with two computer terminals. One terminal is connected to a machine, the other with a non-malicious person Bob. Alice can type questions into both terminals. She is given the task of deciding, after five minutes, which terminal belongs to the machine. The machine passes the test if it can trick Alice at least 30 percent of the time.

While the test is very interesting philosophically, for practical AI, which deals with problem solving, it is not a very relevant test. The reasons for this are similar to those mentioned above related to Braitenberg vehicles.

The AI pioneer and social critic Weizenbaum developed a program named Eliza, which is meant to answer a test subject's questions like a human psychologist. He was in fact able to demonstrate success in many cases. Supposedly his secretary often had long discussions with the program. Today in the internet there are many so-called chatterbots, some of whose initial responses are quite impressive. After a certain amount of time, however, their artificial nature becomes apparent. Some of these programs are actually capable of learning, while others possess extraordinary knowledge of various subjects, for example geography or software development. There are already commercial applications for chatterbots in online customer support and there may be others in the field of e-learning. It is conceivable that the learner and the e-learning system could communicate through a chatterbot. The reader may wish to compare several chatterbots and evaluate their intelligence in Exercise 1.1 on page 14. (Quoted from "Introduction to Artificial Intelligence")

New Words and Expressions

fascination	n.	魅力，魔力
attribute	n.	属性
association	n.	联想，协会
cyborg	n.	赛博格(音译)，改造人
interpretation	n.	解释

scenario	n.	脚本
collision	n.	碰撞
aforementioned	adj.	前述的
configuration	n.	组态，构造
intellectual	adj.	有才智的，理智的
pragmatic	adj.	实际的，务实的
neuroscience	n.	神经科学
precisely	adv.	恰恰，正好
neural	adj.	神经的
goal-oriented	adj.	目标导向性的
encompass	v.	围绕，包含
diagnostic	adj.	诊断的
interdisciplinary	adj.	跨学科的
philosophical	adj.	哲学的
consciousness	n.	意识
pioneer	n.	先驱
terminal	n.	终端
demonstrate	v.	演示，示范
chatterbot	n.	聊天机器人
evaluate	v.	评估

Notes

1. However, the central question for the engineer, especially for the computer scientist, is the question of the intelligent machine that behaves like a person, showing intelligent behavior.

译文：然而，对于工程师而言，尤其是对于计算机科学家而言，核心的问题是如何使智能机器表现得像一个人类，展现出智能化的行为。

2. It would admit for example that a computer with large memory that can save a long text and retrieve it on demand displays intelligent capabilities, for memorization of long texts can certainly be considered as a higher intellectual processing capability of humans, as can for example the quick multiplication of two 20-digit numbers.

译文：举例来说，一台具有大容量内存的计算机，既可以保存长文本并能按照需要进行检索，显示出其具有智能性，对长文本的记忆当然可以被认为是人类的一种更高的智能处理能力，例如快速倍增的两个20位数字。

3. For instance, a person entering an unfamiliar room will recognize the surroundings within fractions of a second, and if necessary, just as swiftly make decisions and plan actions.

译文：例如，一个人进入一个不熟悉的房间，可以在1秒钟内识别周围的环境，并且如果有必要的话，可以迅速做出决定和计划行动。

4. Intelligent systems, in the sense of Rich's definition, cannot be built without a deep understanding of human reasoning and intelligent action in general, because of which neuroscience is of great importance to AI.

译文：根据 Rich 的定义，如果没有对人类的推理和智能行为的深刻理解，智能系统就不可能建立起来，因为神经科学对人工智能来说非常重要。

Text B Smart City Artificial Intelligence Applications and Trends

Thanks to the relative ease with which local governments can now gather real time data, combined with the capabilities of AI, cities are realizing interesting new ways to run more efficiently and effectively.[1]

Improving cities is a pressing global need as the world's population grows and our species becomes rapidly more urbanized. In 1900 just 14 percent of people on earth lived in cities but by 2008 half the world's population lived in urban areas, and the rate continues to grow. There were just 83 cities on earth with more than 1 million residents in 1950, while as of last year there were 512 such cities. In the United States, 3.5 percent of the land now holds 62.7 percent of Americans.

This article will look at how governments and companies are using AI right now in cities. It will mainly focus on three major categories of applications:

① Helping officials learn more about how people use cities;
② Improving infrastructure and optimizing the use of these resources;
③ Improving public safety in cities.

We'll conclude with some of the future implications of these (above) smart city technologies and trends.

The first step in a city becoming a "smart city" is to collect more and better data. There is an old saying in the world of economic modeling: If you put garbage in, you get garbage out. If an organization doesn't start with good data, trying to make predictions about how new government policies will work can end up deeply flawed or even counterproductive. Helping cities gather and process data is one place AI is currently being put to use.

1. AI learns how people use cities

Cities have wealth of possible data sources, such as ticket sales on mass transit, local tax information, police reports, sensors on roads and local weather stations. One huge source of raw data that AI pattern recognition technology is making significantly more manageable are videos and photos. NVIDIA predicted that by 2020 there would be 1 billion cameras deployed on government property, infrastructure, and commercial buildings.

There is far more raw data than that could ever be viewed, processed, or analyzed by humans. This is why only a small fraction of cameras are ever actively monitored by people. This is where deep learning comes in. It can count vehicles and pedestrians. It can read license plates and recognize faces. It can track the speed and movements of millions of vehicles to establish patterns. It can process the huge volume of satellite data to count cars in a parking lot or track road use.

To help cities handle this torrent of video NVIDIA launched Metropolis, their intelligent video analytics platform. NVIDIA has over 50 AI city partner companies providing products and applications that use deep learning on GPUs.

Similarly, AT&T launched their Smart Cities framework in 2015 and formed alliances with Cisco, Deloitte, Ericsson, GE, IBM, Intel, and Qualcomm. Earlier in 2019 AT&T announced a deal to be the exclusive reseller of GE Current's intelligent sensor nodes for connecting cities — a significant deal since GE just announced it will provide San Diego with largest smart city Internet of Things (IoT) sensor platform.[2] There are a huge volume of applications of AI with IoT (some of which we've covered here on Tech Emergence), but few opportunities match the massive scale of smart cities.

GE is going to start by installing 3,200 CityIQ sensor nodes throughout the city and may expand that to over 6,000. The data can be used to identify parking spots for drivers, help first responders, and identify dangerous intersections.

A straightforward application of machine processing video for cities is license plate recognition (LPR), which is used in numerous ways. For example, since 2014 the City of Galveston has been using the company gtechna's Pay by Plate number parking system. Instead of traditional analog meters, people can pay by phone and LPR technology verifies who is parking legally.

The system did not require installing any new infrastructure at the city's historic Seawall, and it reduced deployment costs while preserving the area's aesthetic. The company claims in the first year the system produced $700,000 in new revenue and the city saw an 80 percent increase in collection rates.

Similar parking systems are in use in multiple cities and by large private institutions, which are almost mini cities unto themselves. Stanford University uses VIMOC Technologies' LPR system in its parking lots to quickly check if vehicles parked there have the right permits.

2. AI optimizing infrastructure for cities

A large amount of existing public infrastructure is underutilized, overused, or used inefficiently due to a lack of real time information among individuals, companies, and government agencies. Drivers don't know where parking is available, according to analysis by INRIX New York City drivers spend an average of 107 hours per year looking for parking. Passengers not knowing how long a bus will take have lower ridership than buses they can track. Cities for the most party don't know what the right length for a stop light at every given minute is. These are issues companies and government are addressing.

Anyone who has spent 10 minutes driving in circles in a city trying to find a parking space should be aware of this problem. It is a waste of your time, and circling around increases downtown traffic, wasting other people's time. It may seem like a minor inconvenience, but multiply that by millions of people each day in hundreds of cities, and it adds up to a significant waste of net resources.

Well-known companies are trying to address this issue from the individual's perspective. For example, Waze, acquired by Google back in 2013, used its network of drivers to provide real time data about traffic and accidents to help individuals optimize their routes. Cities are also trying to improve the situation from their end (we covered the specific AI use-case of Waze in our popular "Everyday Examples of AI" article earlier this year).

3. Smart parking garages

VIMOC is using AI to make parking easier in Redwood City. The company installed vehicle detection and reporting in two of the city's large parking garages. The amount of available parking is displayed outside the garages on large LED signs and shared with an open platform for use by App developers.[3] It provides the immediate benefit letting individuals know where parking is available, and in the long term, the wealth of data collected will allow the city to make planning and pricing decisions.

4. Adaptive signal control technology

Adaptive Signal Control Technology allows traffic lights to change their timing based on real time data. According to the Department of Transportation (DOT), "On average [Adaptive Signal Control Technology] improves travel time by more than 10 percent. In areas with particularly outdated signal timing, improvements can be 50 percent or more." Given that traffic congestion costs the country $87.2 billion in wasted fuel and productivity (according the the DOT), there is a strong reason why numerous cities and companies are deploying this technology around the country.

The benefits of this technology where it has already been deployed have been promising. For example, San Diego installed 12 Adaptive Traffic Systems along one of its busiest corridors in the autumn of 2018 and found they reduced travel time by as much as 25 percent and decreased the number of vehicle stops by up to 53 percent during rush hour periods.

Similarly, in 2012 the company Surtrac first deployed intelligent traffic signals at nine intersections in downtown Pittsburgh. It reduced travel times by more than 25 percent on average and wait times by 40 percent on average.

As a result of Surtrac has been expanded to 50 intersections in the city with more planned. Of course, these results come from the technology first being deployed on the busiest roads where it was assumed they would have the biggest impact.

This technology has been widely deployed and proven effective in the last few years in cities like San Antonio, Bellevue and in Los Angeles; but the use of it remains highly limited.

5. Connected public transit technology

This technology allows buses and trains to communicate with each other and the general public. Letting individuals know when buses or trains are coming and if they are going to run late makes them more useful to individuals.

The Massachusetts Bay Transportation Authority was the first agency to make bus locations and arrival-time predictions available, allowing developers to create tracking Apps. Research on the impact of real time information on bus ridership in New York City found that it increased weekday route-level ridership by 1.7 percent.

6. AI improving public safety

Smart cities aren't just about reducing commute times and saving fuel. The same networks of sensors and cameras are being used to save lives and fight crime.

The same LPR technology used to track parking is used by law enforcement to find stolen cars and track criminals. By 2014 LPR was already being used by an overwhelming majority of local law enforcement.

The same intelligent traffic lights normally used to improve traffic flow are utilized by ambulances and fire trucks to get to the scene of an emergency quicker and more safely.

Shotspotter, a company that automatically locates gunfire based on a sensor network, has its technology embedded in GE intelligent street lights. Shotspotter alerted law enforcement to 74,916 gunfire incidents in 2016. In its IPO it received aggregate proceeds of approximately $35.4 million.

The growing body of data gathered by cities is being mined to find out which intersections experience accidents, and importantly exactly how these accidents take place, to prevent them in the future. As part of the Vision Zero effort to eliminate all traffic fatalities, cities are turning to big data to plan and prioritize infrastructure projects. For example, Microsoft and DataKind have partnered with New York, Seattle and New Orleans to use data science to improve safety.

Highly connected cities also provide the ability to give individual hyper localized warnings about possible natural disaster. Doing its unique geography rainfall can vary significantly throughout the city of Seattle. To address this, they created RainWatch which combines radar data with a network of rainfall gauges to monitor rainfall with a high degree of resolution.[4] It allows city maintenance workers to respond more quickly to possible problems and provide more accurate flood warning to residents.

7. Concluding thoughts on AI for smart cities

The grand long-term vision of smart cities is full inter-connectivity: Self driving cars, trucks, and buses all talking with each other as well as with smart highways, traffic lights, and parking garages. The whole system will work together to move people around with an incredible degree of efficiency and safety. A highly connected system that will save lives, save time, and save fuel. A reality that will be made more possible as the federal government moves towards requiring vehicle-to-vehicle communication build into new vehicles in the coming years.

It is also to provide engineers and city planners with an incredible wealth of data that can be used to promote safety, health, and economic growth. Right now, researchers often rely on rough estimates of how people are using most roads and bike paths, but in future they could have access to a minute by minute breakdown of every block.

The important thing is that we don't need to see any new technology developed to see massive gains from cities becoming smarter. We have existing technology proven to be capable of improving parking utilization, safety, and significantly improving traffic. It just hasn't been widely deployed yet.

For example, less than 1 percent of traffic signals in the United States are smart, but the federal government, local governments and many large companies hope to change that.

As a result, the potential for growth for these systems and the companies that make them is significant. It is not surprising, then, that numerous large companies (Siemens, Microsoft, Hitachi, others) have put an increased focus on smart city technology.

Beyond the industries directly providing these services to local governments, the spending on smart cities could impact a range of businesses. Reduced traffic would mean cheaper shipping and technicians being able to spend more time at job sites and less time moving between them. Fewer accidents could result in lower insurance costs for everyone. (Quoted from https://www.techemergence.com/smart-city-artificial-intelligence-applications-trends/[2022-1-21])

8. Key tech policies from China's 20th Communist Party Congress——Push an innovation-driven development strategy

China has recorded major achievements in several core tech sectors and growth in cutting-edge areas such as human spaceflight, supercomputers, deep sea exploration, satellite navigation, quantum information, nuclear power technology, large aircraft manufacturing, and biomedicine.

China needs to improve its technology innovation system, creating an open innovation system with global competitiveness. China declared the establishment of a new innovation-driven development strategy, including conducting original, industry-leading scientific research and making China an attractive country for technological innovation as well as a talent center.

The country plans to implement a number of national major scientific and technological projects to enhance the capacity for independent innovation, with hopes of becoming a global innovation leader by 2035. It will also create a "positive environment" conducive to the growth of tech-based small and medium-sized enterprises.

Above all, innovation is at the "core" of China's modernization.

https://technode.com/2022/10/17/key-tech-policies-from-chinas-20th-communist-party-congress/.[2023-06-04].

New Words and Expressions

capability	n.	能力
implication	n.	启示，意义
counterproductive	adj.	适得其反
infrastructure	n.	基础设施
pedestrian	n.	行人
alliance	n.	联盟
Internet of Things (IoT)		物联网
License Plate Recognition (LPR)		车牌识别
deployment	n.	部署
aesthetic	n.	美学，审美
Department of Transportation (DOT)		交通部
Adaptive Signal Control Technology		自适应信号控制技术

Notes

1. Thanks to the relative ease with which local governments can now gather real time data, combined with the capabilities of AI, cities are realizing interesting new ways to run more efficiently and effectively.

译文：由于地方政府现在可以相对容易地收集到实时数据，结合着人工智能的能力，城市正在以一些有趣的新方式更加高速有效地运行。

2. Earlier in 2019 AT&T announced a deal to be the exclusive reseller of GE Current's intelligent sensor nodes for connecting cities — a significant deal since GE just announced it will provide San Diego with largest smart city Internet of Things (IoT) sensor platform.

译文：2019年年初，AT&T宣布成为GE Current的智能传感器节点连接城市的独家经销商——这是在GE刚刚宣布将为圣地亚哥提供最大的智能城市物联网(IoT)传感器平台后的一个重大交易。

人工神经网络

3. The amount of available parking is displayed outside the garages on large LED signs and shared with an open platform for use by App developers.

译文：可供使用的停车位的数量显示在车库外的大型LED指示牌上，并提供一个开放平台，为应用程序开发人员共享使用。

4. To address this, they created Rain Watch which combines radar data with a network of rainfall gauges to monitor rainfall with a high degree of resolution.

译文：为了解决这个问题，他们开发了 Rain Watch，它可以将雷达数据与降雨量测量网络相结合，以高分辨率监测降雨量。

Lesson Three Optoelectronic Technology and Its Circuit

Text A   Introduction to Optoelectronics

Optoelectronics is the interaction between optics and circuitry. Throughout my life I have been exposed to applications which require these two mediums to communicate with each other, yet never really understood how it was accomplished. I was aware that a signal was sent and a receiver in turn gathered data, but how? What physical properties allowed the circuitry to interpret the data?

The connection between optics and electronics will be discussed along with the applications brought about by them. Several applications for optoelectronics use a few basic principles which are well founded in electronics. The first section will review some of the characteristics electrical devices have which enable them to distinguish between different lighting conditions. The second section will discuss commonly used interactions between optics and the digital medium. In the last section the common interfaces in optoelectronics are used in applications.

1. An introduction of sending and receiving

The sending and receiving ends of an electronic device make up the majority of an optoelectronic system. The sending end can be any light source depending on the application. An electronic device like a light emitting diode (LED), a non-electronic device like a lantern, or a natural source like the sun can be used as the light source for a receiving device. Of the mentioned devices the LED is used in several applications, because the device can be turned off and on numerous times but will consume a small amount of current and require little voltage.[1] Further explanation of sources will be given within specific applications later on. The receiving device is a temperature sensitive electronic device. When light reaches an electric device, the temperature in the device may change which can affect the circuit the device is within. In other words, the change in temperature on a device can be used to trigger reactions in a circuit. In addition, different devices have different sensitivities to light which can be used to isolate and distinguish what light is sensed by the detector. A company selling a device will state the range of the wavelength or frequency range that the device will send or detect.

2. What electrical devices are used for detection and why

Of the receiving devices resistors, diodes, and transistors are some of the most commonly used. A Light Dependent Resistor (LDR), shown in Fig.1, is often used to sense the general change in light over a few seconds. When light hits a resistor made of Cadmium Sulphide (CdS) or another highly light sensitive material, the resistance is greatly reduced thereby changing the state of the circuit it is in.[2] The presence of a diode and a phototransistor within a circuit are also greatly diminished when they are hit by light. A diode has a far greater response time then a resistor but is in turn far more sensitive to light. Increased sensitivity to light increases the likelihood of interference from an undesirable light source. In turn a transistor has a faster response time to light than a diode, but again is far more susceptible to stray light interfering. In order to increase the effectiveness of a transistor a phototransistor is used. A phototransistor is a regular transistor with a larger base that is exposed. For an additional increase in speed a Darlington phototransistor can be used to increase the reaction time by a factor of ten.

Fig.1　LDR

Traditionally resistors, diodes, and transistors built with silicon have always been susceptible to heat. In order to solve the problem integrated circuit devices are shielded to reduce the effects of heat and other elements. As a result photo-resistors, photodiodes, and phototransistors are basically traditional Integrated Circuit (IC) devices with packaging designed to capture light instead of fend it off.[3] The following diagram, Fig.2 shows the objects and symbols of photodetector.

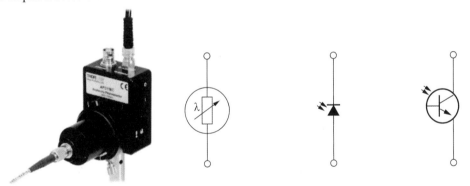

Fig.2　The objects and symbols of photodetector

3. Basic interaction between optics and electronics

There are a few powerful combinations of optics and electronics which serve several applications. Each of these principles will be introduced in this section and then explained within a few common applications later on.

1) Reducing stray light & increasing the power of detection

One of the most common sending devices is a diode, yet diodes emit light in a number of directions. In order to direct the light emitted from the LED a black cylindrical object called a light shield is used. The receiving end of an optical system can also reduce the impact of stray light by using a light shield. Adding a lens within the light shield will focus the light onto the photodetector. The following figure (Fig.3) displays a light shield around a phototransistor.

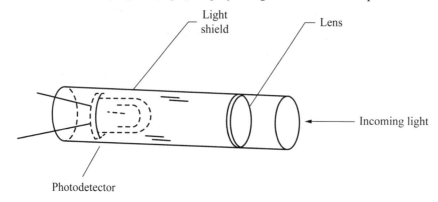

Fig.3   Light collimator

Another common sending device is a laser diode. A laser diode charges its P and N layers to create light which is then bounced between the two surfaces until it exits the device in a waveform. The following figure (Fig.4) displays the physical and principle of a semiconductor laser diode.

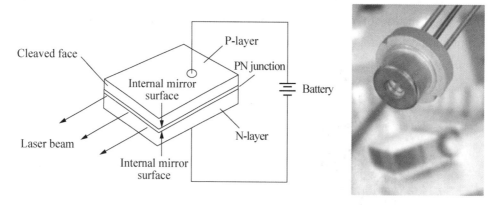

Fig.4   The physical and principle of a semiconductor laser diode

2) Light beam system

A light beam system has one or more sets of sensors and detectors used to set up an array or arrays of light. The detector is constantly polling light originating from the sensor for a break in the system. When a break occurs, the circuit the detector is in does something. Light-beam systems are commonly used in security systems and assembly lines in factories.

There are an infinite number of ways the light can travel between the sending and receiving end of the system. The sensor and detector can be facing each other as they often do in factors or mirrors can be used to bounce the light around before it enters the sensor to increase the area beams cover. Note the more a beam is bounced around the slower the detection time. If lenses are added to the system the response time will be even slower. Remember if the system needs to react faster, there may be sensors which take less time to react, but in turn will be more sensitive to light. When additional sensors and detectors are added, redundancy can be added into the circuit to require multiple light rays to be tripped before something happens. A dual light beam system as seen in Fig.5 can be used to deter false alarms.

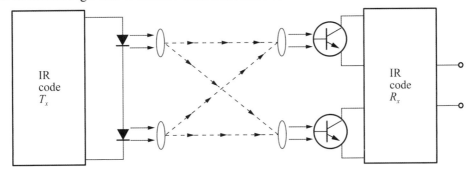

Fig.5 Dual light beam system

3) Optocouplers

The optocoupler is used in numerous devices as a means of one digital device talking to another. In short, an optocoupler is a sensor and receiver in close proximity to each other within an enclosed environment. This allows the sender and receiver to communicate with each other without interference. Optocouplers are commonly used when two devices need to communicate, but most not transfer any voltage, current, or other properties from one circuit to the next.[4] The physical and principle of optocoupler are shown in Fig.6.

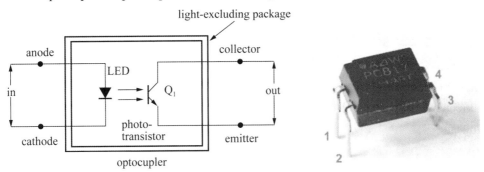

Fig.6 The physical principle of optocoupler

Optocouplers can include several senders and receivers, but there is a limitation on the voltage for parallel components.

4) Optical film strip switch

This device is an optocoupler with an object between the sensor and detector. When the object is removed, a connection between the sensor and the connector is made. The main application to an optical film strip switch is an alarm system for windows, door, and other objects requiring one object to be moved always from another. The following diagram (Fig.7) is an optical film strip switch.

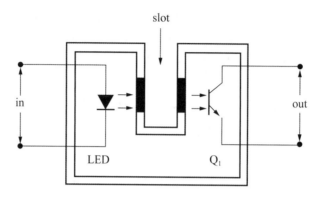

Fig.7 Optical film strip switch

5) Light from a natural source and detectors

Detectors can be used to determine natural light and heat. A series of sensitive detectors designed to receive different wavelengths can be used to sense what light is coming in based on frequencies. In turn a series of detectors can determine how cold or hot a room is using highly temperature sensitive sensors. Another method to gauging light and heat is to have one highly sensitive detector and have different responses to various voltage levels near the circuit. (Quoted from "Introduction to Optoelectronics")

New Words and Expressions

optoelectronics	n.	光电子学
optics	n.	光学
physical property		物理性质
electronics	n.	电子学
Light Emitting Diode (LED)		发光二极管
current	n.	电流
voltage	n.	电压
trigger	v.	触发
isolate	v.	隔离,绝缘
detector	n.	探测器
wavelength	n.	波长
resistor	n.	电阻器
diode	n.	二极管
transistor	n.	晶体管
Light Dependent Resistor(LDR)		光敏电阻
Cadmium sulfide (CdS)		硫化镉
phototransistor	n.	光电晶体管
silicon	n.	硅
Integrated Circuit (IC)		集成电路

| light beam system | | 光束系统 |
| optocoupler | n. | 光电耦合器 |

Notes

1. Of the mentioned devices the LED is used in several applications, because the device can be turned off and on numerous times but will consume a small amount of current and require little voltage.

译文：在上述被提及的器件中，LED可以用于多种应用中，因为该器件能开合无数次，并且仅仅消耗少量的电流，需要的电压也很小。

2. When light hits a resistor made of Cadmium Sulphide (CdS) or another highly light sensitive material, the resistance is greatly reduced thereby changing the state of the circuit it is in.

译文：由硫化镉或其他光敏度高的材料所制成的电阻器在被光线照射时，电阻会大大降低，其所处电路的状态也会因此发生改变。

3. As a result photo-resistors, photodiodes, and phototransistors are basically traditional Integrated Circuit (IC) devices with packaging designed to capture light instead of fend it off.

译文：因此，光敏电阻，光电二极管和光电晶体管都是传统的集成电路器件，封装的目的在于捕获光线而不是抵挡光线。

4. Optocouplers are commonly used when two devices need to communicate, but most not transfer any voltage, current, or other properties from one circuit to the next.

译文：光耦合器通常用于两个设备需要进行通信时，但大多数不会从一个电路向下一个电路传递电压、电流或者其他属性。

Text B Optoelectronic Devices &Their Applications

Optoelectronic is an interesting branch of electronics that combines electronics and optics. Optoelectronic devices find varied applications in telecommunications, military services, medical field, and automatic control systems. Let's check out how they work.

Light is emitted from a material when it is stimulated by the incident energy. If the energy is in the form of photons, photoluminescence is produced. Optoelectronic devices produce electrical energy when exposed to incident light energy. They utilize energy in the visible and infrared regions of the electromagnetic spectrum.

Solid-state devices like sensors, IR emitters, and laser emitters are used for optoelectronic applications. Optoelectronic devices can be classified into photoconductive and photovoltaic devices.

Photoconductive devices such as photo resistors are widely used in counting systems, twilight switches, house security systems, etc. These detect variations in the light intensities and activate or deactivate electronic circuits. Photodiodes and phototransistors also fall in this category. These utilize the reverse biased junctions for generating current when illuminated.

Photovoltaic devices produce a voltage when these are exposed to light. The light energy produces a potential difference across the p-n junction depending on the intensity of the incident light. Solar cells and photovoltaic cells are widely used in various applications to generate electricity.

1. The p-n junction as a voltage source

The controlled diffusion of impurities into such materials as germanium and silicon produces semiconductors. The process of introducing impurities into a pure semiconductor material is known as "doping" Phosphorous, arsenic, boron, and aluminium are some of the materials used as impurities for doping. By means of sophisticated processes, it is possible to produce p-type and n-type junctions within the same slice of silicon or germanium. The resulting junction is called p-n junction. Within the p-n junction there is movement of electrons and holes (as shown in Fig.8).

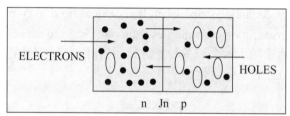

Fig.8 Diffusion of electrons and holes across the p-n junction

From the n-region electrons diffuse across the junction into the p-region and combine with the holes present in p-type material. Similarly, some of the holes present in the p-type material move across the junction to the n-region and combine with the electrons present in the n-region. The process continues and creates a region on either side of the junction with no free charges. This region is known as "depletion layer" (referred by Fig.9). The continuous movement of electrons and holes results in an equilibrium, with the p-region acquiring a small negative charge and the n-region acquiring a small positive charge.[1] This creates a small potential across the p-n junction equivalent to a small voltage.

When an external voltage having a polarity opposite to that of the p-n junction is applied to the p-n junction, it effectively negates the internal potential difference and reduces the width of the depletion layer. As the external voltage is increased, the depletion layer becomes zero, and this causes easy diffusion of charge carriers across the junction. Electrons move from n-region to p-region and the junction is forward biased (referred by Fig.10). A large of current flows from the p-region (anode) to the n-region (cathode). If the external potential has the same polarity as that of the junction, no current flows, as the depletion layer widens and inhibits the flow of charge carriers.

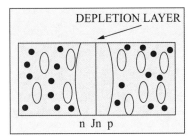

Fig.9   Depletion layer with no free charges on either side of the junction

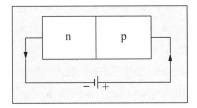

Fig.10   Forward biased p-n junction

2. Photovoltaic cells

Photoelectric transducers generate electric current when exposed to light. A photovoltaic cell consists of many p-n junctions connected in series. One of the junctions is very thin, so light can easily pass through it. When light passes, charge carriers such as holes and electrons are produced proportional to the incident light. Photovoltaic cells are used in various applications to generate electricity where mains power is not available. Examples include solar cells (referred by Fig.11) and solar batteries, which are used in satellites.

The solar energy incident on the p-n junction of the solar cell collides with the valence electrons. This causes the formation of electron-hole pairs, which cross the p-n junction in an opposing manner and create a voltage across the p-n junction. The voltage generated per cell is approximately 0.6V. Large arrays of solar cells are used in series and parallel combinations to produce a large of voltage.

3. Photoconductive cells

Photoconductive cells use a semiconductor material whose electrical conductivity varies with the intensity of the incident light. Light Dependent Resistors (LDRs) (referred by Fig.12) are typical photoconductive cells. When light falls on the semiconductor material, its conductivity increases. Normally, Cadmium Sulphide (CdS) is used in LDRs and their resistance depends on the intensity of light. CdS cells have a sensitive area that contains small amounts of silver, antimony, or indium impurities. The electron-hole pairs produced by the incident light increase its conductivity and cause increase in current flow. Besides CdS, lead sulphide or cadmium selenide are also used in photoconductive cells.

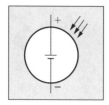
Fig.11 Solar cell

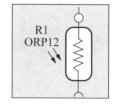
Fig.12 Light dependent resistor

In absolute darkness the resistance of an LDR is a few mega-ohms, while it reduces to as low as a few ohms when fully illuminated. The LDR is made up of a thin film of semiconductor material enclosed in a transparent case. The glass window permits entry of light into the semiconductor. Primary advantages of CdS are their high dissipation capacity, excellent sensitivity in the visible spectrum, low resistance in light, etc.[2] It can handle many watts, so a relay can be directly operated using an LDR. LDRs are used as switching devices in the presence or absence of light. Counters, twilight switches, camera control systems etc. utilize this property of LDR.

4. Photodiodes

Photodiodes (Fig.13) are high-impedance devices that are usually reverse biased for improved performance. These are high-speed sensors which generate a tiny current (in μA) proportional to the amount of incident light. The photodiode consists of a relatively large silicon p-n junction, which is illuminated by the incident light. Light photons impinging on the junction have sufficient energy to rupture a number of covalent bonds in the junction, thereby producing electron-hole pairs. This causes the flow of current in the diodes. As the illumination increases, additional electron-hole pairs are released and the diode current increases.

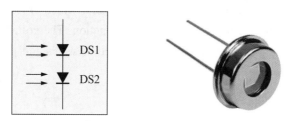
Fig.13 Photodiode

5. Phototransistor

Phototransistors employ the principle of photodiodes, but the amplifying action of the transistor makes these devices more sensitive. Phototransistors are duo diodes having two junctions in the same device separated by a wide base region, thus forming an n-p-n junction (Fig.14).

第 2 章　　**Application and Appreciation**

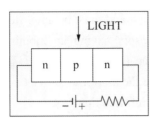

Fig.14　The working principle and object of the phototransistor

The n-p junction is slightly forward biased and the p-n junction is reversed biased. Light energy striking the n-p junction liberates electron-hole pairs. The released electrons diffuse out of the p-region towards the junction. The holes, however, are trapped in the p-region and form a positive surface charge. This causes an increase in forward bias of n-p junction, increasing the current flow. Phototransistor is usually connected in common-emitter configuration with an open base. Photons are focused to the junction through a lens system. Only two leads (collector and emitter) of the phototransistor are usually used in circuit connections. The base current is created by the photons falling on the base-collector junction. The current in the phototransistor depends on the intensity of incident light and is less affected by the voltage in the circuit. Darlington n-p-n phototransistors are widely used in light-detection devices, light-operated systems, counters, and house security systems.

6. Infrared diodes

Infrared (IR) diodes are photodiodes that emit a beam of infrared light when their p-n junction is forward biased. The p-n junction in IR diodes (Fig.15) is made up of gallium arsenide. The p-n junction consists of a recombination region between p-type and n-type materials. When a potential difference is applied between the anode and the cathode of the IR diode, the p-n junction is energised and electrons move from the n-region and combine with the holes present in the p-region.[3] The recombination of electrons and holes takes place in the recombination region. The recombination restores the equilibrium of the p-n junction, leading to the emission of photons in the form of infrared rays. These rays have a wavelength of 900 nm. IR diodes are used in TV remotes, remote switching burglar alarms, etc.

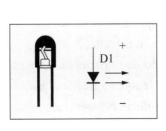

Fig.15　IR diode

7. IR sensor modules

The photo current from a photodiode is very small and must be amplified for activating the circuit. IR sensors (Fig.16) are high-efficiency sensors having an inbuilt phototransistor or photodiode and a transistor amplifier consisting of an n-p-n transistor or FET. These are 3-pin light-to-voltage converters with provision to improve the amplifier's offset voltage stability. The output voltage is directly proportional to the incident infrared light.

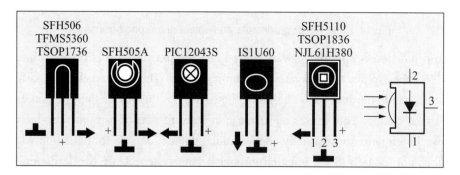

Fig.16　IR sensors

IR sensors simplify the circuit design as these require no external component for amplifying the signal. Some of these produce digital outputs. IR sensors are sensitive to infrared rays only and strong sunlight or fluorescent lamps may affect their functioning. Most IR sensors require a pulsating IR beam for maximum performance. The pulsating IR ray allows the sensor to keep the sensing ability and reduce the response to visible light. IR sensor modules are used in TV/VCR remote systems and remote switching controls.

8. Laser diodes and their applications

Laser is a long narrow beam of photons emitted from specially made diodes called laser diodes. Like infrared diodes or LEDs, laser diodes (Fig.17) convert electrical energy into light energy. The most common lasers used are semiconductor or injection lasers. These lasers are based on the fact that a population of inversion electrons is produced when a voltage is applied across the p-n junction. The p-n junction is doped with gallium arsenide. Laser beam is available from the doped semiconductor from the near UV to well into infrared regions. The p-n junction of the laser diode has polished ends so that the emitted photons reflect back and forth to cause more recombination of electrons and holes in the p-n junction and new photons are emitted with the same phase.[4] The photons come out from the p-n junction in the form of a long-range narrow beam. All the photons in the laser beam are coherent and in phase.

Lasers are of prime importance in optical memories, fiber-optic communications, military applications, surgical procedures, and also in CD players. Besides gallium arsenide lasers, helium-neon lasers, argon-ion lasers, and carbon-dioxide lasers are also used in various applications.

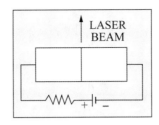

Fig.17   The working principle of a laser diode

9. Lasers and CD players

CD players use laser technology to read the optically recorded data in the form of bits and pits on a CD. A CD is made up of a polycarbonate plastic known as polymethyle metacrylite. The surface of the CD is coated with a thin film of aluminium and protected by a coating of lacquer. About 20,000 tracks are found in a disk's recording surface. The digital information is defined as the length of pits and distance between them. The pits and reflective surface represent logic 0 and 1.

When a laser beam is focused onto the disk, because of a difference between the depth of the pits and wavelength of the laser beam, a phase difference develops between the light reflected from the pits and the reflecting surface.[5] The reflected light is then modulated by the detector system.

The laser diode-lens assembly and the sensor form the optical system of the CD player. The lens system focuses the laser beam reflected onto the disk and reflected back light is collected by the objective lens and transmitted to the detector system. Before passing to the detector, the reflected laser beam is polarised and aligned to 90 degrees. The detector is a photosensor that produces corresponding electrical signals, which are then amplified and separated into corresponding video and audio signals.

New Words and Expressions

telecommunication	n.	电信
military service		军事服务
stimulate	v.	刺激，激发
photon	n.	光子
photoluminescence	n.	光致发光
incident light		入射光
IR emitter		红外发射器
laser emitter		激光发射器
photoconductive	adj.	光电导的
photovoltaic	adj.	光伏的
reverse biased junction		反向偏置结
potential difference		电位差
solar cell		太阳能电池

photovoltaic cell		光伏电池
semiconductor	n.	半导体
arsenic	n.	砷
boron	n.	硼
germanium	n.	锗
hole	n.	空穴
charge	n.	电荷
depletion layer		耗尽层
charge carrier		载流子
anode	n.	阳极
cathode	n.	阴极
series	n.	串联
electrical conductivity		导电率
silver	n.	银
antimony	n.	锑
indium	n.	铟
relay	n.	继电器
covalent bond		共价键
electron-hole pair		电子空穴对
IR sensor		红外传感器
infrared ray		红外线
fluorescent lamp		日光灯
laser diode		激光二极管
gallium arsenide		砷化镓
fiber-optic communication		光纤通信
helium-neon laser		氦氖激光器
argon-ion laser		氩离子激光器
carbon-dioxide laser		二氧化碳激光器
lens	n.	透镜

Notes

1. The continuous movement of electrons and holes results in an equilibrium, with the p-region acquiring a small negative charge and the n-region acquiring a small positive charge.

译文：电子和空穴的连续运动会产生一个平衡，即 p 区域聚集着小的负电荷，而 n 区域聚集着小的正电荷。

2. Primary advantages of CdS are their high dissipation capacity, excellent sensitivity in the visible spectrum, low resistance in light, etc.

译文：硫化镉的主要优点包括散热能力强、可见光灵敏度高、电阻值低等。

3. When a potential difference is applied between the anode and the cathode of the IR diode, the p-n junction is energised and electrons move from the n-region and combine with the holes present in the p-region.

译文：在红外二极管的阴阳两极之间施加电势差时，p-n 结就会被激发，电子从 n 区开始移动并与 p 区中存在的空穴相结合。

4. The p-n junction of the laser diode has polished ends so that the emitted photons reflect back and forth to cause more recombination of electrons and holes in the p-n junction and new photons are emitted with the same phase.

译文：激光二极管的 p-n 结具有抛光端面，使得发射的光子可以来回反射，这样 p-n 结中电子和空穴将产生更多的结合，并且新光子也以相同的相位来发射。

5. When a laser beam is focused onto the disk, because of a difference between the depth of the pits and wavelength of the laser beam, a phase difference develops between the light reflected from the pits and the reflecting surface.

译文：当激光束聚焦到磁盘上时，由于不同的凹陷深度和激光束波长，凹陷处反射的光与反射表面反射的光之间会产生相位差。

Exercises

Lesson Four　Design Patterns

Text A　Intro to Design Patterns (Ⅰ)

1. Someone has already solved your problems

In this chapter, you'll learn why (and how) you can exploit the wisdom and lessons learned by other developers who've been down the same design problem road and survived the trip. Before we're done, we'll look at the use and benefits of design patterns, look at some key Object Oriented (OO) design principles, and walk through an example of how one pattern works. The best way to use patterns is to load your brain with them and then recognize places in your designs and existing applications where you can apply them. Instead of code reuse, with patterns you get experience reuse.[1]

2. It started with a simple SimuDuck App

Joe works for a company that makes a highly successful duck pond simulation game, SimuDuck. The game can show a large variety of duck species swimming and making quacking sounds. The initial designers of the system used standard OO techniques and created one Duck superclass from which all other duck types inherit. The class diagram shows as Fig.1.

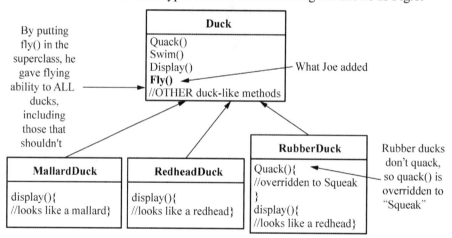

Fig.1　Class diagram of SimuDuck application

In the last year, the company has been under increasing pressure from competitors. After a week-long off-site brainstorming session over golf, the company executives think it's time for a big innovation. They need something really impressive to show at the upcoming shareholders meeting in Maui next week.[2]

3. But now we need the ducks to FLY

The executives decided that flying ducks is just what the simulator needs to blow away the other duck simulation competitors. And of course Joe's manager told them it'll be no problem for

Joe to just whip something up in a week. "After all", said Joe's boss, "He's an OO programmer…, how hard can it be?"

Joe: I just need to add a fly() method in the Duck class and then all the ducks will inherit it. Now it is my time to really show my true OO genius.

The new class diagram is shown in Fig.2.

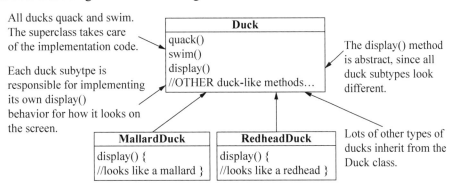

Fig.2　The new class diagram

4. But something went horribly wrong

The boss telephoned Joe: "Joe, I'm at the shareholder's meeting. They just gave a demo and there were rubber ducks flying around the screen. Was your idea of a joke? You might want to spend some time on Monster.com…"

5. What happened

Joe failed to notice that not all subclasses of duck should fly. When Joe added new behavior to the Duck superclass, he was also adding behavior that was not appropriate for some Duck subclasses. He now has flying inanimate objects in the SimuDuck program.

Joe: OK, so there's a slight flaw in my design. I don't see why they can't just call it a "feature". It's kind of cute…

What he thought was a great use of inheritance for the purpose of reuse hasn't turned out so well when it comes to maintenance.

6. Joe thinks about inheritance

Joe: I could always just override the fly() method in rubber duck, the way I am with the quack() method. But then what happens when we add wooden decoy ducks to the program? They aren't supposed to fly or quack…

Here's another class in the hierarchy; notice that like RubberDuck, it doesn't fly, but it also doesn't quack.

7. Sharpen your pencil

Which of the following are disadvantages of using inheritance to provide Duck behavior? (Choose all that apply.)

A. Code is duplicated across subclasses.
B. Runtime behavior changes are difficult.
C. We can't make ducks dance.
D. Hard to gain knowledge of all duck behaviors.
E. Ducks can't fly and quack at the same time.
F. Changes can unintentionally affect other ducks.

8. How about an interface

Joe realized that inheritance probably wasn't the answer, because he just got a memo that says the executives now want to update the product every six months (in ways they haven't yet decided on). Joe knows the spec will keep changing and he'll be forced to look at and possibly override fly() and quack() for every new Duck subclass that's ever added to the program… forever.[3]

So, he needed a cleaner way to have only some (but not all) of the duck types fly or quack.

Joe: I could take fly() out of the Duck superclass, and make a Flyable() interface with a fly() method. That way, only the ducks that are supposed to fly will implement that interface and have a fly() method. And I might as well make a Quackable, too, since not all ducks can quack. The new design is shown in Fig.3. What do you think about this design?

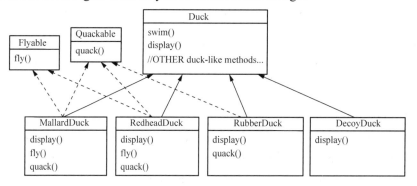

Fig.3　The new design by interface

9. What would you do if you were Joe

We know that not all of the subclasses should have flying or quacking behavior, so inheritance isn't the right answer. But while having the subclasses implement Flyable and /or Quackable solves part of the problem (no inappropriately flying rubber ducks), it completely destroys code reuse for those behaviors, so it just creates a different maintenance nightmare. And of course there might be more than one kind of flying behavior even among the ducks that do fly…

At this point you might be waiting for a Design Pattern to come riding in on a white horse and save the day. But what fun would that be? No, we're going to figure out a solution the old-fashioned way—by applying good OO software design principles.[4]

Joe: Wouldn't it be dreamy if only there were a way to build software so that when we need to change it, we could do so with the least possible impact on the existing code? We could spend less time reworking code and more time making the program do cooler things…

10. The one constant in software development

Okay, what's the one thing you can always count on in software development?

No matter where you are working, what you are building, or what language you are programming in, what's the one true constant that will always be with you ?

No matter how well you design an application, over time an application must grow and change or it will die.[5] (An example of program designed see Fig.4.)

(use a mirror to see the answer)

Fig.4　The constant of programming

11. Sharpen your pencil

Lots things can drive change. List some reasons you've had to change code in your applications (We put in a couple of our own to get you started).

(1) My customers or users decide they want something else, or they want new functionality.

(2) My company decided it is going with another database vendor and it is also purchasing its data from another supplier that uses a different data format Argh!

12. Zeroing in on the problem

So we know using inheritance hasn't worked out very well, since the duck behavior keeps changing across the subclasses, and it's not appropriate for all subclasses to have those behaviors. The Flyable and Quackable interface sounded promising at first—only ducks that really do fly will be Flyable, etc.—except Java interfaces have no implementation code, so no code reuse. And that means that whenever you need to modify a behavior, you're forced to track down and change it in all the different subclasses where that behavior is defined, probably introducing new bugs along the way! Luckily, there's a design principle just for this situation. The first design principle is: Identify the aspects of your application that vary and separate them from what stays the same.

Take what varies and "encapsulate" it so it won't affect the rest of your code. The result? Fewer unintended consequences from code changes and more flexibility in your systems! In other words, if you've got some aspect of your code that is changing, say with every new requirement, then you know you've got a behavior that needs to be pulled out and separated from all the stuff that doesn't change. Here's another way to think about this principle: Take the parts that vary and encapsulate them, so that later you can alter or extend the parts that vary without affecting those that don't. As simple as this concept is, it forms the basis for almost every design pattern. All patterns provide a way to let some part of a system vary independently of all other parts. Okay, it's time to pull the duck behavior out of the Duck classes!

13. Separating what changes from what stays the same

Where do we start? As far as we can tell, other than the problems with fly() and quack(), the Duck class is working well and there are no other parts of it that appear to vary or change frequently. So, other than a few slight changes, we're going to pretty much leave the Duck class alone.

Now, to separate "the parts that change from those that stay the same", we are going to create two sets of classes (totally apart from Duck), one for fly and one for quack. Each set of classes will hold all the implementations of their respective behavior. For instance, we might have one class that implements quacking, another that implements squeaking, and another that implements silence.

We know that fly() and quack() are the parts of the Duck class that vary across ducks.

To separate these behaviors from the Duck class, we'll pull both methods out of the Duck class and create a new set of classes to represent each behavior. Please look at Fig.5.

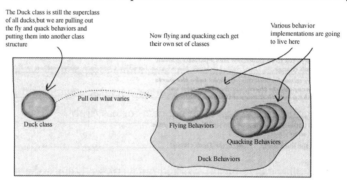

Fig.5　Separate what changes from that stays the same

14. Designing the duck behaviors

So how are we going to design the set of classes that implement the fly and quack behaviors? We'd like to keep things flexible; after all, it was the inflexibility in the duck behaviors that got us into trouble in the first place. And we know that we want to assign behaviors to the instances of Duck. For example, we might want to instantiate a new MallardDuck instance and initialize it with a specific type of flying behavior. And while we're there, why not make sure that we can change the behavior of a duck dynamically? In other words, we should include behavior setter methods in the Duck classes so that we can, say change the MallardDuck's flying behavior at runtime.

Given these goals, let's look at our second design principle: Program to an interface, not an implementation.

From now on, the Duck behaviors will live in a separate class—a class that implements a particular behavior interface.

That way, the Duck classes won't need to know any of the implementation details for their own behaviors.

We'll use an interface to represent each behavior—for instance, FlyBehavior (see Fig.6) and QuackBehavior—and each implementation of a behavior will implement one of those interfaces.

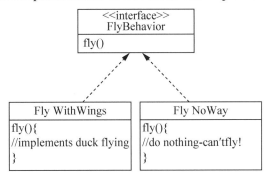

Fig.6　The FlyBehavior interface

So this time it won't be the Duck classes that will implement the flying and quacking interfaces. Instead, we'll make a set of classes whose entire reason for living is to represent a behavior (fox example, "squeaking"), and it's the behavior class, rather than the Duck class, that will implement the behavior interface.

This is in contrast to the way we were doing things before, where a behavior either came from a concrete implementation in the superclass Duck, or by providing a specialized implementation in the subclass itself. In both cases we were relying on an implementation. We were locked into using that specific implementation and there was no room for changing out the behavior (other than writing more code).

With our new design, the Duck subclasses will use a behavior represented by an interface (FlyBehavior and QuackBehavior), so that the actual implementation of the behavior (in other words, the specific concrete behavior coded in the class that implements the FlyBehavior or QuackBehavior) won't be locked into the Duck subclass.

Joe: I don't see why you have to use an interface for FlyBehavior. You can do the same thing with an abstract superclass. Isn't the whole point to use polymorphism?

15. "Program to an interface" really means "Program to a supertype"

The world interface is overloaded here. There's the concept of interface, but there's also the Java construct interface. You can program to an interface, without having to actually use a Java interface. The point is to exploit polymorphism by programming to a supertype so that the actual runtime object isn't locked into the code. And we could rephrase "program to a supertype" as "the declared type of the variables should be a supertype, usually an abstract class or interface, so that the objects assigned to those variables can be of any concrete implementation of the supertype, which means the class declaring them doesn't have to know about the actual object types!"

This is probably old news to you, but just to make sure we're all saying the same thing, here's a simple example of using a polymorphic type—imagine an abstract class Animal, with two concrete implementations, Dog and Cat.

Programming to an implementation would be:

```
    Dog d=new Dog();    //Declaring the variable "d" as type Dog (a concrete
implementation
    d.bark();        // of Animal forces us to code to a concrete implementation
```

But programming to an interface/supertype would be:

```
Animal animal=new Dog();    //We know it's a Dog, but we can now use the animal
Animal.makeSound();         //reference polymorphically
```

Even better, rather than hard-coding the instantiation of the subtype (like new Dog()) into the code (see Fig.7).

Assign the concrete implementation object at runtime:

```
    a=getAnimal();    //we don't know what the actual animal subtype is… all
we care about
    animal.makeSound();  //is that it knows how to respond to makeSound()
```

Implement the Duck Behavior see Fig.8.

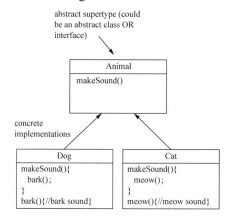

Fig.7　Program to supertype

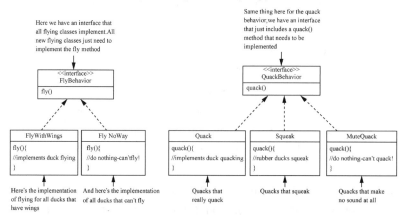

Fig.8　Implement the Duck Behavior

New Words and Expressions

design pattern		设计模式
exploit	v.	充分利用
lesson	n.	教训
superclass	n.	超类；父类
inherit	vt.	继承
competitor	n.	竞争者
brainstorming	n.	头脑风暴
executive	n.	经理主管人员
innovation	n.	改革；创新
impressive	adj.	给人印象深刻的
shareholders meeting		股东大会
blow away		吹走，驱散
OO		面向对象的
horribly	adv.	可怕的；非常的
subclass		子类
inanimate	adj.	没有生命的
quack	v.	(指鸭)嘎嘎地叫
nightmare	n.	梦魇；噩梦；可怕的事物
encapsulate	vt.	封装
dynamically	adv.	动态地

Notes

1. The best way to use patterns is to load your brain with them and then recognize places in your designs and existing applications where you can apply them. Instead of code reuse, with patterns you get experience reuse.

译文：使用设计模式最好的办法是将它们装进你的脑袋里，然后在你设计的现有程序中找到合适的地方把它们放进去。它不是代码复用，使用模式是经验复用。

2. In the last year, the company has been under increasing pressure from competitors. After a week-long off-site brainstorming session over golf, the company executives think it's time for a big innovation. They need something really impressive to show at the upcoming shareholders meeting in Maui next week.

译文：去年，公司的竞争压力加剧。在为期一周的高尔夫假期兼头脑风暴会议之后，公司主管认为该是创新的时候了，他们需要在下周毛伊岛股东会议上展示一些"真正"让人印象深刻的东西来振奋人心。

3. Joe realized that inheritance probably wasn't the answer, because he just got a memo that says the executives now want to update the product every six months (in ways they haven't yet decided on). Joe knows the spec will keep changing and he'll be forced to look at and possibly override fly() and quack() for every new Duck subclass that's ever added to the program…forever.

译文：Joe 认识到继承可能不是答案，因为他刚刚拿到来自主管的备忘录，希望以后每 6 个月更新一次产品(至于更新的方法，他们还没想到)。Joe 知道规格会常常改变，每当有新的鸭子子类出现，他就要被迫检查并可能需要覆盖 fly()和 quark()…这简直是无穷无尽的噩梦。

4. At this point you might be waiting for a Design Pattern to come riding in on a white horse and save the day. But what fun would that be? No, we're going to figure out a solution the old-fashioned way—by applying good OO software design principles.

译文：此时，你可能正期盼着设计模式能骑着白马来解救你离开苦难的一天。但是，如果直接告诉你答案，这有什么乐趣？我们会用老方法找出一个解决之道——采用良好的面向对象软件设计原则。

5. No matter where you are working, what you are building, or what language you are programming in, what's the one true constant that will always be with you?

No matter how well you design an application, over time an application must grow and change or it will die.

译文：不管你在何处工作，构建些什么，用何种编程语言，在软件开发上，一直伴随你的那个不变真理是什么？

不管当初软件设计得有多好，一段时间之后，它总是需要成长与改变，否则软件会"死亡"。

Exercises

Text B Intro to Design Patterns (Ⅱ)

1. Implementing the Duck Behaviors

Here we have the two interfaces, FlyBehavior and QuackBehavior along with the corresponding classes that implement each concrete behavior. Please look at Fig.8. With this design, other types of objects can reuse our fly and quack behaviors because these behaviors are no longer hidden away in our Duck classes!

And we can add new behaviors without modifying any of our existing behavior classes or touching any of the Duck classes that use flying behaviors.

So we get the benefit of REUSE without all the baggage that comes along with inheritance.

2. Dumb Questions

Q: Do I always have to implement my application first, see where things are changing, and then go back and separate & encapsulate those things?

A: Not always; often when you are designing an application, you anticipate those areas that are going to vary and then go ahead and build the flexibility to deal with it into your code. You'll find that the principles and patterns can be applied at any stage of the development lifecycle.

Q: Should we make Duck an interface too?

A: Not in case. As you'll see once we've got everything hooked together, we do benefit by having Duck be a concrete class and having specific ducks, like MallardDuck, inherit common properties and methods. Now that we've removed what varies from the Duck inheritance, we get the benefits of this structure without the problems.

Q: It feels a little weird to have a class that's just a behavior. Aren't classes supposed to represent things? Aren't classes supposed to have both state and behavior?

A: In an OO system, yes, classes represent things that generally have both state (instance variables) and methods. And in this case, the thing happens to be a behavior. But even a behavior can still have stage and methods; a flying behavior might have instance variables representing the attributes for the flying (wing beats per minute,max altitude and speed, etc.) behavior.

3. Integrating the Duck Behaviors

Integrating the Duck Behaviors see Fig.9. The key is that a Duck will now delegate its flying and quacking behavior, instead of using quacking and flying methods defined in the Duck class (or subclass). Here is how.

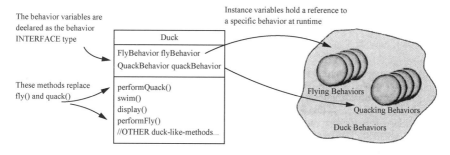

Fig.9 Integrating the Duck Behaviors

(1) First we'll add two instance variables to the Duck class called FlyBehavior and QuackBehavior, those are declared as the interface type (not a concrete class implementation type). Each duck object will set these variables polymorphically to reference the specific behavior type it would like at runtime (FlyWithWings, Squeak, etc.).

We'll also remove the fly() and quack() methods from the Duck class (and any subclasses) because we've moved this behavior out into the FlyBehavior and QuackBehavior classes.

We'll replace fly() and quack() in the Duck class with two similar methods, called performFly() and performQuack(); you'll see how they work next.

(2) Now we implement performQuack().

```
Public class Duck{
    QuackBehavior quackBehavior; //Each Duck has a reference to something that
                                 //more implement the QuackBehavior interface
    Public void performQuack(){ //Rather than handling the quack behavior itself,
        quackBehavior.quack();  //the Duck object delegates that behavior to the
    }                           //object referenced by quackBehavior
}
```

Pretty simple, huh? To perform the quack, a Duck just allows the object that is referenced by quackBehavior to quack for it.

In this part of the code we don't care what kind of object it is, all we care about is that it knows how to quack()!

(3) Okay, it's time to worry about how the flyBehavior and quackBehavior instance variables are set. Let's take a look at the MallardDuck class.

```
Public class MallardDuck extends Duck{
    Public MallardDuck(){              //A Mallard Duck uses the Quack class to handle
        quackBehavior=new Quack();     //its quack, so when performQuack is called, the
        flyBehavior=new FlyWithWings();//responsibility for the quack is delegated to the
    }       //Quack object and we get a real quack and it uses FlywithWings as its
            //FlyBehavior type Remember, MallardDuck inherits the quackBehavior
            //and flyBehavior instance variables from class Duck.
    Public void display(){
        System.out.println("I'm a real Mallard duck");
    }
}
```

So MallardDuck's quack is a real live duck quack, not a squeak and no a mute quack. So what happens here? When a MallardDuck is instantiated, its constructor initializes the MallardDuck's inherited quackBehavior instance variable to a new instance of type Quack (a QuackBehvior concrete implementation class).

And the same is true for the duck's flying behavior—the MallardDuck's constructor initializes the flyBehavior instance variable with an instance of type FlyWithWings (a

FlyBehavior concrete implementation class).

Good catch, that's exactly what we're doing… for now.

Later in the book we'll have more patterns in our toolbox that can help us fix it.

Still, notice that while we are setting the behaviors to concrete classes (by instantiating a behavior class like Quack or FlyWithWings and assigning it to our behavior reference variable), we could easily change that at runtime.

So, we still have a lot of flexibility here, but we're doing a poor job of initializing the instance variables in a flexible way. But think about it, since the quackBehavior instance variable is an interface type, we could (through the magic of polymorphism) dynamically assign a different QuackBehavior implementation class at runtime.

Take a moment and think about how you would implement a duck so that its behavior could change at runtime. (You'll see the code that does this a few pages from now.)

4. The Big Picture on Encapsulated Behaviors

Okay, now that we've done the deep dive on the duck simulator design, it's time to come back up for air and take a look at the Big Picture.[1]

Fig.10 is the entire reworked class structure. We have everything you'd expect: ducks extending Duck, fly behaviors implementing FlyBehavior and quack behaviors implementing QuackBehavior.

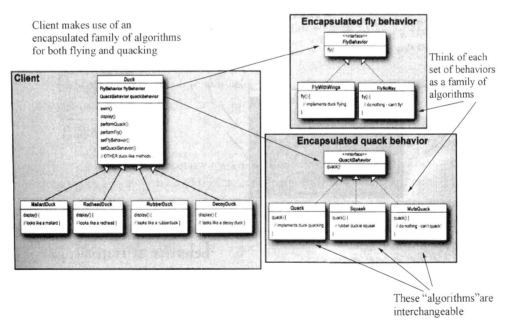

Fig.10　The Big Picture on Encapsulated Behaviors

Notice also that we've started to describe things a little differently. Instead of thinking of the duck behaviors as a set of behaviors, we'll start thinking of them as a family of algorithms. Think about it: in the SimuDuck design, the algorithms represent things a duck would do (different ways of quacking or flying), but we could just as easily use the same techniques for a set of classes that implement the ways to compute state sales tax by different states.

Pay careful attention to the relationships between the classes. In fact, grab your pen and write the appropriate relationship (IS-A, HAS-A and IMPLEMENTS) on each arrow in the class diagram.

5. HAS-A can be better than IS-A

The HAS-A relationship is an interesting one: each duck has a FlyBehavior and a QuackBehavior to which it delegates flying and quacking.

When you put two classes together like this you're using composition. Instead of inheriting their behavior, the ducks get their behavior by being composed with the right behavior object.

This is an important technique; in fact, we've been using our third design principle: Favor composition over inheritance.

As you've seen, creating systems using composition gives you a lot more flexibility. Not only does it let you encapsulate a family of algorithms into their own set of classes, but it also lets you change behavior at runtime as long as the object you're composing with implements the correct behavior interface.[2]

Composition is used in many design patterns and you'll see a lot more about its advantages and disadvantages throughout the book.

Brain Power: A duck call is a device that hunters use to mimic the calls (quacks) of ducks. How would you implement your own duck call that does not inherit from the Duck class?

6. Master and Student

Master: Grasshopper, tell me what you have learned of the object-Oriented ways.

Student: Master, I have learned that the promise of the object-oriented way is reuse.

Master: Grasshopper, continue…

Student: Master, through inheritance all good things may be reused and so we will come to drastically cut development time like we swiftly cut bamboo in the woods.

Master: Grasshopper, is more time spent on code before or after development is complete?

Student: The answer is after, Master. We always spend more time maintaining and changing software than initial development.

Master: So Grasshopper, should effort go into reuse above maintainability and extensibility?

Student: Master, I believe that there is truth in this.

Master: I can see that you still have much to learn. I would like for you to go and meditate on inheritance further. As you've seen, inheritance has its problems, and there are other ways of achieving reuse.

7. Speaking of design patterns

You just applied your first design pattern—the Strategy Pattern. That's right, you used the Strategy Pattern to rework the SimuDuck App. Thanks to this pattern, the simulator is ready for any changes those execs might cook up on their next business trip to Vegas.

Now that we've made you take the long road to apply it, here's the formal definition of this pattern.

The strategy pattern defines a family of algorithms, encapsulates each one, and makes them interchangeable. Strategy lets the algorithm vary independently from clients that use it.[3]

Use this definition when you need to impress friends and influence key executives.

8. Overheard at the local diner

Alice: I need a Cream cheese with jelly on white bread, a chocolate soda with vanilla ice cream, a grilled cheese sandwich with bacon, a tuna fish salad on toast, a banana split with ice cream & sliced bananas and a coffee with a cream and two sugars,…oh, and put a hamburger on the grill.

Flo: Give me a C.J. White, a black & white, a Jack Benny, a radio, a house boat, a coffee regular and burn one!

What's the difference between these two orders? Not a thing! They're both the same order, except Alice is using twice the number of words and trying the patience of a grumpy short order cook.

What's Flo got that Alice doesn't? A shared vocabulary with the short order cook. Not only is it easier to communicate with the cook, but it gives the cook less to remember because he's got all the diner patterns in his head.

Design Patterns give you a shared vocabulary with other developers. Once you've got the vocabulary you can more easily communicate with other developers and inspire those who don't know patterns to start learning them. It also elevates your thinking about architectures by letting you think at the pattern level, not the nitty gritty object level.[4]

9. Overheard in the next cubicle

Rick: So I created this broadcast class. It keeps track of all the objects listening to it and anytime a new piece of data comes along it sends a message to each listener. What's cool is that the listeners can join the broadcast at any time or they can even remove themselves. It is really dynamic and loosely-coupled!

Joe: Rick, why didn't you just say you were using the Observer pattern?

Jack: Exactly. If you communicate in patterns, then other developers know immediately and precisely the design you've describing. Just don't get Pattern Fever…You'll know you have it when you start using patterns for Hello World…

Brain Power: Can you think of other shared vocabularies that are used beyond OO design and diner talk?(Hint: how about auto mechanics, carpenters, gourmet chefs, air traffic control?) What qualities are communicated along with lingo? Can you think of aspects of OO design that get communicated along with pattern names? What qualities get communicated along with the name "Strategy Pattern"?

10. The power of a shared pattern vocabulary

When you communicate using patterns you are doing more than just sharing lingo.

Shared pattern vocabularies are powerful. When you communicate with another developer or your team using patterns, you are communicating not just a pattern name but a whole set of qualities, characteristics and constraints that the pattern represents.

Patterns allow you to say more with less. When you use a pattern in a description, other developers quickly know precisely the design you have in mind.

"We've using the strategy pattern to implement the various behaviors of our ducks." This tells you the duck behavior has been encapsulated into its own set of classes that can be easily expanded and changed, even at runtime if needed.

Talking at the pattern level allows you to stay "in the design" longer. Talking about software systems using patterns allows you to keep the discussion at the design level, without having to dive down to the nitty gritty details of implementing objects and classes.[5]

How many design meetings have you been in that quickly degrade into implementation details?

Shared vocabularies can turbo charge your development team. A team well versed in design patterns can move quickly with less room for misunderstanding.

As your team begins to share design ideas and experience in terms of patterns, you will build a community of patterns users.

Shared vocabularies encourage more junior developers to get up to speed. Junior developers look up to experienced developers. When senior developers make use of design patterns, junior developers also become motivated to learn them. Build a community of pattern users at your organization.

Think about starting a patterns study group at your organization, maybe you can even get paid while you're learning…

11. How do I use design patterns

We've all used off-the-shelf libraries and frameworks. We take them, write some code against their APIs, compile them into our programs, and benefit from a lot of code someone else has written. Think about the Java APIs and all the functionality they give you: network, GUI, IO, etc. Libraries and frameworks go a long way towards a development model where we can just pick and choose components and plug them right in. But… they don't help us structure our own applications in ways that are easier to understand, more maintainable and flexible. That's where Design Patterns come in.

Design patterns don't go directly into your code, they first go into your brain. Once you've loaded your brain with a good working knowledge of patterns, you can then start to apply them to your new designs, and rework your old code when you find it's degrading into an inflexible mess of jungle spaghetti code. Fig.11 shows how design patterns work.

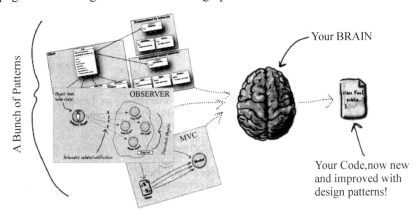

Fig.11　How design patterns work

New Words and Expressions

composition	n.	合成
overhear	vt.	无意中听到；偷听
jelly	n.	果子冻；一种果冻甜品
vanilla	n.	[植]香草；香子兰
bacon	n.	咸肉；熏肉
grill	n.	烤架；铁格子；烤肉
grumpy	adj.	脾气坏的；性情乖戾的；脾气暴躁的
inspire	vt.	鼓舞；感动；激发
elevate	vt.	举起；提拔；提升
cubicle	n.	小隔挡
constraint	n.	约束
dive down		压低
nitty	adj.	多虱卵的；多小虫卵的
gritty	adj.	多砂的；粗砂质的
spaghetti	n.	意大利式细面条

Notes

1. Okay, now that we've done the deep dive on the duck simulator design, it's time to come back up for air and take a look at the big picture.

译文：好，我们已经深入研究了鸭子模拟器的设计，该是将头探出水面，呼吸空气的时候了。现在就来看看整体的格局。

2. As you've seen, creating systems using composition gives you a lot more flexibility. Not only does it let you encapsulate a family of algorithms into their own set of classes, but it also lets you change behavior at runtime as long as the object you're composing with implements the correct behavior interface.

译文：如你所见，使用组合建立系统具有很大的弹性，不仅可将算法封装成类，更可以"在运行时动态地改变行为"，只要组合的行为对象符合正确的接口标准即可。

3. The strategy pattern defines a family of algorithms, encapsulates each one, and makes them interchangeable. Strategy lets the algorithm vary independently from clients that use it.

译文：策略模式定义了一组算法，将每个算法封装起来，并使其可以互换。策略模式使得算法可以独立于使用它们的客户变化。

4. Design patterns gives you a shared vocabulary with other developers. Once you've got the vocabulary you can more easily communicate with other developers and inspire those who don't know patterns to start learning them. It also elevates your thinking about architectures by letting you think at the pattern level, not the nitty gritty object level.

译文：设计模式让你和其他开发人员之间有共享的词汇，一旦懂得这些词汇，和其他开发人员之间沟通就很容易，也会促使那些不懂的程序员想开始学习设计模式。设计模式也可以把你的思考架构的层次提高到模式层面，而不是停留在琐碎的对象上。

5. Talking at the pattern level allows you to stay "in the design" longer. Talking about software systems using patterns allows you to keep the discussion at the design level, without having to dive down to the nitty gritty details of implementing objects and classes.

译文：将说话的方式保持在模式层次，可让你待在"设计圈子"久一点。使用模式谈论软件系统，可以让讨论话题保持在设计层面，不会被压低到对象与类这种琐碎的事情上面。

Exercises

第 2 章　Application and Appreciation

Lesson Five　RF Technology and Its Circuits

Text A　What Is RF?

1. Historical basis of definition

What does RF exactly mean? We all know that RF is an abbreviation for radio frequency. Although it can be used as a noun (as in, "RF is King!"), it is mostly used as a qualifier: RF circuit, RF engineer, RF interference, RF spectrum, etc. If RF is primarily a qualifier, then its purpose is to distinguish things that are RF from those that are not. So what distinguishing features or characteristics does this qualifier imply? The answer to that question keeps shifting with time due to the changes in technology. For example, once upon a time, an amplifier made with electron tubes would qualify as an RF amplifier if its pass-band extended above 600 kHz into the "radio" broadcast band.[1] Today, an operational amplifier having a pass-band from dc to 2 GHz, is called an analog, rather than an RF component. There seem to be several bases on which the distinction between RF and other objects has been based in the past, each with its own shortcoming. Here are some of them.

1) Bandwidth-based definition

A generation of radio engineers from a half century ago, Fredric E. Terman's Electronic and Radio Engineers, treats RF amplifiers as synonymous with tuned amplifiers. The implication is that RF circuits are necessarily narrowband circuits, having bandwidths that are a small fraction of the center frequency. Conversely, broadband circuits would not qualify as RF. Such a definition would not pass muster today; we routinely design circuits with multi-decade frequency pass-bands. Indeed, increasing the bandwidth of your RF design would carry with it the risk that the design would no longer remain RF!

2) Frequency-based definition

Sometimes, handbooks define RF as the range of electromagnetic waves lying between the low-frequency bands (LF and below) and the microwave frequency bands (UHF and above), thus encompassing the CCIR-designated bands MF (300kHz～3MHz), HF (3MHz～30MHz), and VHF (30MHz-300MHz). This is the frequency range that the microwave engineers of earlier years condescendingly referred to as "dc" Given that the integrated circuits in the UHF region are now routinely called RFICs, we may have to shift the UHF band out of the microwave basket and add it to the RF group. How times have changed! I personally knew some of the practitioners of that high art form called microwave engineering who proudly declared themselves to be "microwave plumbers" and would have been offended if someone had called them a mere "RF engineer".

3) Application-based definition

Communication system engineers sometimes distinguish RF from other frequency ranges on the basis of the role in which the signals at those frequencies serve. Historically, RF signals were not "information" but were used as carriers of the information-bearing signals in radio broadcasting and other radio (i.e., wireless) applications.[2] By tradition, in the AM radio band (where actual information-bearing signals extend from approximately 50Hz to 6kHz), a preamplifier that extends from 600 to 1600 kHz would be considered an RF amplifier because it operates on the carrier signals in that frequency range. On the other hand, a video amplifier having a pass-band from 50Hz to 6MHz is not an RF amplifier because the information-bearing video signal itself occupies that frequency range. Since most information-bearing signals start out at base-band, this definition makes the qualifier RF almost an antonym of the qualifier "base-band". There are many problems with this definition, of course. For example, optical signals are used as carriers too, but the practice of referring to them as RF has not become widespread, at least as yet. Then there is the problem that some information-bearing signals are not base-band, and many a digital information-bearing signal may contain frequency components extending all the way up to the carrier frequency.

4) Size-Based Definition

An object (component, circuit, module, product, etc.) used to process electronic signals is sometimes defined as being RF provided the phase-shift of that signal, occurring over the extent of that object, is not negligible.[3] This is equivalent to the assertion that, for RF hardware, size is not negligible compared to the wavelength of the electromagnetic (EM) waves that they process. However, this definition of RF elements appears to be synonymous with that of distributed circuit elements and leaves the so-called "lumped RF components", such as chip capacitors and spiral inductors, in a precarious position. There are also several other difficulties with it: We should compare the wavelength with the size of the entire system, or the smallest critical dimension in it; what if the size is much larger than the wavelength (at the optical end of the spectrum); what about the use of the qualifier RF for non-tangible items, such as RF software, RF data, RF methodology, etc., that have no inherent "size" of their own, or that may be applicable for designing objects having a variety of sizes.

2. Finding a consistent basis for definition

It is clear that the historical definitions of RF are no longer adequate. However, current usage is no more logical or consistent. We find the phrase being used to convey more than one sense. On the one hand, the qualifier RF is frequently used to refer to the frequency range lying just below the microwave frequency range. This use is inconsistent with the use of the term RFIC for integrated circuits operating at millimeter and submillimeter wave frequencies. On the other hand, we find the phrase RF being used in the literature to refer to signals ranging in frequency from the AM broadcast band to the submillimeter wave and even infrared (IR) region.[4] But if that is accepted, RF includes the microwave region as a subset and the wildly popular phrase "RF and microwave" is meaningless.

The widespread use of the phrase "RF and microwaves" is problematic in itself. There are several reasons for its current popularity.

1) Fuzzy thinking

Today, we sometimes use the phrase "RF and microwave" the way laymen use the phrase "science and technology"—as if they were one and the same. Maybe we are just too lazy to think precisely and choose the appropriate word. A fuzzy phrase serves us well. Often it is used where we would have used the term microwave in an earlier era.

2) Glamorous Association

Popular press has glamorized the term RF by calling it one of the most promising commercial technologies of the decade, which gives it the image of being an up-to-the-minute, exciting field. By contrast, microwaves are an "established" (read "older") technology that has a historical association with military work and a cyclical nature of marketability. So an association with RF makes microwaves more respectable.

3) Political Correctness

As a result of the current trend of political correctness that has crept into our language, we constantly try to be all-inclusive. The phrase "RF and microwave" clearly has a wider scope and meets this subconscious need.

4) Pompous Writing

Lawyers are known to routinely add a lot of near-synonymous words to important phrases, in an attempt to make a document air-tight—for example, cease and desist; covenants, conditions, and restrictions; as amended, revised, modified, or supplemented; and sell, exchange, transfer, or otherwise dispose. Of course, the resulting legalese is known to be stuffy and formal, but others have copied this habit for emphasis or simply to make their writing appear important. The phrase "RF and microwave" has this ring of being a well-considered, profound term.

It seems that the question, "What is RF?" cannot be satisfactorily answered by an etymological or historical analysis of the name RF. Such an analysis would only show that it is the incessant advancement of technology that makes it hard for us to define the qualifier RF. Point out a precise boundary line to a creative engineer, and he/she will find a way to make it fuzzy by inventing objects that straddle the boundary. Once we recognize technology as the culprit that makes definitions imprecise, we might also look to it for guidance. Like technology itself, the meaning of the qualifier RF changes with time, and like many other technological ideas, it is a concept whose understanding requires a familiarity with the technology to which it relates. In fact, the most rational basis for defining RF, and one that evolves with time to stay forever current, may be based on the distinguishing features of the RF technology itself. Then, RF refers to a way of looking at the world that is somehow distinct from audio, video, optical, and various other world views.

3. Distinguishing features of RF

What confers upon a component a membership in the RF class? It seems that the distinction between the RF and the non-RF objects arises from the different design considerations that required the attention of their designers. RF designs need attention to some (or several) of the following.

1) Phase Shift

Concern with signal phase shift over the extent of the component caused by a component size that is nonnegligible compared to wavelength. This concern manifests itself through the use of

- compact designs, so as to minimize unintended phase-shifts.
- explicit accounting and utilization of phase shift due to propagation delays.
- distributed (i.e., transmission-line) models for circuit elements.

2) Reactances

Concern with presence of nonnegligible parasitic (i.e., unintended) reactive (i.e., energy-storing) elements and its various consequences, such as resonances.

3) Dissipation

Concern with signal dissipation in the circuit, not merely due to the resulting loss of signal power, but primarily due to its impact on

- frequency selectivity, or Q, in a narrow-band operation.
- thermal noise generated in dissipative elements.

4) Noise

Concern with internally generated noise, which tends to dominate over other external sources of noise—both natural and man-made—in the RF range.

5) Radiation

Concern with electromagnetic radiation of energy from the circuit, either

- for minimizing the unintentional radiation of energy, (e.g., to reduce unwanted coupling).
- for enhancing the effectiveness of intentional radiation (typically by incorporating radiating structures).

6) Reflections

Concern with impedance matching, primarily for minimizing the resulting reflections, rather than the resulting loss of transferred power.

7) Non-linearity

Concern with non-linearity in the context of frequency translation and spurious generation.

It seems RF will remain a popular phrase for some time to come. Components and circuits whose design share a number of these concerns are RF, regardless of the numerical value of the frequency or bandwidth of electromagnetic signals involved. With a definition based on the designers' mind-set, we can include many kinds of components under the umbrella of RF at virtually any frequency from LF to IR. How's that for all-inclusive, politically correct terminology? (Quoted from "What Is RF?")

New Words and Expressions

abbreviation	*n.*	缩写
qualifier	*n.*	修饰词
pass-band		通频带

bible	n.	圣经；有权威性的书籍
synonymous	adj.	类似的，相近的
tuned amplifier		调谐放大器
bandwidth	n.	带宽
narrowband	n.	窄带
broadband	n.	宽带
electromagnetic wave		电磁波
condescendingly	adv.	谦逊地
preamplifier	n.	前置放大器
antonym	n.	反义词
phase-shift		相移
precarious	adj.	不稳定的
chip capacitor		片式电容器
spiral inductor		螺旋电感器
critical dimension		临界尺寸
logical	adj.	符合逻辑的
submillimeter	n.	亚毫米
subset	n.	子集
fuzzy	adj.	模糊的
precisely	adj.	精确地
glamorized	v.	粉饰，美化
up-to-the-minute		最新的
marketability	n.	市场性
resonance	n.	共振
dissipation	n.	消耗
thermal noise		热噪声
radiation	n.	辐射

Notes

1. For example, once upon a time, an amplifier made with electron tubes would qualify as an RF amplifier if its pass-band extended above 600 kHz into the "radio" broadcast band.

译文：例如，在以前，一个用电子管制成的放大器，如果它的通频带超过 600kHz 到达"无线电"广播频段，就有资格作为射频放大器。

2. Historically, RF signals were not "information" but were used as carriers of the information-bearing signals in radio broadcasting and other radio (i.e., wireless) applications.

译文：历史上，射频信号不是"信息"，而是在无线电广播和其他无线电(即无线)应用中，作为承载信息的载体。

3. An object (component, circuit, module, product, etc.) used to process electronic signals is

sometimes defined as being RF provided the phase-shift of that signal, occurring over the extent of that object, is not negligible.

译文：用于处理电子信号的对象(如组件、电路、模块、产品等)有时被定义为 RF，因为该对象中发生的信号相移是不可忽略的。

4. On the other hand, we find the phrase RF being used in the literature to refer to signals ranging in frequency from the AM broadcast band to the submillimeter wave and even infrared (IR) region.

译文：另一方面，我们发现在文献中使用的短语 RF，是指从 AM 广播频带到亚毫米波甚至是红外波段，这一频率范围内的信号。

Text B Active Components in RF Circuits

As with passive components, the active components used in RF circuits share many characteristics with active components typically found in lower-frequency analog systems.[1] However, there are certain components that are highly specific to RF design. Furthermore, different semiconductor technologies are often employed to ensure that RF components maintain adequate performance at very high frequencies.

1. Amplifiers

Amplifier circuits, often built around an operational amplifier, are extremely common in both low-frequency and high-frequency analog design. In RF systems, there are two fundamental types of amplifiers: power amplifiers and low-noise amplifiers. The former is used to increase the power level of an RF signal prior to transmission, and the latter are used to amplify the (often very small) signals received by the antenna.

2. Power amplifiers

The power amplifier, or PA, is used to increase the power level of the signal before it is sent to the antenna. A similar situation is found in audio circuits: the audio signal's amplitude may be perfectly adequate in terms of voltage, but a power amplifier is needed to supply large amounts of current to the speaker coil. In audio, more current corresponds to more power, and this in turn corresponds to more volume. In RF, higher power means longer range.

3. Low-noise amplifiers

There are many non-RF applications that require low-noise amplification, but the specific phrase "low-noise amplifier" is common only in the context of RF. Actually, we usually hear the abbreviated version of the term, i.e., LNA.

The received signal delivered by an antenna can be of very low magnitude, and furthermore, it is buried in noise. This signal needs to be amplified for further processing, but it is also important to minimize further degradation of the signal-to-noise ratio. Thus, a low-noise amplifier is designed to provide high voltage gain while contributing minimal noise.

The noise performance of an LNA is quantified via the "noise figure" (NF), which corresponds to the amount of SNR degradation (in dB) created by the amplifier.[3] Thus, an ideal amplifier would have NF = 0 dB, and as noise performance declines, NF increases.

4. Mixers

Another fundamental RF component is the mixer. This name can be misleading; an RF mixer does not combine signals as an audio mixer does. Rather, an RF mixer takes two input frequencies and generates a third output frequency via multiplication. In other words, a mixer performs frequency translation.

Mixers allow signals to be shifted to higher or lower frequencies in a way that maintains the details of the signal. For example, an information-carrying (i.e., modulated) baseband signal can be shifted to a higher frequency that is suitable for wireless transmission, and the transmitted signal will retain the important modulation details that were present in the baseband signal.[4]

5. Phase-locked loops

The actual generation of a periodic signal is more closely related to the domain of passive components, but active components are used to manipulate these periodic signals. A phase-locked loop (PLL), shown in Fig.1, is actually a system of sub-components at minimum, a phase detector, a low-pass filter, a voltage-controlled oscillator (VCO), and a frequency divider—that allows a wide variety of output frequencies to be generated from one input frequency.

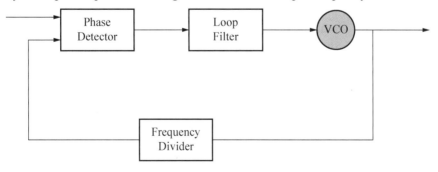

Fig.1 PLL

Combining a PLL with a high-precision temperature-compensated oscillator converts a highly accurate but fixed reference frequency into a system that can produce highly accurate yet variable output frequencies.[5] An oscillator combined with a PLL is referred to as a synthesizer, i.e., a component that can generate a range of frequencies.

This ability to adjust the oscillator frequency is very important in RF design. A particular system may need to operate on different channels in order to avoid interference, and thus the oscillation circuitry must be adjustable with respect to frequency. Furthermore, the frequency spacing between adjacent channels may be relatively small, and thus the adjustments must be precise.

6. Data converters

Though not standard components in the context of historical RF engineering, it is important to recognize that analog-to-digital converters (ADCs) and digital-to-analog converters (DACs) are increasingly important in many RF systems. ADCs and DACs allow RF systems to benefit from the special capabilities offered by digital-signal-processing techniques and from the general flexibility and convenience associated with software-based solutions.

The term "software-defined radio" (SDR), shown in Fig.2, refers to wireless communication systems that rely on software to implement important portions of the RF signal chain. Data converters are critical components in such systems—for example, a DAC could be used to directly generate a baseband waveform, or an ADC could be used to digitize a received baseband waveform (followed by further analysis in a digital signal processor).

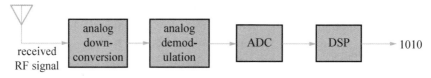

Fig.2 SDR

SDRs can introduce additional design complexity, but they also offer advantages that are particularly valuable in certain applications.

7. RF semiconductors

Silicon is still the dominant material in semiconductor manufacturing. However, other materials are more compatible with the high signal frequencies present in RF systems. Three alternative materials that are used in RF semiconductors are gallium nitride (GaN), gallium arsenide (GaAs), and silicon germanium (SiGe). Specialized semiconductor technologies make it possible to fabricate devices that maintain adequate performance at extremely high frequencies, i.e., above 100 GHz.

8. Inside the IC

As with low-frequency devices, the fundamental active component in RF integrated circuits is the transistor. However, thus far we have used the word "component" to refer to devices that may consist of numerous transistors. It is important to understand the justification for this: designing high-performance, high-frequency RF components is extremely challenging and not within the skill set of many RF engineers. Practical RF engineering is focused on combining these components into functional circuits and then dealing with the various complicated issues that arise. (Quoted from https://www.allaboutcircuits.com/textbook/radio-frequency-analysis-design/rf-principles-components/active-components-in-rf-circuits/[2022-1-25])

New Words and Expressions

passive component		无源元件
active component		有源元件
adequate	*adj.*	足够的
operational amplifier		运放
level	*n.*	电平
speaker	*n.*	扬声器
volume	*n.*	音量
magnitude	*n.*	量级
signal-to-noise		信噪比
noise figure (NF)		噪声系数
mixer	*n.*	混频器
via	*prep.*	通过，经过
frequency translation		频率转换
phase-locked loop(PLL)		锁相环
phase detector	*n.*	鉴相器
low-pass filter		低通滤波器
voltage-controlled oscillator(VCO)		压控振荡器
frequency divider		分频器
synthesizer	*n.*	合成器
analog-to-digital converter(ADC)		模数转换器
software-defined radio(SDR)		软件定义无线电
gallium nitride		氮化镓
silicon germanium		硅锗
fabricate	*v.*	制造，装配
complicated	*adj.*	复杂的

Notes

1. As with passive components, the active components used in RF circuits share many characteristics with active components typically found in lower-frequency analog systems.

译文：和无源器件一样，射频电路中使用的有源器件与低频模拟系统中常见的有源器件类似，具有很多共同的特性。

2. The former are used to increase the power level of an RF signal prior to transmission, and the latter are used to amplify the (often very small) signals received by the antenna.

译文：前者用在传输之前，目的是增加 RF 信号的功率电平，而后者目的是放大天线接收(通常非常小)的信号。

3. The noise performance of an LNA is quantified via the "noise figure" (NF), which corresponds to the amount of SNR degradation (in dB) created by the amplifier.

译文：通过"噪声系数"对低噪声放大器的噪声性能进行量化，该噪声系数就对应于放大器造成的信噪比衰减的量级(以 dB 为单位)。

4. For example, an information-carrying (i.e., modulated) baseband signal can be shifted to a higher frequency that is suitable for wireless transmission, and the transmitted signal will retain the important modulation details that were present in the baseband signal.

译文：例如，载有信息的(已调制的)基带信号可以被搬移到适合无线传输的高频上，并且所传输的信号将保留基带信号中的重要调制细节。

5. Combining a PLL with a high-precision temperature-compensated oscillator converts a highly accurate but fixed reference frequency into a system that can produce highly accurate yet variable output frequencies.

译文：锁相环与高精度温度补偿振荡器结合后，可将高精度但参考频率固定的系统转换为高精度且输出频率可变的系统。

Exercises

第 2 章　Application and Appreciation

Lesson Six　5G Communication and Standards

Text A　5G Wireless Communication Systems

1. What is 5G?

5G radio access technology will be a key component of the Networked Society. It will address high traffic growth and increasing demand for high-bandwidth connectivity. It will also support massive numbers of connected devices and meet the real-time, high-reliability communication needs of mission-critical applications.

5G will provide wireless connectivity for a wide range of new applications and use cases, including wearables, smart homes, traffic safety/control, critical infrastructure, industry processes and very-high-speed media delivery.[1] As a result, it will also accelerate the development of the Internet of Things.

The overall aim of 5G is to provide ubiquitous connectivity for any kind of device and any kind of application that may benefit from being connected.

5G networks will not be based on one specific radio-access technology. Rather, 5G is a portfolio of access and connectivity solutions addressing the demands and requirements of mobile communication beyond 2020.

The specification of 5G will include the development of a new flexible air interface, NX, which will be directed to extreme mobile broadband deployments. NX will also target high-bandwidth and high-traffic-usage scenarios, as well as new scenarios that involve mission-critical and real-time communications with extreme requirements in terms of latency and reliability.

In parallel, the development of Narrow-Band IoT (NB-IoT) in 3GPP is expected to support massive machine connectivity in wide area applications. NB-IoT will most likely be deployed in bands below 2GHz and will provide high capacity and deep coverage for enormous numbers of connected devices.

Ensuring interoperability with past generations of mobile communications has been a key principle of the ICT industry since the development of GSM and later wireless technologies within the 3GPP family of standards. In a similar manner, LTE will evolve in a way that recognizes its role in providing excellent coverage for mobile users, and 5G networks will incorporate LTE access [based on Orthogonal Frequency Division Multiplexing (OFDM)] along with new air interfaces in a transparent manner toward both the service layer and users.[2]

Around 2020, much of the available wireless coverage will continue to be provided by LTE, and it is important that operators with deployed 4G networks have the opportunity to transition some (or all) of their spectrum to newer wireless access technologies. For operators with limited spectrum resources, the possibility of introducing 5G capabilities in an interoperable way — thereby allowing legacy devices to continue to be served on a compatible carrier — is highly beneficial and, in some cases, even vital.

At the same time, the evolution of LTE to a point where it is a full member of the 5G family of air interfaces is essential, especially since initial deployment of new air interfaces may not operate in the same bands. The 5G network will enable dual-connectivity between LTE operating within bands below 6GHz and the NX air interface in bands within the range 6GHz to100GHz, shown in Fig.1. NX should also allow for user-plane aggregation, i.e. joint delivery of data via LTE and NX component carriers. This books explain the key requirements and capabilities of 5G, along with its technology components and spectrum needs.

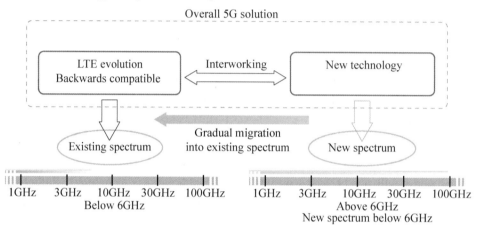

Fig.1　The overall 5G wireless-access solution consisting of LTE evolution and new technology

2. 5G 一 requirements and capabilities

In order to enable connectivity for a very wide range of applications with new characteristics and requirements, the capabilities of 5G wireless access must extend far beyond those of previous generations of mobile communication.[3] These capabilities will include massive system capacity, very high data rates everywhere, very low latency, ultra-high reliability and availability, very low device cost and energy consumption, and energy-efficient networks.

1) Massive system capacity

Traffic demands for mobile-communication systems are predicted to increase dramatically. To support this traffic in an affordable way, 5G networks must deliver data with much lower cost per bit compared with the networks of today. Furthermore, the increase in data consumption will result in an growing energy footprint from networks. 5G must therefore consume significantly lower energy per delivered bit than current cellular networks.

The exponential increase in connected devices, such as the deployment of billions of wirelessly connected sensors, actuators and similar devices for massive machine connectivity, will place demands on the network to support new paradigms in device and connectivity management that do not compromise security. Each device will generate or consume very small amounts of data, to the extent that they will individually, or even jointly, have limited impact on the overall traffic volume. However, the sheer number of connected devices seriously challenges the ability of the network to provision signaling and manage connections.

2) Very high data rates everywhere

Every generation of mobile communication has been associated with higher data rates compared with the previous generation. In the past, much of the focus has been on the peak data rate that can be supported by a wireless-access technology under ideal conditions. However, a more important capability is the data rate that can actually be provided under real-life conditions in different scenarios.

(1) 5G should support data rates exceeding 10Gbps in specific scenarios such as indoor and dense outdoor environments.

(2) Data rates of several 100Mbps should generally be achievable in urban and suburban environments.

(3) Data rates of at least 10Mbps should be accessible almost everywhere, including sparsely populated rural areas in both developed and developing countries.

3) Very low latency

Very low latency will be driven by the need to support new applications. Some envisioned 5G use cases, such as traffic safety and control of critical infrastructure and industry processes, may require much lower latency compared with what is possible with the mobile communication systems of today.

To support such latency-critical applications, 5G should allow for an application end-to-end latency of 1ms or less, although application-level framing requirements and codec limitations for media may lead to higher latencies in practice.[4] Many services will distribute computational capacity and storage close to the air interface. This will create new capabilities for real-time communication and will allow ultra-high service reliability in a variety of scenarios, ranging from entertainment to industrial process control.

4) Ultra-high reliability and availability

In addition to very low latency, 5G should also enable connectivity with ultra-high reliability and ultra-high availability. For critical services, such as control of critical infrastructure and traffic safety, connectivity with certain characteristics, such as a specific maximum latency, should not merely be "typically available." Rather, loss of connectivity and deviation from quality of service requirements must be extremely rare. For example, some industrial applications might need to guarantee successful packet delivery within 1 ms with a probability higher than 99.9999 percent.

5) Very low device cost and energy consumption

Low-cost, low-energy mobile devices have been a key market requirement since the early days of mobile communication. However, to enable the vision of billions of wirelessly connected sensors, actuators and similar devices, a further step has to be taken in terms of device cost and energy consumption. It should be possible for 5G devices to be available at very low cost and with a battery life of several years without recharging.

6) Energy-efficient networks

While device energy consumption has always been prioritized, energy efficiency on the network side has recently emerged as an additional KPI, for three main reasons.

(1) Energy efficiency is an important component in reducing operational cost, as well as a driver for better dimensioned nodes, leading to lower total cost of ownership.

(2) Energy efficiency enables off-grid network deployments that rely on medium-sized solar panels as power supplies, thereby enabling wireless connectivity to reach even the most remote areas.

(3) Energy efficiency is essential to realizing operators' ambition of providing wireless access in a sustainable and more resource-efficient way. The importance of these factors will increase further in the 5G era, and energy efficiency will therefore be an important requirement in the design of 5G wireless access.

New Words and Expressions

massive	adj.	大规模的
wearables	n.	可穿戴设备
accelerate	v.	加快、加速
ubiquitous	adj.	无处不在的
interface	n.	接口
latency	n.	延迟
capacity	n.	容量
enormous	adj.	庞大的，巨大的
coverage	n.	覆盖范围(或方式)
interoperability	n.	互用性，互操作性
spectrum	n.	频谱
legacy device		传统设备
compatible	adj.	兼容的
essential	adj.	至关重要的
aggregation	n.	聚合
energy-efficient	adj.	高能效的
dramatically	adv.	急剧地
consumption	n.	消耗
footprint	n.	(尤指计算机)占用的空间
exponential	adj.	指数的
paradigm	n.	范例
prioritize	v.	优先考虑
solar panel		太阳能板

Notes

1. 5G will provide wireless connectivity for a wide range of new applications and use cases, including wearables, smart homes, traffic safety/control, critical infrastructure, industry processes and very-high-speed media delivery.

译文：5G 将为范围广泛的新应用和用例提供无线连接，包括可穿戴设备、智能家居、交通安全/控制、关键性的基础设施、工业过程和超高速媒体传输。

2. In a similar manner, LTE will evolve in a way that recognizes its role in providing excellent coverage for mobile users, and 5G networks will incorporate LTE access [based on Orthogonal Frequency Division Multiplexing (OFDM)] along with new air interfaces in a transparent manner toward both the service layer and users.

译文：以类似的方式，LTE 将以为移动用户提供良好覆盖的方式演进，并且 5G 网络将 LTE 接入[基于正交频分复用(OFDM)]与新的空中接口相结合以透明的方式面向服务层和用户。

3. In order to enable connectivity for a very wide range of applications with new characteristics and requirements, the capabilities of 5G wireless access must extend far beyond those of previous generations of mobile communication.

译文：为了确保大量应用的连接性可以满足新特性和要求，5G 无线接入的能力必须远远超过前几代移动通信。

4. To support such latency-critical applications, 5G should allow for an application end-to-end latency of 1ms or less, although application-level framing requirements and codec limitations for media may lead to higher latencies in practice.

译文：为了支持这样的延迟关键型应用，5G 应该要满足 1ms 或更短的端到端延迟，尽管在实际中可能会因应用层的框架要求和编解码器的限制导致更高的延迟。

Text B 5G Key Technologies: Identifying Innovation Opportunity

1. Introduction

Today, changes in the realm of telecommunication technology have occurred and will remain happening. Mobile telecommunication grows from first generation, known as 1G, to 2G, 3G, and now to the fourth generation that still in implementation stage in several countries, 4G. Every generation of technology have several differences and innovations.

5G is a terminology that is used for the 5th generation mobile technology. Telecommunication companies or standardization bodies of telecommunication such as 3GPP, WiMax Forum, or ITU-R haven't issued the official standard for 5G. The absence of official standard makes the 5G have limitless possibilities. However, several expectations have been raised about how 5G should and will be.

The 5G technology is expected to complete the 4G technology and provide solutions to the shortage arising from 4G technology. This technology will be a new technology that makes users able to access different Radio Access Technologies (RATs) using one mobile. 5G has been proposed to assemble the existing wireless and wired communication techniques into an all IP (Internet Protocol) high performance world wide network. 5G technology will help perfecting World Wide Wireless Web (WWWW). WWWW itself is an attempt to create a circumstance where subscriber can savor the great quality and quick access of internet, dynamic movement, favorable Bit Error Ratio (BER) and great security as on wired communications in their wireless communication devices.[1] Limitations of frequency resources making 5G shall have a technical development, which uses other resources than frequency/time resources in order to increase a capacity of the system.

In this paper, we try to identify innovation opportunity of the 5G technological development. It explored the fundamental literature framework to answer a question: in which technological area one may contribute to the innovation? The answer shall benefit countries, firms, universities and research institute which intends to contribute to the formulation of official 5G standard.

The second section of this paper provides the review of the key technologies of 5th generation mobile communication technology (5G). The third section presents our identification of technological challenges, focusing on the issues related to security and problems to deal with limited frequency spectrum resources. In the fourth section, we mapped the innovation opportunity based on technological area which is recently published in research article.

2. Review of 5G key technologies

There are several key technologies which are expected to help fulfilling the need of improvement for 5G. Those are Flat IP Based Network and Cognitive Radio (CR).

1) Flat IP based network

Previous works by Toni Janevski from University Sv Kiril I Metodij define the basic concept of 5G mobile network which is seen as user-centric concept instead of operator-centric as in 3G or service-centric concept as seen for 4G. The 5G mobile phone is designed as an open platform on different layers, from physical layer up to the application.

The network layer at 5G networks will be divided into several sub-layers to provide all-IP connectivity anywhere and anytime. The use of the Internet Protocol (IP) in the network layer is inevitable, given the IP system is the best and most used system to support and expand the network layer nowadays. All IP Network (AIPN) system has started well since the development of LTE.

All IP Network (AIPN) system has started well since the development of LTE as an evolution of the 3GPP system. Flat IP Network is a key concept that is expected to make 5G acceptable to all kinds of technology. Flat IP architecture provides a way to identify each device using symbolic names, unlike the hierarchical architecture commonly used in the usual IP address. With the shift to flat IP architectures, mobile operators will be able to:

- Reduce the number of network elements in the data path, thereby reducing operations costs and capital expenditure.

- Splitting the cost of service delivery from the amount of data that is sent to equate infrastructure capabilities to the requirements of emerging applications.

- Minimize system latency and enable applications with a lower tolerance for delay; upcoming latency enhancements on the radio link can also be fully realized.

- Evolve radio access and packet core networks independently of each other to achieve greater development and make better flexibility in network planning and deployment.

- Develop a flexible core network that can be the basis of innovative services for mobile and generic IP access network.

Create a platform that will enable mobile broadband operators to be competitive with wired networks in terms of price and performance.

IPv6 is the best possible system that can support a flat IP network for technology implementation 5G later. IPv6 is the latest revision of the IP system is expected to overcome the shortcomings of the predecessor version of IPv4. Each device will then have a fixed IPv6 address, and multiple addresses Care of Address (CoA). The number of CoA for the device is according to the number of access networks where device is connected. There are 3 sub-layers of the network layer, the lower network layer, middleware layer and the upper network layer. Lower network layer use CoA, middleware network layer translates CoA into IPv6 so the upper network layer using IPv6 addresses.

Device is expected to be provided by a variety of options in order to get the best wireless connection in accordance with the type of device and current network conditions. QoS parameters such as delay time, jitter, bandwidth, reliability and so on will be stored in a database that can be used for training intelligent algorithms in a mobile terminal, thus the 5G technology can choose the best connections for the device at the given time and condition.[2]

2) Cognitive radio

For mobile and wireless communications technologies, since the 4G, interoperability was an important thing, as it is also applied for 5G(Fig.2). Interoperability system means any system with different technologies can work together and communicate with each other. The network architecture for 5G mobile system consists of a user terminal and a number of independent, autonomous radio access technologies. Within each of the terminals, each of the radio access technologies is seen as the IP link to the outside Internet world. With the use of cognitive radio terminal, 5G can achieve interoperability and still have a good quality of service. In the cognition system, the system recognizes the location, position and condition to determine the best option for network. With this system, users can choose a suitable network for communication and different wireless networks will be able to integrate and communicate with each other via cognitive radio devices.

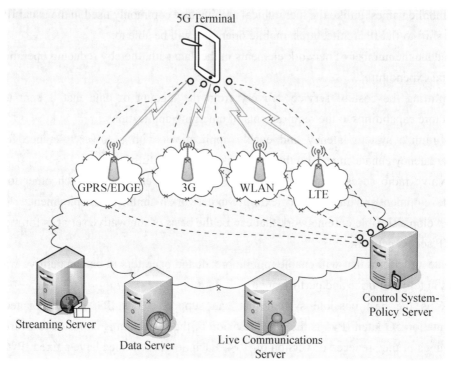

Fig.2　5G interoperability

Cognitive radio is an intelligent communication system that is aware of its surrounding environment (i.e., outside world), and uses the methodology of understanding-by-building to learn from the environment and adapt its internal states to statistical variations in the incoming RF stimuli by making corresponding changes in certain operating parameters (e.g., transmit-power, carrier-frequency, and modulation strategy) in real-time, with two primary objectives in mind: highly reliable communication whenever and wherever needed; efficient utilization of the radio spectrum.

By that definition, the cognitive terminal is a smart terminal with intelligence to choose the proper network from all the existing wireless networks. The choice is based on some information such as time, demand, and resource. The 5G technology proposes a universal terminal, which should include all of the radio predecessors features into a single device. This terminal convergence is strongly sustained by the users' needs and demands; therefore, cognitive radio becomes the ideal 5G terminal candidate.

3. Technological challenges

By understanding the key technologies of 5G, we identified the technological challenges which mainly lie on the problems concerning security as well as limited frequency resources.

1) Security

Being able to scan the available spectrum, select from a wide range of operating frequencies, adjust modulation wave forms, and perform adaptive resource allocation — all of these in real-time — these new Cognitive Radio technology will be able to adapt to a wide variety of radio interference conditions and adaptively select the most efficient communication mechanisms.[3] However, in addition to the advantages and potential of the cognitive radio technology, there are a number of challenges related to security, especially in cognitive radio terminals. The paradigm of cognitive radio systems poses a new threat on security, such as selfish misbehaviors, harmful interference, licensed user emulation, competition between licensed users and eavesdropping.

There is an opportunity and need to develop a system that able to prevent the misuse in the highly open and granular control which is provided to the radio interface. One of them was proposed by with a framework known as TRIESTE which is short term for Trusted Radio Infrastructure for Enforcing Spectrum Etiquettes. TRIESTE will be able to ensure that radio devices are only able to access and use the spectrum in a manner that conforms to their privileges.

2) Limited frequency spectrum resources

Limited spectrum resources yielded a major challenge for mobile and wireless technologies. Those limited frequency and time are divided to be used among multiple users. Due to this condition, it is expected to improve efficiency in order to enhance the capacity and quality of the system. To achieve this, several multiple access techniques used today, for example, Time Division Multiple Access (TDMA), Frequency Division Multiple Access (FDMA), Code Division Multiple Access (CDMA), Orthogonal Frequency Division Multiple Access (OFDMA), etc. However, in all of multiple access system that are used nowadays, the capacity of a mobile communication system depends on time and frequency. This generates a challenge to develop a multiple access system which is able to resolve the dependencies of capacity to the limited frequency spectrum. Korean research and development has suggested BDMA as a radio interface for 5G, which is not depended on frequency/time resources.

The BDMA technique of the present invention divides an antenna beam according to locations of the mobile stations to allow the mobile stations to give multiple accesses, thereby significantly increasing the capacity of the system. In such a concept, mobile stations and a base station are in a Line of Sight (LOS) state, so they exactly know each other's positions. In this condition they will be able to transmit beams which direct to each other's position to communicate without interfering with mobile stations at cell edge.

For adapting the BDMA system into 5G, the development of the phase array antenna is required. The smart antenna with the ability to switch its beam is needed. Switched beam antennas support radio positioning via Angle of Arrival (AOA) information collected from base and mobile stations. The use of adaptive antenna arrays is one area that shows opportunity for improving the capabilities.

4. Innovation opportunities

Opening up innovations opportunity means to discover the technical area as the guidance to conduct research work on such particular technological agenda. We monitored the spread of technical issues related to 5G in various scientific and engineering journals. There are 18 research articles which have stated 5G as the main corresponding topic in their research work. Those publications include 7 conference papers, 7 journal papers, 3 conference reviews and 1 document review.

Subsequently, we map the technical area based on 40 keywords mentioned in those 18 research articles. Table 1 lists the keywords and the corresponding number of research articles. In general, it mainly indicates that technical area is not yet heavily concentrated on certain technological agenda. However, more researches were conducted concerning topics of relay selection, mobile ad hoc network and one hop cooperative MAC, while other topics are equally distributed.

We identified that the keywords are likely relevant to three technological agenda, i.e. security, network, and technological implementation and applications issues.

Security technological agenda spreads over collision avoidance, Denial of Service (DoS), blacklisting, etc. Meanwhile, network technological agenda consists of protocol, all IP network, ad hoc network, etc. Some other technological agenda that remain being the most researched topic are frequency hopping topic, MIMO system, space time codes, relay selection techniques, multi hop systems, etc. There are also a few of topics other those main topics, which are covering about implementation of the proposed 5G applications, such as implanted medical devices, remote monitoring and telemedicine.

Based on those findings, we may formulate the concept to exploit opportunity on certain technological agenda. Researchers may work on those specific areas, which can lead to new innovation on 5G. Such a concept is mainly benefit the developing country which intends to increase their innovation and technological competitiveness. For example, since relay selection has been frequently researched, a new researcher may establish the cooperative work with other researchers working on that field. As in the future, wireless network is expected to be able to support the relay-based communication, where the relay node is well-placed to receive messages from the source node, process it, and then forward it to the node of its intended destination.[4] Alternatively, developing country can put more concentration on another topic such as spatial diversity, AODV, or technique to improve collision avoidance, since the works on those fields are relatively less conducted.

As the continuous upgrading of wireless technologies, the basic concept of 5G is to open up all the doors of possible methods, technologies and techniques used to leverage telecommunication for human life. Combining with the perspective of 5G key technologies, in particular about flat based IP and cognitive radio, any researchers may contribute to the development of relevant standard. Such research activities are not only to improve faster data access, but also to create innovation on many technical areas as shown in Table 1.

Table1　Keywords on 5G research publications

Keywords on the research articles	Number of research publications
Relay selection	4
Mobile Adhoc Networks (MANETS)	3
One-hop cooperative MAC	3
Ad hoc On-Demand Distance Vector (AODV)	2
Architecture for humanity	2
Blacklsiting	2
Dnynamic Source Routing (DSR)	2
Error Vector Magnitude (EVM)	2
GNU Radio	2
Multihop wireless network	2
Orthogonal space time codes	2
Prognoses	2
Remote monitoring	2
Two-hop cooperative communication	2
Universal Software Radio Peripheral(USRP)	2
Wireless optics	2
All IP networks	1
Collision avoidance	1
Constellation sizes	1
Cooperative protocols	1
Core networks	1
Denial of Service(Dos)	1
Dense network	1
Heterogeneous networking	1
Linear complexity	1
MIMO channels	1
Modulation technique	1
Multi-hops	1
Network achitecture	1
OFDM systems	1
Packet delivery ratio	1
Parallel transmission	1
Piraeus	1
Service oriented architecture	1
Space diversity	1
Space time code	1
Spatial diversity	1
Spectrum efficiency	1
Throughput improvement	1
Ubiquitous and pervasive computing	1

Finally, it is commonly known that technological development of preceding standards (1G, 2G and 3G) were dominantly controlled by developed countries such as USA, Japan and some European countries. Therefore, in current and future time, developing countries should contribute to 5G technological development by utilizing innovation opportunities. Results of research works on 5G can be made into technical submission to the international standardization bodies, such as ITU. Meanwhile, developing countries can also push their national industries to develop patents and to create innovation on relevant 5G technical areas. It is believed that those schemes may influence the global standards development and increase the country's competitiveness.

5. Conclusions

Key technologies in the seam of 5G has been reviewed, i.e. Flat IP Based Network and Cognitive Radio. The key technologies help us to spot the 5G technological challenges. The challenges mainly exist in the security area and the limited frequency resources problem.

We have identified innovation opportunity regarding the technological development of 5G standards from understanding technological challenges and exploring fundamental literature framework. There is an opportunity and demand to develop a system that will be able to prevent the misuse of control, maintain the security and enhance the capacity of system. As the result of exploring literature framework, we conclude three technological agenda in which one may contribute to, i.e. security, network, and technological implementation and applications issues. Accordingly, researchers can make new research focusing on those technical area and make new innovation for the 5G technological development. It is expected that research works may result a relevant submission to the international standardization bodies. On the other hand, innovation can be also made by pushing national industries to develop patents and to create innovation on such relevant 5G technical areas. (Quoted from "5G Key Technologies: Identifying Innovation Opportunity")

New Words and Expressions

terminology	n.	术语
Cognitive Radio (CR)		认知无线电
sub-layer		子层
All IP Network (AIPN)		全 IP 网络
hierarchical architecture		分层架构
enhancement	n.	增强
flexibility	n.	灵活性
innovative	adj.	创新的
operator	n.	运营商
Care of Address (CoA)		转交地址
transmit-power		发射功率
carrier-frequency		载波频率
modulation strategy		调制方式
eavesdropping	n.	窃听
granular	adj.	颗粒状的

第 2 章　Application and Appreciation

privilege	n.	特权
Line of Sight (LoS)		视线
Angle of Arrival (AoA)		到达角
relay	n.	中继
implanted	adj.	(医学)植入的
remote monitoring		远程监控
telemedicine	n.	远程医疗
spatial diversity		空间分集

Notes

1. WWWW itself is an attempt to create a circumstance where subscriber can savor the great quality and quick access of internet, dynamic movement, favorable Bit Error Ratio (BER) and great security as on wired communications in their wireless communication devices.

译文：全球无线网络本身就是企图创造一种应用环境，即用户在使用无线通信设备时，能有与有线通信方式类似的优质体验，如能快速访问互联网、能动态移动、良好的误码率以及极高的安全性。

2. QoS parameters such as delay time, jitter, bandwidth, reliability and so on will be stored in a database that can be used for training intelligent algorithms in a mobile terminal, thus the 5G technology can choose the best connections for the device at the given time and condition.

译文：服务质量参数，如延迟时间、抖动、带宽、可靠性等，将被存储在用于训练智能算法的一个移动终端数据库中，因此在给定的时间和条件下，5G 技术可以为设备选择最佳的连接。

3. Being able to scan the available spectrum, select from a wide range of operating frequencies, adjust modulation wave forms, and perform adaptive resource allocation — all of these in real-time — these new Cognitive Radio technology will be able to adapt to a wide variety of radio interference conditions and adaptively select the most efficient communication mechanisms.

译文：扫描可用频谱、从广泛的工作频率中进行选择、调整调制波形并执行自适应性的资源分配，以上所有行为都是实时的，即新的认知无线电技术能在各种各样的无线电干扰条件下，自适应地选择最有效的通信机制。

4. As in the future, wireless network is expected to be able to support the relay-based communication, where the relay node is well-placed to receive messages from the source node, process it, and then forward it to the node of its intended destination.

译文：预测未来的无线网络将能够支持基于中继的通信，其中中继节点能够很好地接收来自源节点的消息，并对其进行处理，然后转发到预期的目的节点。

Exercises

Lesson Seven Industrial Internet

Text A Introduction to Industrial Internet

1. An introduction of Industrial Internet

Today we find ourselves in what is called the fourth industrial revolution: Industry 4.0. This revolution merges the physical world with the virtual one and develops digital models of the system before its construction. Industrial Internet tackles the challenges of the industry: increased functionality in products, more connectivity, high interdisciplinarity, designing for X, more product/process complexity, etc. It is an integrated engineering approach where different software tools are interconnected during the whole lifetime of the project, reducing inconsistencies and developing times.

Industrial Internet is leading in an innovative way of industrialized mutiny from end-to-end networking, industrial equipment, calculating, and users. This is creating different ways to link various sensors and actuators that are inserted in the machines with the help of Internet. The gigantic quantities of data are produced via sensors and are supplementary analyzed to comprehend the functioning and conditioning of the apparatuses and industrial systems, and even authorize independent operations and controlling the complete systems. It is going to influence a wide industrialized spectrum that includes trade, health care, conveyance, power, oil and gas, operation, smart buildings, and cities. The topics that are generally included in this are: industrial cyber-physical systems, industrial communication and schmoozing technologies, industrial cloud and edge computing, industrial robotics and autonomous systems, data management and analytics, security, trust, real-time, privacy, reliability, and safety, industrial big data and AI and applications, test beds, and case studies.

2. Industrial Internet of Things Analytics Framework

The Industrial Internet Consortium (IIC) has recently published an Industrial Internet of Things Analytics Framework (IIAF), as part of their Industrial Internet Reference Architecture (IIRA) series of publications. Industrial IoT (IIoT) targets the integration of industrial assets and machines to enterprise information systems, business processes, and people who operate and use them. The IIAF thus puts a focus on applying analytics to data and control related to Operational Technology (OT). The IIAF provides assistance in how to develop and deploy analytics solutions in an industrial IoT context and provides guidance into business, usage, and technology perspectives according to the IIRA viewpoints. As such, the IIAF is the first work of its kind by an industrial alliance to start the modeling of analytics, AI, and other MI technologies applied to the context of the IoT.

In the work by IIC, analytics is mapped onto the IIRA consisting of the following main functional domains (see Fig.1):

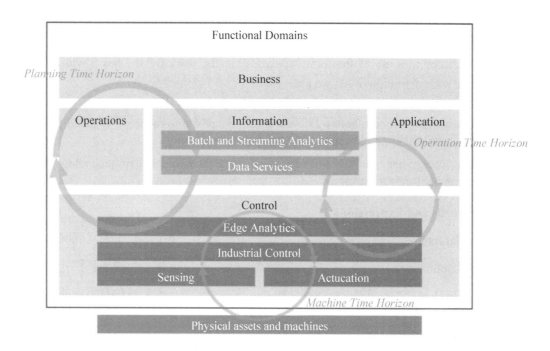

Fig.1　Analytics mapped to the IIC reference architecture (adapted from IIC)

• Control: This domain interfaces the physical assets via sensing and actuation and provides the necessary underlying communications and execution means. It is the collection of functions performed by the industrial assets and associated control systems.

• Information: The information domain performs the collection, transformation, and analysis of data to reach a higher level of intelligence of the system.

• Application: The application domain provides use case-specific logic, rules, and models to deliver system-wide optimization of operations and relies on intelligence from the information domain.

• Business: This domain integrates information across applications and business systems in order to reach the desired business objectives.

• Operations: This last domain ensures the continued operations of assets and the associated control systems.

As can be seen, applying industrial analytics is considered in three main time horizons. The control domain at the edge provides real-time operational insights in the "machine time horizon" which involves sensing–actuation control loops in milliseconds or less which can be typical in factory robot control. Machine fault detection or diagnostics is based on deriving insights from machine data to discover anomalies or understand any changing behavior of the operations. This takes place in the "operation time horizon" which requires responses in seconds or more. Finally, the "planning time horizon" focuses more on business planning, operations planning, and scheduling and also other more long-term engineering processes. This time horizon requires responses in days or more.

The IIAF provides a high level overview of industrial analytics design considerations, deployment models, and different types of analytics including the relation to Big Data and AI. As can be understood, the use of the term "analytics" in the work by IIC has a wider definition, similar to the wide definition of MI we use.

https://www.elsevier.com/books/T/A/9780128144350[2022-1-25]

https://www.elsevier.com/books/27th-european-symposium-on-computer-aided-process-engineering/espuna/978-0-444-63965-3[2022-1-23]

https://www.elsevier.com/books/handbook-of-research-on-blockchain-technology/krishnan/978-0-12-819816-2[2022-1-23]

New Words and Expressions

Industrial Internet		工业互联网
interdisciplinarity	n.	跨学科性
cyber-physical		信息物理的
IIC (Industrial Internet Consortium)	n.	工业互联网联盟
IIAF (Industrial Internet of Things Analytics Framework)	n.	工业物联网分析框架
IIRA (Industrial Internet Reference Architecture)	n.	工业互联网参考体系结构
OT (Operational Technology)		操作技术
end-to-end		端对端的
conveyance	n.	运送
autonomous	adj.	自动的
analytics	n.	解析学
case-specific		特定案例的

Notes

1. Today we find ourselves in what is called the fourth industrial revolution: Industry 4.0. This revolution merges the physical world with the virtual one and develops digital models of the system before its construction.

译文：今天，我们发现自己处于所谓的第四次工业革命：工业4.0。这场革命将物理世界与虚拟世界融合在一起，并在构建系统之前开发了系统的数字模型。

2. It is an integrated engineering approach where different software tools are interconnected during the whole lifetime of the project, reducing inconsistencies and developing times.

译文：这是一种集成工程方法，不同的软件工具在项目的整个生命周期内相互连接，缩小了不一致性、减少了开发时间。

3. Industrial Internet is leading in an innovative way of industrialized mutiny from end-to-end networking, industrial equipment, calculating, and users.

译文：工业互联网正以一种创新的方式引领着端到端网络、工业设备、计算和用户的工业化变革。

4. The IIAF provides a high level overview of industrial analytics design considerations, deployment models, and different types of analytics including the relation to Big Data and AI.

译文：IIAF 提供了工业分析设计考虑因素、部署模型和不同类型分析(包括与大数据和人工智能的关系)的高级概述。

Text B Industrial Internet of Things

1. Industrial Internet of Things

IoT, a general concept, makes anything and everything in the physical world communicate with each other, whereas IIoT is an application of IoT technology in the manufacturing industry. IIoT also requires all the participating devices/machines in the manufacturing setup to be intelligent and communicable. Specific features of IIoT in the manufacturing process are:

• It captures all sensor data from the machines, facilitates machine-to-machine communication, and makes use of automation technologies that have existed in the industrial environment for years.

• It incorporates data analytics, machine learning and big data analysis technology.

• The driving philosophy behind IIoT is that the smart (intelligent and communicable) machines along with human intelligence are better for accurate and consistent data capturing, and subsequent dispatch.

• Analyses of the captured data enable companies to identify invisibility and inefficiency problems quickly in the manufacturing process, save time and money, and support business intelligence efforts.

• It holds great potential for quality control, sustainable practices, supply chain efficiency, operational efficiency, maintenance, and traceability.

2. Future of IIoT

The future of IIoT has the potential to be limitless. The rise of industrial IoT will soon bring the factory of the future to reality. Advances to the industrial internet will be accelerated through increased network agility, integrated artificial intelligence (AI) and the capacity to deploy, automate, orchestrate and secure diverse use cases at hyper-scale. An exciting wave of future IoT applications will emerge, brought to life through intuitive human to machine interactivity. Human 4.0 will allow humans to interact in real time over great distances—both with each other and with machines—and have similar sensory experiences to those that they experience locally. This will enable new opportunities within remote learning, surgery and repair. Immersive mixed reality applications have the potential to become the next platform after mobile—realized through 3D audio and haptic sensations and becoming our main interface to the real world. Bringing future IoT to life will require close synergy between the IoT- and network platforms.

The Ignition IIoT solution greatly improves connectivity, efficiency, scalability, time savings, and cost savings for industrial organizations. It can unite the people and systems on the plant floor with those at the enterprise level. It can also allow enterprises to get the most value from their system without being constrained by technological and economic limitations.

To gain the upper-edge on these looming forces, executing on an IIoT strategy is becoming invaluable in industrial enterprises. These adopters will benefit from extensive IIoT solutions quickly solving their business needs of today and capable of scaling to meet future requirements of tomorrow. The competencies of IIoT providers will become more apparent as these projects grow and these shifting requirements need solutions from providers with the right mix of technology, domain knowledge, and a partnership ecosystem to fill the gaps. Successful IIoT deployments in manufacturing and operations functions will continue to span across organizational hierarchies enabling synchronized operations with IIoT touch points ranging from the CXO to front-line worker.

Myriad global forces are causing organizations to become more "digital" at a rapid pace to avoid disruption, become more efficient, and capitalize on new opportunities. This digital transformation means different things to different industries. In manufacturing it comes back to operational efficiencies and becoming more flexible and agile.

The Industrial Internet of Things will drastically change the future, not just for industrial systems, but also for the many people involved. From wrist watches to smart appliances, we can already see this trend come to fruition. If we can achieve the full potential of the Industrial IoT vision, many people will have an opportunity to better their careers and standards of living because the full potential of this vision will lead to countless value creation opportunities. This always happens when new "revolutions" get set into motion.

The full potential of the Industrial IoT will lead to smart power grids, smart healthcare, smart logistics, smart diagnostics, and numerous other "smart" paradigms. Material handling, manufacturing, product distribution and supply chain management will all be automated to a degree in the years to come. In the future, experts suggest that industrial IoT will enhance production levels even further and become the driving force behind various types of innovation (including the utilization of innovative fuels). It will enable manufacturing ecosystems driven by smart systems that have autonomic self-* properties such as self-configuration, self-monitoring, and self-healing. Think of a "Terminator" style technology. Instead, this is technology that will allow us to achieve unprecedented levels of operational efficiencies and accelerated growth in productivity.

While an array of adoption challenges will still have to be overcome, predictive analysis suggested that the world would have 50 billion connected devices by 2020. It would be a pity for such a massive network to remain unutilized in attempts to enhance industrial processes. Remember that industrial IoT is not about smart product development. Rather, it will help for a higher level of efficiency and predictive rather than reactionary interventions—a main problem industries across the world are struggling with today.

https://www.sciencedirect.com/science/article/abs/pii/S0065245819300634

New Words and Expressions

philosophy	*n.*	哲学
synergy	*n.*	协同作用
scalability	*n.*	可扩展性
ecosystem	*n.*	生态系统
agile	*adj.*	敏捷的
drastically	*adv.*	猛烈地
fruition	*n.*	完成，取得成果
reactionary	*adj.*	反动的，保守的；[化] 反应的
hyper-scale		超大规模的
self-configuration		自配置
self-monitoring		自我监控的
self-healing		自我修复的

Notes

1. IIoT also requires all the participating devices/machines in the manufacturing setup to be intelligent and communicable.

译文：IIoT 还要求制造设置中的所有参与设备/机器具有智能性和可通信性。

2. It captures all sensor data from the machines, facilitates machine-to-machine communication, and makes use of automation technologies that have existed in the industrial environment for years.

译文：它从机器上捕获所有传感器数据，促进机器之间的通信，并利用工业环境中存在多年的自动化技术。

3. It holds great potential for quality control, sustainable practices, supply chain efficiency, operational efficiency, maintenance, and traceability.

译文：它在质量控制、可持续实践、供应链效率、运营效率、维护和可追溯性方面具有巨大潜力。

4. If we can achieve the full potential of the Industrial IoT vision, many people will have an opportunity to better their careers and standards of living because the full potential of this vision will lead to countless value creation opportunities.

译文：如果我们能够实现工业物联网愿景的全部潜力，许多人将有机会改善他们的职业和生活水平，因为这一愿景的全部潜力将带来无数的价值创造机会。

Exercises

Lesson Eight　Intelligent Transportation Systems

什么是智能交通

Text A　Introduction to Intelligent Transportation Systems

1. An introduction of Intelligent Transportation Systems

Intelligent Transportation Systems (ITS) technologies include state-of-the-art wireless, electronic, and automated technologies. Collectively, these technologies have the potential to integrate vehicles (transit, trucks, and personal vehicles), system users, and infrastructure (roads and transit). Automated and in-vehicle technologies include precision docking for buses, automated guideways, and collision avoidance systems. Many ITS technologies can help to optimize trips (route guidance), diminish unnecessary miles traveled, increase other mode use, reduce time spent in congestion, reduce dependence on foreign oil, and improve air quality. Furthermore, when ITS technologies are applied to system management (transit and highways) and vehicle design, they can reduce fuel consumption by the following:

• facilitating optimal route planning and timing;

• smoothing accelerations/decelerations and stop-and-go driving;

• reducing congestion;

• enabling pricing and demand management strategies;

• increasing the attractiveness of public transportation mode use;

• adjusting vehicle transmission for varying road conditions and terrain;

• facilitating small platoons of closely spaced vehicles (i.e., safer vehicles could enable weight reduction without compromising occupant safety).

Although ITS technologies are still in the early phase of deployment, many have shown the potential to reduce energy use. During the past 10 years or so, fuel consumption impacts of the following ITS technologies have been studied: ① traffic signal control, ② traffic management and surveillance (e.g., ramp metering), ③ incident management, ④ Electronic Toll Collection (ETC), ⑤ traveler information, ⑥ transit management, ⑦ Commercial Vehicle Operations (CVO), and ⑧ vehicle control technologies. Nevertheless, ITS impacts, including benefits, unintended consequences, and aggregate effects, are still not well understood.

Information technologies and intelligent transportation systems offer some promise for reducing freight transportation's external costs. Intelligent freight transportation uses advanced technologies and intelligent decision making to make existing infrastructure for freight transportation more efficient. ITS has two key elements: intelligence and integration. The first is characterized by knowledge discovery made possible by better access to data and advanced data-analysis techniques, and the second by an understanding of how to use that data to manage the elements of the system more efficiently. Freight ITS benefits from reduced delay and congestion costs because of the development of integrated systems. Containerized cargo is the main focus in some intelligent freight transportation because it reduces handling cost and loading and unloading time, increases storage efficiency, and increases average payloads.

Crainic et al. reviewed freight ITS, including advances in two-way communication, location and tracking devices, Electronic Data Interchange (EDI), advanced planning, and operation decision-support systems and classified them into two groups: CVO and advanced fleet management systems (AFMS). The first group includes systemwide, regional, national, or continental applications, and the second group is more concerned about the operations of a particular firm or group of firms. Both groups require e-business activities to be partially integrated across firms, and both are the result of adopting EDI in freight transportation. EDI is a two-way communication and vehicle and cargo location and tracking technology. Of course, the original motivation for development of these technologies was not reducing externalities but increasing the efficiency of the freight-transportation system, which can indirectly decrease externalities.

2. The way forward

ITS needs more in-depth and systematic research in policy making. Autonomous vehicles will revolutionize the transport sector with numerous significant policy suggestions. Further research is required to measure how much ITS can lessen the bottlenecks and contamination and thus make a better sustainable ecology. Also, similar in-depth research is required to enhance safer and more effectual rail systems to improve the expedition efficacy and cross-border enablement. The secretariat of the Economic and Social Commission for Asia and the Pacific could also bring out additional investigations into mixed mode commuting and interconnected transport systems, with a vision to promote smooth trade in possessions and the development of tourism in the province. A similar study should also be done in domestic waterways, navigation, air traffic control, and maritime transport.

https://www.sciencedirect.com/science/article/pii/B012176480X001911[2022-1-23]

https://www.sciencedirect.com/science/article/pii/B9780128182871000139[2022-1-23]

3. Key tech policies from China's 20th Communist Party Congress——Transition to green and low-carbon development

China needs to find a development model that also protects the environment, pursuing economic growth while cutting carbon emissions, reducing pollution, expanding green development, protecting ecology, and conserving resources.

Other major efforts under Beijing's climate initiative include carefully promoting hydropower facilities given their large environmental impact, actively developing nuclear power safely and orderly, improving the official CO_2 emissions calculation tool, and establishing a national carbon trading scheme. In addition, China continues to head toward carbon neutrality by shifting toward green energy vehicles. China vowed to promote a low-carbon lifestyle and step up the green revolution in the transportation sector.

In 2021, China's ambition to become a leader in global climate actions faced major setbacks as operations of heavy industries such as steelmaking experienced a widespread power crunch. At this year's congress, the central government addressed concerns around economic stability and strength, that China will steadily reach peak carbon and carbon neutrality, implementing control measures "in a planned and step-by-step manner".

The country would continue to speed up the establishment of a clean energy revolution while enhancing the "clean and efficient use of coal" given its natural resource restraints. The strategy is meant to see a gradual reduction of total emissions as well as carbon intensity, which refers to the amount of energy consumed per unit of economic growth.

https://technode.com/2022/10/17/key-tech-policies-from-chinas-20th-communist-party-congress/.[2023-06-06].

New Words and Expressions

ITS (Intelligent Transportation Systems)		智能交通系统
state-of-the-art		最先进的
Electronic Toll Collection (ETC)		电子收费系统
Commercial Vehicle Operations (CVO)		商用车量营运系统
Electronic Data Interchange (EDI)		电子数据交换
cross-border		跨国的
externalities	n.	外部效应
systemwide	adj.	全系统的
surveillance	n.	监察

Notes

1. Autonomous vehicles will revolutionize the transport sector with numerous significant policy suggestions.

译文：自动驾驶汽车将通过众多重大政策建议彻底改变交通部门。

2. Information technologies and intelligent transportation systems offer some promise for reducing freight transportation's external costs.

译文：信息技术和智能交通系统为降低货运的外部成本提供了一些希望。

3. Intelligent freight transportation uses advanced technologies and intelligent decision making to make existing infrastructure for freight transportation more efficient.

译文：智能货运使用先进的技术和智能决策，使现有的货运基础设施更加高效。

4. Many ITS technologies can help to optimize trips (route guidance), diminish unnecessary miles traveled, increase other mode use, reduce time spent in congestion, reduce dependence on foreign oil, and improve air quality.

译文：许多 ITS 技术可以帮助优化出行(路线指引)，减少不必要的行驶里程，增加其他交通方式的使用，减少拥堵时间，减少对外国石油的依赖，以及改善空气质量。

Text B Applications of Intelligent Transportation Systems

1. Traffic Control

ITS allows for traffic control systems that are more advanced than traditional timed traffic signals. One type of control device is intelligent traffic lights, which use traffic data collected at the local intersection, as well as future traffic information provided by RSUs, to create a dynamic time schedule to maximize the flow of traffic through an intersection. Another control system is variable speed limits. These systems work to minimize traffic density in congested areas by dynamically changing the speed limit of roads based on weather conditions, road conditions, or the presence of congestion areas. Lastly, dynamic lanes can be used to provide more inbound or outbound lanes depending on the flow of traffic as traffic in many metropolitan areas is not symmetric.

2. ITS Big Data Application and Service Platform

The ITS Big Data application and service platform is based on ITS Big Data and the ITS cloud computing supporting platform. It adopts the "central data storage and processing" and "local application and service" mode. The real-time transportation information is grabbed from ITS Big Data and analyzed together with the historical data. Intelligent predictions are made on the platform to provide decision support for users.

The ITS Big Data application and service platform mainly provides services for the government, enterprises, and public users. The platform structure is shown in Fig.1. The government can use the platform for the management of transportation law enforcement. Multiple services are available, including accurate geoinformation, traffic management, emergency response, on-road parking space management, and public transit supervision. Enterprises can use the platform for the accurate acquisition of geoinformation, assistance in decision-making, and the analysis of commercial data. In addition, mobile applications are developed for the public users to provide them with transportation information services. The data of public trip behavior can be gathered through the APPs (Applications). And in return the public users get improved services like accurate geoinformation, real-time traffic conditions, driving and parking guidance, etc.

Based on this platform, the industry data, computation resources, and characterized intelligence analysis results can be shared by different kinds of users. In this way, system resources and costs can be saved, and at the same time efficiency can be improved significantly.

3. Smart transportation systems (STSs) in critical conditions

In the context of smart transportation systems (STSs) in smart cities, the use of applications that can help in case of critical conditions is a key point. Examples of critical conditions may be natural-disaster events such as earthquakes, hurricanes, floods, and manmade ones such as terrorist attacks and toxic waste spills. Disaster events are often combined with the destruction of the local telecommunication infrastructure, if any, and this implies real problems to the rescue operations.

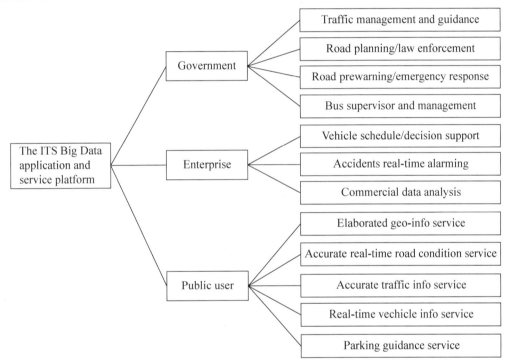

Fig.1 The platform structure

The quick deployment of a telecommunication infrastructure is essential for emergency and safety operations as well as the rapid network reconfigurability, the availability of open source software, the efficient interoperability, and the scalability of the technological solutions. The topic is very hot and many research groups are focusing on these issues. Consequently, the deployment of a smart network is fundamental. It is needed to support both applications that can tolerate delays and applications requiring dedicated resources for real-time services such as traffic alert messages, and public safety messages. The guarantee of Quality of Service (QoS) for such applications is a key requirement.

https://www.sciencedirect.com/science/article/abs/pii/S0065245816300304.[2023-06-06].

https://www.sciencedirect.com/science/article/pii/B9780128120132000083.[2023-06-06].
https://www.sciencedirect.com/science/article/pii/B9780128034545000146.[2023-06-06].

4. Recursive traffic percolation on urban transportation systems

Researchers from Fudan University and Shanghai University of Electric Power in China proposes a recursive traffic percolation framework to capture the dynamics of cascading failures and analyze potential overloaded bottlenecks. In particular, compared to current work, the influence of external flow is considered, providing a new perspective for the study of regional commuting. Finally, they present an empirical study to verify the accuracy and effectiveness of their framework. Further analysis indicates that external flows from different regions affect the network. Their work requires only primary data and verifies the improvement of the functional network.

This research sits at the intersection of physics and information science and is an innovative model involving the study of smart cities. The model uses a modified form of percolation theory, widely used to understand flow of liquids through porous media, such as soil and gels. When liquid flows through a network of pores, it is occasionally blocked in much the same way the flow of vehicles through roads can be blocked.

In constructing their model, the investigators considered the existing road network and population distribution in Shanghai. They generated trips between various population centers, assigning those trips to roads that provided the shortest travel distance.

"The urban area is an open system where, in addition to intraregional flows, there is also an exchange of flows between external regions. To simulate the effect of commuting, we increased the population of bordering regions," author Yugang Ma said.

The traffic load on each road was converted to a velocity. When the flow of traffic reached an unacceptably low velocity on a given road, that road was deemed dysfunctional and removed from the model. Framework of the traffic modeling procedure is shown in Fig.2.

By repeating this process in a recursive fashion, the investigators discovered that a massive cascading failure of the urban transportation system occurred in a sudden and discontinuous fashion, much the way a phase transition occurs suddenly when ice melts or water boils.

Author and project leader Dingding Han said, "We used publicly available maps for the Yangpu District in Shanghai and identified four roads that serve as major commuting thoroughfares. By applying our recursive traffic percolation model, we were able to identify one particular thoroughfare, Zhonghuan Road, as a potential bottleneck that could lead to cascading failure of the entire urban traffic system."

When Zhonghuan Road becomes blocked, traffic flows into side streets that are eventually unable to handle the flow of vehicles. This leads to additional blockages and a breakdown of the entire system. When this occurs, the network of roads breaks into disconnected fragments.

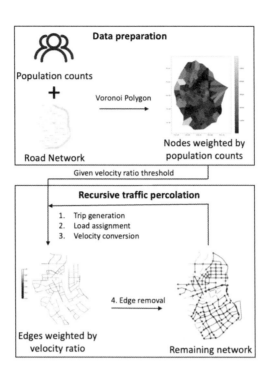

Fig.2　Framework of the traffic modeling procedure

"It is worth noting that the Zhonghuan Road bottleneck was found during the fifth round of road removal in our model," author Jianghai Qian said. "Through the dynamic process of cascading failure, the hidden bottleneck was discovered."

https://www.eurekalert.org/news-releases/983138.[2023-06-06].

https://publishing.aip.org/publications/latest-content/cascading-failures-in-urban-traffic-systems-tied-to-hidden-bottlenecks/.[2023-06-06].

https://news8plus.com/cascading-failures-in-urban-traffic-systems-tied-to-hidden-bottlenecks;
https://www.sciencedaily.com/releases/2023/03/230321112656.htm.[2023-06-06].

https://wwwnewswise.com/articles/cascading-failures-in-urban-traffic-systems-tied-to-hidden-bottlenecks.[2023-06-06].

New Words and Expressions

symmetric	*adj.*	对称的
geoinformation	*n.*	地理信息
natural disaster		自然灾害
terrorist	*n.*	恐怖主义者
spills	*n.*	漏损
QoS (Quality of Service)		服务质量

SDN (Software Defined Networking)		软件定义网络
deployment	n.	部署
reconfigurability	n.	可重构性
manmade	adj.	人造的
toxic	adj.	有毒的

Notes

1. Lastly, dynamic lanes can be used to provide more inbound or outbound lanes depending on the flow of traffic as traffic in many metropolitan areas is not symmetric.

译文：最后，动态车道可用于根据交通流量提供更多的入站或出站车道，因为许多大都市地区的交通是不对称的。

2. Multiple services are available, including accurate geoinformation, traffic management, emergency response, on-road parking space management, and public transit supervision.

译文：提供多种服务，包括准确的地理信息、交通管理、应急响应、道路停车位管理和公共交通监管。

3. And in return the public users get improved services like accurate geoinformation, real-time traffic conditions, driving and parking guidance, etc.

译文：作为回报，公众用户可以得到更好的服务，如准确的地理信息、实时交通状况、驾驶和停车指导等。

4. The quick deployment of a telecommunication infrastructure is essential for emergency and safety operations as well as the rapid network reconfigurability, the availability of open source software, the efficient interoperability, and the scalability of the technological solutions.

译文：电信基础设施的快速部署对于应急和安全操作以及快速网络重新配置、开放源代码软件的可用性、高效互操作性和技术解决方案的可扩展性至关重要。

Exercises

第 2 章　Application and Appreciation

Lesson Nine　Complex Networks and Its Applications

Text A　Exploring Complex Networks (Ⅰ)

Networks are on our minds nowadays. Sometimes we fear their power — and with good reason. On 10 August, 1996, a fault in two power lines in Oregon led, through a cascading series of failures, to blackouts in 11 US states and two Canadian provinces, leaving about 7 million customers without power for up to 16 hours. The Love Bug worm, the worst computer attack to date, spread over the Internet on 4 May, 2000 and inflicted billions of dollars of damage worldwide.

In our lighter moments we play games about connectivity. "Six degrees of Marlon Brando"[1] broke out as a nationwide fad in Germany, as readers of *Die Zeit* tried to connect a falafel vendor in Berlin with his favourite actor through the shortest possible chain of acquaintances. And during the height of the Lewinsky scandal, the *New York Times* printed a diagram of the famous people within "six degrees of Monica".

Meanwhile scientists have been thinking about networks too. Empirical studies have shed light on the topology of food webs(Fig.1(a)), electrical power grids(Fig.1(b)), cellular and metabolic networks(Fig.1(c)), the World-Wide Web, the Internet backbone, the neural network of the nematode worm. *Caenorhabditis elegans*, telephone call graphs, co-authorship and citation networks of scientists.

(a) Food web of Little Rock Lake

(b) New York State electric power grid

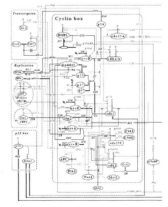

(c) A portion of the molecular interaction map for the regulatory network that controls the mammalian cell cycle

Fig.1　Wiring diagrams for complex networks

These databases are now easily accessible, courtesy of the Internet. Moreover, the availability of powerful computers has made it feasible to probe their structure; until recently, computations involving million-node networks would have been impossible without specialized facilities.[2]

Why is network anatomy so important to characterize? Because structure always affects function. For instance, the topology of social networks affects the spread of information and disease, and the topology of the power grid affects the robustness and stability of power transmission.

From this perspective, the current interest in networks is part of a broader movement towards research on complex systems. In the words of E. O. Wilson, "The greatest challenge today, not just in cell biology and ecology but in all of science, is the accurate and complete description of complex systems.[3] Scientists have broken down many kinds of systems. They think they know most of the elements and forces. The next task is to reassemble them, at least in mathematical models that capture the key properties of the entire ensembles".

But networks are inherently difficult to understand, as the following list of possible complications illustrates.

(1) Structural complexity: the wiring diagram could be an intricate tangle.

(2) Network evolution: the wiring diagram could change over time. On the World-Wide Web, pages and links are created and lost every minute.

(3) Connection diversity: the links between nodes could have different weights, directions and signs. Synapses in the nervous system can be strong or weak, inhibitory or excitatory.

(4) Dynamical complexity: the nodes could be nonlinear dynamical systems. In a gene network or a Josephson junction array, the state of each node can vary in time in complicated ways.

(5) Node diversity: there could be many different kinds of nodes. The biochemical network that controls cell division in mammals consists of a bewildering variety of substrates and enzymes, only a few of which are shown in Fig.1(c).[4]

(6) Meta-complication: the various complications can influence each other. For example, the present layout of a power grid depends on how it has grown over the years — a case where network evolution (2) affects topology (1). When coupled neurons fire together repeatedly, the connection between them is strengthened; this is the basis of memory and learning. Here nodal dynamics (4) affect connection weights (3).

To make progress, different fields have suppressed certain complications while highlighting others. For instance, in nonlinear dynamics we have tended to favour simple, nearly identical dynamical systems coupled together in simple, geometrically regular ways. Furthermore we usually assume that the network architecture is static. These simplifications allow us to sidestep any issues of structural complexity and to concentrate instead on the system's potentially formidable dynamics.[5]

Laser arrays provide a concrete example. In the single-mode approximation, each laser is characterized by its time-dependent gain, polarization, and the phase and amplitude of its electric field. These evolve according to four coupled, nonlinear differential equations. We usually hope the laser will settle down to a stable state, corresponding to steady emission of light, but periodic pulsations and even chaotic intensity fluctuations can occur in some cases. Now suppose that many identical lasers are arranged side by side in a regular chain or ring, interacting with their neighbours by evanescent coupling or by overlap of their electric fields. Will the lasers lock their phases together spontaneously, or break up into a standing wave pattern, or beat each other into incoherence? From a technological standpoint, self-synchronization would be the most desirable outcome, because a perfectly coherent array of N lasers would produce N^2 times as much power as a single one. But in practice, semiconductor laser arrays are notoriously prone to both spatial and temporal instabilities. Even for a simple ring geometry, this problem is dynamically complex.

The first part of this article reviews what is known about dynamical complexity in regular networks of nonlinear systems. I offer a few rules of thumb about the impact of network structure on collective dynamics, especially for arrays of coupled limit-cycle oscillators.

The logical next step would be to tackle networks that combine dynamical and structural complexity, such as power grids or ecological webs. Unfortunately they lie beyond our mathematical reach — we do not even know how to characterize their wiring diagrams. So we have to begin with network topology.

By a happy coincidence, such architectural questions are being pursued in other branches of science, thanks to the excitement about the Internet, functional genomics, financial networks, and so on. The second part of this article uses graph theory to explore the structure of complex networks, an approach that has recently led to some encouraging progress, especially when combined with the tools of statistical mechanics and computer simulations.

Needless to say, many other topics within network science deserve coverage here. The subject is amazingly rich, and apologies are offered to those readers whose favourite topics are omitted.

New Words and Expressions

complex network		复杂网络
blackout	n.	毁灭；出故障
inflict	v.	予以(打击等)；使受(痛苦等)
empirical study		实证研究
courtesy	n.	礼貌，谦恭
intricate	adj.	复杂的，难懂的
weight	n.	权重

synapse	n.	突触
dynamical complexity		动力学复杂性
substrate	n.	基质
enzyme	n.	酶
sidestep	v.	回避

Notes

1. Six degrees of Marlon Brando，这是一个著名的小世界网络实验，俗称"六度分离"。它是社会学家在研究社交网络(social networks)时提出的一个概念。该问题源于社会学家、哈佛大学的心理学教授 Stanley Milgram(1934—1984)在 1967 年做的实验："追踪美国社交网络中的最短路径。"他要求每个参与者设法寄信给一个住在波士顿附近的"目标人物"，规定每个参与者只能转发给一个他们认识的人。Milgram 发现完整的链平均长度为 6 个人。

2. Moreover, the availability of powerful computers has made it feasible to probe their structure; until recently, computations involving million-node networks would have been impossible without specialized facilities.

译文：而且，强大的计算机的使用使我们有可能探明它们的结构；至今，百万节点网络的计算仍旧离不开专业设备的辅助。

3. The greatest challenge today, not just in cell biology and ecology but in all of science, is the accurate and complete description of complex systems.

译文：当今最大的挑战是对复杂系统做精确、完整的分析，这不只存在于细胞生物学和生态学，而是整个科学领域。

4. The biochemical network that controls cell division in mammals consists of a bewildering variety of substrates and enzymes, only a few of which are shown in Fig.1(c).

译文：正如图 1(c)所示的，控制着哺乳动物细胞分裂的生化网络就包含各种各样的基质和酶。

5. These simplifications allow us to sidestep any issues of structural complexity and to concentrate instead on the system's potentially formidable dynamics.

译文：这些简化使我们能够回避结构上的复杂性，从而将重点放在系统潜在的强大的动力学行为上。

Exercises

第 2 章 Application and Appreciation

Text B Exploring Complex Networks (Ⅱ)

1. Complex Network Architectures

All the network topologies discussed so far — chains, grids, lattices and fully-connected graphs — have been completely regular (Fig.2(a),(b)). Those simple architectures allowed us to focus on the complexity caused by the nonlinear dynamics of the nodes, without being burdened by any additional complexity in the network structure itself. Now I take the complementary approach, setting dynamics aside and turning to more complex architectures. A natural place to start is at the opposite end of the spectrum from regular networks, with graphs that are completely random.[1]

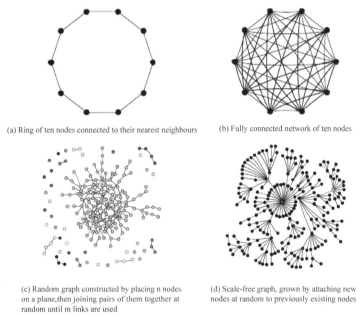

(a) Ring of ten nodes connected to their nearest neighbours

(b) Fully connected network of ten nodes

(c) Random graph constructed by placing n nodes on a plane, then joining pairs of them together at random until m links are used

(d) Scale-free graph, grown by attaching new nodes at random to previously existing nodes

Fig.2 Schematic illustration of regular and random network architectures

2. Random Graphs

Imagine $n \gg 1$ buttons strewn across the floor. Pick two buttons at random and tie them together with thread. Repeat this process m times, always choosing pairs of buttons at random. (If m is large, you might eventually select buttons that already have threads attached. That is certainly allowed; it merely creates clusters of connected buttons.) The result is a physical example of a random graph with n nodes and m links (Fig.2(c)). Now slowly lift a random button off the floor. If it is tied to other buttons, either directly or indirectly, those are dragged up too. So what happens? Are you likely to pull up an isolated button, a small cluster or a vast meshwork?

Erdös and Rényi studied how the expected topology of this random graph changes as a function of m. When m is small, the graph is likely to be fragmented into many small clusters of nodes, called components. As m increases, the components grow, at first by linking to isolated nodes and later by coalescing with other components. A phase transition occurs at $m = n/2$, where many clusters crosslink spontaneously to form a single giant component. For $m > n/2$, this giant component contains on the order of n nodes (more precisely, its size scales linearly with n, as $n \to \infty$), while its closest rival contains only about log n nodes. Furthermore, all nodes in the giant component are connected to each other by short paths: the maximum number of "degrees of separation" between any two nodes grows slowly, like log n.

In the decades since this pioneering work, random graphs have been studied deeply within pure mathematics. They have also served as idealized coupling architectures for dynamical models of gene networks, ecosystems and the spread of infectious diseases and computer viruses.[2]

3. Small-world Networks

Although regular networks and random graphs are both useful idealizations, many real networks lie somewhere between the extremes of order and randomness. Watts and Strogatz studied a simple model that can be tuned through this middle ground: a regular lattice where the original links are replaced by random ones with some probability $0 \leqslant \phi \leqslant 1$. They found that the slightest bit of rewiring transforms the network into a "small world", with short paths between any two nodes, just as in the giant component of a random graph. Yet the network is much more highly clustered than a random graph, in the sense that if A is linked to B and B is linked to C, there is a greatly increased probability that A will also be linked to C (a property that sociologists call "transitivity").

Watts and Strogatz conjectured that the same two properties — short paths and high clustering — would hold also for many natural and technological networks. Furthermore, they conjectured that dynamical systems coupled in this way would display enhanced signal propagation speed, synchronizability and computational power, as compared with regular lattices of the same size. The intuition is that the short paths could provide high-speed communication channels between distant parts of the system, thereby facilitating any dynamical process (like synchronization or computation) that requires global coordination and information flow.

Research has proceeded along several fronts. Many empirical examples of small-world networks have been documented, in fields ranging from cell biology to business. On the theoretical side, small-world networks are turning out to be a Rorschach test — different scientists see different problems here, depending on their disciplines.

Computer scientists see questions about algorithms and their complexity. Walsh showed that graphs associated with many difficult search problems have a small-world topology. Kleinberg introduced an elegant model of the algorithmic challenge posed by Milgram's original sociological experiment — how to actually find a short chain of acquaintances linking yourself to a random target person, using only local information — and he proved that the problem is easily solvable for some kinds of small worlds, and essentially intractable for others.[3]

Epidemiologists have asked how local clustering and global contacts together influence the spread of infectious disease, with implications for vaccination strategies and the evolution of virulence. Neurobiologists have wondered about the possible evolutionary significance of small-world neural architecture. They have argued that this kind of topology combines fast signal processing with coherent oscillations, unlike either regular or random architectures, and that it may be selected by adaptation to rich sensory environments and motor demands.

4. Scale-free Networks

In any real network, some nodes are more highly connected than others are. To quantify this effect, let p_k denote the fraction of nodes that have k links. Here k is called the degree and p_k is the degree distribution.

The simplest random graph models predict a bell-shaped Poisson distribution for p_k. But for many real networks, p_k is highly skewed and decays much more slowly than a Poisson. For instance, the distribution decays as a power law $p_k \sim k^{-\gamma}$ for the Internet backbone, metabolic reaction networks, the telephone call graph and the World-Wide Web (Fig.3(a)). Remarkably, the exponent $\gamma \approx 2.1$–2.4 for all of these cases. Taken literally, this form of heavy-tailed distribution would imply an infinite variance. In reality, there are a few nodes with many links (Fig.2(d)). For the World-Wide Web, think Yahoo; for metabolic networks, think ATP. Barabási, Albert and Jeong have dubbed these networks "scale-free", by analogy with fractals, phase transitions and other situations where power laws arise and no single characteristic scale can be defined.

The scale-free property is common but not universal. For coauthorship networks of scientists, p_k is fit better by a power law with an exponential cutoff (Fig.3(b)); for the power grid of the western United States, p_k is an exponential distribution (Fig.3(c)); and for a social network of Mormons in Utah, p_k is gaussian (Fig.3(d)).

Nevertheless, the scale-free case has stimulated a great deal of theorizing. The earliest work is due to Simon in 1955, now independently rediscovered by Barabási, Albert and Jeong. They showed that a heavy-tailed degree distribution emerges automatically from a stochastic growth model in which new nodes are added continuously and attach themselves preferentially to existing nodes, with probability proportional to the degree of the target node. Richly connected nodes get richer, and the result is $p_k \sim k^{-3}$. More sophisticated models include the effects of adding or rewiring links, allowing nodes to age so that they can no longer accept new links, or varying the form of preferential attachment. These generalized models predict exponential and truncated power-law p_k in some parameter regimes, as well as scale-free distributions.

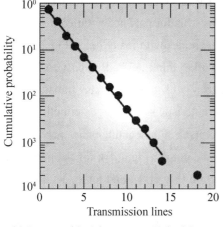
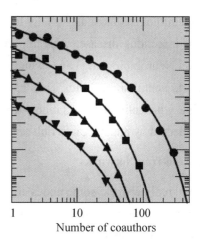
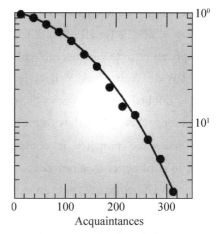

(a) World-Wide Web. Nodes are web pages; links are directed URL hyperlinks from one page to another. The log–log plot shows the number of web pages that have a given in-degree (number of incoming links)

(b) Coauthorship networks. Nodes represent scientists; an undirected link between two people means that they have written a paper together

(c) Power grid of the western United States and Canada. Nodes represent generators, transformers and substations; undirected links represent high-voltage transmission lines between them

(d) Social network. Nodes are 43 Mormons in Utah; undirected links represent acquaintances with other Mormons

Fig.3 Degree distributions for real networks

Could there be a functional advantage to scale-free architecture? Albert, Jeong and Barabási suggested that scale-free networks are resistant to random failures because a few hubs dominate their topology (Fig.2(d)). Any node that fails probably has small degree (like most nodes) and so is expendable. The flip side is that such networks are vulnerable to deliberate attacks on the hubs. These intuitive ideas have been confirmed numerically and analytically by examining how the average path length and size of the giant component depend on the number and degree of the nodes removed. Some possible implications for the resilience of the Internet, the design of therapeutic drugs, and the evolution of metabolic networks have been discussed.

5. Outlook

In the short run there are plenty of good problems about the nonlinear dynamics of systems coupled according to small-world, scale-free or generalized random connectivity. The speculations that these architectures are dynamically advantageous (for example, more synchronizable or error-tolerant) need to be sharpened, then confirmed or refuted mathematically for specific examples. Other ripe topics include the design of self-healing networks, and the relationships among optimization principles, network growth rules and network topology.

In the longer run, network thinking will become essential to all branches of science as we struggle to interpret the data pouring in from neurobiology, genomics, ecology, finance and the World-Wide Web. Will theory be able to keep up? Time to log back on to the Internet...

New Words and Expressions

regular network		规则网络
cluster	*n.*	团簇，集群
spontaneously	*adv.*	自然地；本能地
transitivity	*n.*	传递性
acquaintance	*n.*	交往；相识
vaccination strategy		疫苗接种策略

Notes

1. A natural place to start is at the opposite end of the spectrum from regular networks, with graphs that are completely random.

译文：一个很自然的出发点就是从规则网络图谱到完全随机的图谱。

2. They have also served as idealized coupling architectures for dynamical models of gene networks, ecosystems and the spread of infectious diseases and computer viruses.

译文：它们还为动态基因网络、生态网络、传染病及计算机病毒传播提供了理想的耦合模型。

3. Kleinberg introduced an elegant model of the algorithmic challenge posed by Milgram's original sociological experiment — how to actually find a short chain of acquaintances linking yourself to a random target person, using only local information — and he proved that the problem is easily solvable for some kinds of small worlds, and essentially intractable for others.

译文：为了解决 Milgram 的原始社会学实验中所存在的算法难题(如何仅仅根据本地信息找到自己和一个随机目标人物之间的最短人际关系链)，Kleinberg 引入了一个可靠的模型，而且他还证明尽管大多数情况下这个问题难以处理，但对于一些小世界而言是易于解决的。

Lesson Ten Cloud Computing

Text A An Introduction to Cloud Computing (Ⅰ)

1. Executive Summary

Cloud computing is a consequence of economic, commercial, cultural and technological conditions that have combined to cause a disruptive shift in Information Technology (IT) towards a service-based economy. The underlying driver of this change is the commoditization of IT.[1]

While there are many well-documented benefits of cloud computing from economies of scale to acceleration of speed to market, there are also three main groups of risks associated with it; the risk of doing nothing, transitional risks related to this disruptive change in our industry and the general risks of outsourcing.

Canonical's view is that open source technology will help solve many of these latter concerns by not only enabling enterprises to deploy, experiment and test cloud computing concepts behind the firewall, but also by encouraging the formation of competitive marketplaces based around standards.

Canonical is therefore launching Ubuntu Enterprise Cloud, an open source system, based on Eucalyptus, that enables our users to build their own private clouds that match the popular emerging standard of Amazon's Elastic Compute Cloud (EC2).[2]

By using Ubuntu Enterprise Cloud, an enterprise can gain and experiment with many of the benefits of cloud computing while keeping the service behind the firewall and running on its own infrastructure. It's cloud computing that the enterprise controls. By matching emerging industry standards, Canonical aims to simplify any future migration to an external provider. By providing an open source system, Canonical intends to foster an ecosystem so that when the enterprise chooses to move outside the firewall, it will have a choice of service providers.

In summary, Canonical aims to give Enterprise IT a mechanism to prepare for a future life in the clouds along with a simple path for migration between clouds.[3]

Ubuntu Enterprise Cloud is currently provided as a technology preview in the Ubuntu 9.04 Server Edition distribution.

2. Introduction

Today it feels as though IT is under assault from a heady mix of terminology such as utility computing, disruptive technologies, innovation, network effects, open source, agile development, software as a service (SaaS), mashups, web 2.0, web 3.0 and commoditization … the list goes on. It's easy to start drowning as wave after wave of new concepts crash onto the scene. The latest wave is cloud computing.

To some, cloud computing is a future where you won't host your own infrastructure. To others, the cloud is an electricity grid of utility software. While there has been much debate over what cloud computing means, the reality is the term generic. It describes a combination of business and technological factors that are causing a change to our industry and is no more precise than the term "industrial revolution".

Sorting through the tangled mess of today means first getting a clear understanding of what is causing this change. This article is an explanation of the underlying processes behind this onslaught. It aims to provide the reader with a simple pattern to help make sense of the maelstrom. We will examine the fundamental forces behind change, what cloud computing really is, the benefits and disadvantages of cloud computing and why open source matters. Finally, we will also cover how Canonical plans to help you safely navigate this storm.

3. The fundamental forces behind change

Back in the 1990s, Paul Strassmann demonstrated that there was no link between IT spending and business value. While there has been some argument over the validity of the research, Strassmann's work created an idea that rapidly spread. This idea was that not all IT is the same, not all IT has value and some IT has commoditized.

Commoditization is a neologism that describes how a rare and poorly-understood innovation becomes well-defined and ubiquitous in the eyes of the consumer. In other words, it's a transition that describes how a once-exciting and new activity (an innovation) becomes commonplace and standardized (more of a commodity).[4]

The most often-quoted example of this is the electricity industry and how this innovation led to the formation of national grids in the 1930s. Today, to most consumers, electricity is something you get from a plug and few companies describe their use of electricity as a source of competitive advantage.

In Fig.1, we plot business activities against an axis of ubiquity (how common something is) and certainty (how well-defined and understood something is). The data is derived from the TV, radio and telephony industries and it suggests that an S-Curve relationship exists between the ubiquity and certainty of an activity.

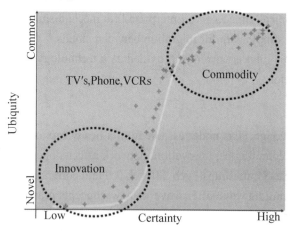

Fig.1 A path for how a rare and poorly-understood innovation becomes a common and well-defined commodity

All business activities are somewhere on that path and all of them are moving-commoditization never stops and IT activities are no exception. However, the journey of an innovation to ubiquity is not an easy one and some of the changes can be disruptive to an existing industry. This is especially true as any activity moves from the product to the services stage of its journey.[5]

Such a disruptive change is occurring in IT today. A quick glance at the current list of hot topics brings up subjects such as Service-oriented Architecture (SoA), web services and mashing-up services. All of these contain a strong service theme. The computing stack, which for brevity I'll characterize into the three layers of application, platform and infrastructure, is slowly shifting away from products towards standard components provided as Internet services.

This shift requires 4 simultaneously occurring factors.

(1) The suitability of activities to change (for example, an activity that is widespread and well-defined).

(2) The technology to support such a change.

(3) The concept of service provision to spread in the industry.

(4) The willingness of consumers to adopt such a shift (for example, more of IT being seen and treated as a commodity).

The last thing to note is that you have no choice when it comes to commoditization. If you treat an activity as an innovation while everyone else uses standard services, then you are only likely to create a competitive disadvantage for yourself. Any company needs to continuously adapt to changes in the surrounding market just to retain its competitive position. Doing nothing is a risk in itself.[6]

Commoditization is a continual process that can be highly disruptive. You have to continuously adapt to this change and it is happening in IT today.

4. What is cloud computing

云计算

A combination of business attitude and technology, together with certain activities becoming common and well-defined, has led to a situation whereby some parts of IT are now suitable for service provision through volume operations. This is not confined to one particular layer of the computing stack but across all layers. This transition has given rise to the "as a Service" industry which includes the following.

(1) Infrastructure (or Hardware) as a Service providers such as Amazon and FlexiScale.

(2) Platform (or Framework) as a Service providers like Ning, BungeeLabs and Azure.

(3) Application (or Software) as a Service providers like Salesforce, Zoho and Google Apps.

Supporting this transition is a range of technologies from clustering to virtualization. In essence, these have provided an effective means of balancing the supply of computing resources to match the demand for volume operations.

While the concept of offering computing resources through utility-like service providers dates back to John McCarthy in the 1960's, many early attempts were unsuccessful as they tried to apply such ideas to activities that lacked both ubiquity and definition.[7] Over the years, as numerous IT activities were widely adopted, they became more suitable for outsourcing to service providers. Managed hosting led the second wave of change and the new breed of volume operations specialists such as Amazon are leading this third wave.

The disruptive transition of the computing stack from a product to a service economy, the growth of a new breed of volume-based service providers and the underlying technologies supporting this change have been grouped together under the heading of cloud computing.

New Words and Expressions

commoditization	n.	商品化
outsourcing	n.	外包；外购；外部采办
marketplace	n.	市场；市场环境；商场；市集
foster	vt.	培养；养育，抚育；抱(希望等)
mechanism	n.	机制；原理，途径；进程；机械装置；技巧
migration	n.	迁移；移民；移动
mashup	n.	混搭程式；混搭网站；混合；聚合；糅合技术
infrastructure	n.	基础设施；公共建设；下部构造
maelstrom	n.	大漩涡；极度混乱；不可抗的破坏力
validity	n.	有效性；正确；正确性
neologism	n.	新词；新义；新词的使用
ubiquity	n.	普遍存在；到处存在
cluster	n.	群；簇；丛；串
	vi.	群聚；丛生
	vt.	使聚集；聚集在某人的周围
virtualization	n.	虚拟化，虚拟化技术
stack	n.	堆，堆叠
	vt.	使堆叠，把……堆积起来
	vi.	堆积，堆叠
disruptive shift		剧变
economies of scale		规模经济
Ubuntu Enterprise Cloud		乌班图企业云
open source system		开源服务系统
emerging industry		新兴产业
derived from		来源于
volume operation		卷操作；并联工作；批量操作
in essence		本质上；其实；大体上

Notes

1. Cloud computing is a consequence of economic, commercial, cultural and technological conditions that have combined to cause a disruptive shift in Information Technology (IT) towards a service-based economy. The underlying driver of this change is the commoditization of IT.

译文：当今经济、商业、文化和工艺条件等因素联合起来导致信息技术(IT)不断向以服务业为基础的经济转变，这种剧变导致了云计算的产生。而这种变化的根源则是信息技术产业的商品化。

2. Canonical is therefore launching Ubuntu Enterprise Cloud, an open source system, based on Eucalyptus, that enables our users to build their own private clouds that match the popular emerging standard of Amazon's Elastic Compute Cloud (EC2).

译文：因此，Canonical 正在开设乌班图企业云服务，一种基于 Eucalyptus 技术的开源服务系统。它可以允许用户建立自己的私人云端以便匹配亚马逊弹性计算云(EC2)的新服务标准。

3. In summary, Canonical aims to give Enterprise IT a mechanism to prepare for a future life in the clouds along with a simple path for migration between clouds.

译文：总之，Canonical 的目的在于，为信息技术企业提供一种机制，这种机制可以作为在未来云环境中进行简单云端资源切换的准备。

4. Commoditization is a neologism that describes how a rare and poorly-understood innovation becomes well-defined and ubiquitous in the eyes of the consumer. In other words, it's a transition that describes how a once-exciting and new activity (an innovation) becomes commonplace and standardized (more of a commodity).

译文：商品化在用户的眼中被赋予了一种新义，即一种罕见的、鲜为人知的创新技术变得无处不在、人人皆知。换句话说，是一种技术(革新)从新鲜刺激、不断升级到普遍应用、标准完备的转变(不仅仅作为一种商品存在)。

5. However, the journey of an innovation to ubiquity is not an easy one and some of the changes can be disruptive to an existing industry. This is especially true as any activity moves from the product to the services stage of its journey.

译文：然而，新兴产业走向普及化的道路并不平坦，一些变革对于已经存在的产业来说可能是破坏性的，这一点在任何产业从产品生产阶段到企业服务阶段的转变过程中尤为凸显。

6. Any company needs to continuously adapt to changes in the surrounding market just to retain its competitive position. Doing nothing is a risk in itself.

译文：对于公司企业而言亦是如此，它们都需要不断地适应周围市场的变化来维持自己的竞争地位，而无为本身就是一种风险。

7. While the concept of offering computing resources through utility-like service providers dates back to John McCarthy in the 1960's, many early attempts were unsuccessful as they tried to apply such ideas to activities that lacked both ubiquity and definition.

译文：然而通过使用服务供应商来提供计算资源的观念要追溯到20世纪60年代，John McCarthy 在这方面做过了很多尝试，但由于他将这种观念赋予了那些既不普及也没有标准规范的产业，所以这些尝试均以失败告终。

Text B   An Introduction to Cloud Computing (Ⅱ)

1. Benefits and risks of cloud computing

The shift of the computing stack provides an opportunity to eliminate complexities, cost and capital expenditure in much the same way that using an electricity provider removes the need for every company to build power generators.[1]

The main benefits of cloud computing are therefore economies of scale through volume operations, pay-per-use through utility charging, a faster speed to market through componentisation and the ability to focus on core activities through the outsourcing of that which is not core(including scalability and capacity planning).[2]

Providing self-service IT while simultaneously reducing costs may be highly attractive but it creates a competitive risk to doing nothing.

However, it should be remembered that we are in a disruptive transition at this moment. This transition creates commonly-repeated concerns covering management, legal, compliance and trust of service providers. A Canonical survey of 7,000 companies and individuals found that, while over 60 percent of respondents thought that the cloud was ready for mission-critical workloads, less than 30 percent are planning to deploy any kind of workload to the cloud.

In addition to these transitional risks, there also exist the normal considerations for outsourcing any common activity, including whether the activity is suitable for outsourcing, what the second-sourcing options are and whether switching between providers is easy.

Though service level agreements (SLAs) can help alleviate some concerns, any fears can only be truly overcome once customers can easily switch between providers through a marketplace. This already occurs in many industries from electricity to telephony and it is this switching, which has created competitive markets with competitive price pressures. Until such markets appear, it is probable that many corporations will continue to use home-grown solutions, particularly in industries that have already expended capital to remove themselves from lock-in, which is widespread in the product world.[3]

While the cloud lacks any functioning marketplaces today, it is entirely possible that ecosystems of providers will emerge based on easy switching and competition through price and quality of service. In such circumstances, many of the common concerns regarding the uncertainty of supply will be overcome.

While the benefits of cloud computing are many and obvious, there exist the normal concerns associated with the outsourcing of any activity, combined with additional risks due to the transitional nature of this change.

2. Why open source matters

Open source companies give away their products freely while competing on services. Hence this disruptive shift of the computing stack is not only beneficial to them, they are also the companies least likely to be held back through a product mentality. Many of the winners in the cloud computing space are likely to come from an open source background.

It is also likely that open source will lead the way in creating defector standards in the cloud in much the same way that Apache became the standard for the web. An open source reference implementation of a potential standard provides a fast means for multiple parties to operationally implement a standard without sacrificing strategic control to a technology vendor.[4] The use of open source also encourages ecosystems to develop around a technology and, while there currently exists a plethora of different cloud offerings for the same activity (such as infrastructure provision), none have created a widespread ecosystem. Successful creation of an ecosystem is the difference between becoming the TCP/IP of the cloud computing world or the Banyan Vines.

As outlined above, the solution to many of the risks of cloud computing depends on the formation of viable ecosystems containing marketplaces of providers with easy switching between them. Such marketplaces depend on standards and understanding this issue is key for any reader wishing to explore the potential future of cloud computing.

In the analogy of the electricity industry, a power plant is used by a provider to create electricity as a standardized output. In the computing industry, while physical hardware is the equivalent of a power plant, the output is the three layers of the computing stack. To standardize this would mean that providers would need to offer the same outputs. For example, a marketplace of application providers would need to consolidate around standardized applications. Competition, in such a marketplace, would be around price and quality of service for the provision of the same application.

For a product-based industry, this creates a fundamental shift in mindset to competition on service rather than feature differentiation. Such a change is inevitable as it is only those activities, which are well-defined and commonplace that are suitable for service provision. The ubiquity and feature-completeness of those activities means there is little advantage to the end consumer through further feature differentiation.

However, standardized output is not in itself enough as the analogy of computing to the electricity industry contains a flaw. In the electricity industry, you have no relationship with your provider. In the case of cloud computing, you do, it's called your data. Hence any future marketplaces will require not only standardized outputs and competition on service, but also freedom of data and, as a result, easy switching.

While many will argue that such effects can be created through agreed and open specifications (known as open standards), the historical problem has always been not what is in the standard but how providers seek to extend beyond it. In the service world, such extensions or feature differentiations are the antithesis of portability and would severely limit the growth of any ecosystem. While a service provider might consider it to be an advantage to lock in a consumer, it is these very same concerns that continue to slow user adoption.

In a service world, it makes little sense for the code that describes an activity to be anything other than open source or at least based on an open source reference implementation that ensures portability between providers. In such a world, service providers will need to seek competitive advantages through operations and not feature differentiation.

As a general rule of thumb, the future of open source and the development of cloud computing appear to go hand in hand. We've already seen the first shoots of this future with the Distributed Management Task Force's (DMTF's) proposals for a standard to enable portability between virtual machines and the creation of open source systems such as Eucalyptus.[5]

Eucalyptus, a system developed by University of California Santa Barbara (UCSB), is an open source environment that enables you to create and build your own cloud that matches the Amazon EC2 application program interface (API). Creating your own internal cloud is a way of testing, deploying and experimenting with the benefits of cloud computing without the need to venture outside of the corporate firewall.

It is Canonical's view that the open source Eucalyptus system will help to create an ecosystem of providers and is likely to develop into a de facto standard for cloud computing at the infrastructure layer of the stack.

Open source is likely to feature strongly in the future of cloud computing and the development of any standards.

3. What is Canonical doing about the cloud

Canonical supports and sponsors Ubuntu, the fastest-growing Linux-based operating system with over 10 million users and a huge community of developers. As a service-focused company that specializes in the free provision of software for common activities, Canonical is well positioned to compete in this cloud computing world.

The software we provide is used for everything from customer relationship management (CRM) to databases. We focus on those common workloads and those commodity-like activities, which have become ubiquitous in IT. Our approach of providing standardized open source components is specifically aimed at enabling companies to quickly implement standard services, which can be used to support more innovative activities.

In our recent survey, 85 percent of respondents said they would use Ubuntu on the cloud. For this reason, we have introduced Ubuntu Server Edition onto Amazon EC2 (see www.ubuntu.com/ec2) to enable our users to take advantage of the benefits that cloud computing can create.

While we are aware that as the cloud industry develops, many of the adoption issues will be resolved, we also realize that our users need specific support in this time of transition. We take the view that many of our users and enterprise customers wish to experiment with cloud computing but within the confines of their own environments.

For this reason, we will be releasing Ubuntu Enterprise Cloud, which includes Eucalyptus in the Ubuntu distribution. We will also be working on supporting efforts to ensure the portability of infrastructure between different service providers. This will minimise any future impact on our users due to migration. As part of these efforts, we will be looking to build a consortium of providers and management tools to help promote open source in the cloud computing space.

Our aim is to support the growth of both private and public clouds based around an entirely open source stack, and to provide portability between both environments. Canonical will also be offering commercial support for internal clouds along with technical consultancy for installation.

Canonical will be providing open source cloud computing systems in the Ubuntu distribution. This will give Enterprise IT a mechanism to deal with common workloads while preparing for a life in the clouds.

4. Summary

云服务器

Cloud computing is a disruptive change, caused by the underlying commoditization of IT. Canonical expects to see a future dominance of the open source model in cloud computing, which will solve the major adoption concerns for users.[6]

At this moment in time, IT is in transition from "as a product" to "as a service" for common workloads and activities. Unsurprisingly the cloud currently lacks standards and there remain several unresolved legal, management and compliance questions. This is on top of the normal concerns raised by the outsourcing of a common activity including: whether the activity is suitable for outsourcing, whether second-sourcing options exist and whether there is easy switching between providers.

To support our users in this time of transition, Canonical will be launching Ubuntu Enterprise Cloud by including Eucalyptus in the Ubuntu distribution. This will provide our users with an open source system that enables them to build their own private clouds, which match the current emerging standard of the Amazon EC2 API.

Canonical views this system as a stepping stone on the road to a future marketplace of external cloud providers. Hence, we are also providing Ubuntu for use with leading cloud providers and promoting infrastructure portability between clouds.

New Words and Expressions

componentization	n.	构件化，元件化，组件化
scalability	n.	可扩展性，可伸缩性；可量测性

simultaneously	adv.	同时地，同时发生地
compliance	n.	顺从，服从；承诺
respondent	adj.	回答的；应答的
	n.	应答者
deploy	vt.	配置；展开；使疏开
	vi.	调配；部署；展开
	n.	部署
mentality	n.	心态；智力；精神力；心理素质
de facto		事实上的，实际上的
		事实上
vendor	n.	卖主，供应商
plethora	n.	过多；过剩
consolidate	vt.	巩固，使固定；联合，合并
	vi.	巩固，加强
flaw	n.	瑕疵；裂纹；缺点
antithesis	n.	对立面；对照
portability	n.	可移植性；轻便；可携带；可调动性
consortium	n.	联合；结合
pay-per-use		按每次使用计费；付费；使用付费；量计价
service level agreements (SLAs)		服务水平协议
easy switching		轻松切换
feature-completeness		功能完整性
make sense		有意义，讲得通，言之有理
as a rule of thumb		根据经验，一般说来
private cloud		私有云，私有云端，私人云端

Notes

1. The shift of the computing stack provides an opportunity to eliminate complexities, cost and capital expenditure in much the same way that using an electricity provider removes the need for every company to build power generators.

译文：IT产业的转型为企业带来了消除复杂度、成本和基建费用的机遇，这就与每一个企业都有电力供应商而不需要使用电力发电机差不多。

2. The main benefits of cloud computing are therefore economies of scale through volume operations, pay-per-use through utility charging, a faster speed to market through componentization and the ability to focus on core activities through the outsourcing of that which is not core(including scalability and capacity planning).

译文：云计算服务的主要优势在于，批量业务操作的规模经济、按使用付费、组件化快速投入市场以及通过外包非核心产业使企业能够更加致力于核心产业(包括可扩展性和产能规划)的建设。

3. Until such markets appear, it is probable that many corporations will continue to use home-grown solutions, particularly in industries that have already expended capital to remove themselves from lock-in, which is widespread in the product world.

译文：这样的市场一经出现，很多公司很有可能继续使用自有的服务措施，尤其对于那些已经花费了成本用于解除价格压力的公司来说更会如此，接着这种市场效应就会蔓延到产品生产层面。

4. An open source reference implementation of a potential standard provides a fast means for multiple parties to operationally implement a standard without sacrificing strategic control to a technology vendor.

译文：一项带有潜在标准的开源系统参考运行提供了一种多方在不丧失对技术供应商战略性控制的情况下快速完成操作上执行标准的方法。

5. As a general rule of thumb, the future of open source and the development of cloud computing appear to go hand in hand. We've already seen the first shoots of this future with the Distributed Management Task Force's (DMTF's) proposals for a standard to enable portability between virtual machines and the creation of open source systems such as Eucalyptus.

译文：以一般的经验角度来说，未来开源技术以及云计算服务的发展将会齐头并进。我们已经看到这种未来发展的第一枝萌芽，那就是为了实现虚拟机和建立像 Eucalyptus 这样的开源系统之间相互调度而创立的分布式管理任务组建议的提出。

6. Cloud computing is a disruptive change, caused by the underlying commoditization of IT. Canonical expects to see a future dominance of the open source model in cloud computing, which will solve the major adoption concerns for users.

译文：IT 产业的潜在商品化使得云计算成为颠覆性的变革。Canonical 认为，未来云计算中占据支配地位的将是开源模型，这些模型将解决用户关心的大部分问题。

Exercises

第 3 章　科技论文写作的基础知识

3.1　概　　述

　　现代科学技术工作已经趋于综合化、社会化。科技工作与社会各方面的联系十分密切。在某一科学技术领域中往往是一群人在进行各个不同方向(或者是相同方向、相同课题)的研究，这就需要彼此联系、交流和借鉴。这种联系、交流和借鉴主要是通过科技工作者发表论文的形式进行的。论文的写作与发表，是科技工作者之间进行科学思想交流的永久记录，也是科学的历史，它记载了探索真理的过程，记载了各种观测结果和研究结果，而科学技术研究是一种承上启下的连续性的工作，一项研究的结束可能是另一项研究的起点。因此，科技工作者通过论文写作与发表的形式进行学术交流，从而促进研究成果的推广和应用。党的二十大报告也指出，要"深化文明交流互鉴，推动中华文化更好走向世界。"

　　很多作者往往把写论文当成课题研究最后阶段的事来做，因而常常听到他们说："等课题完了再写吧！"其实，写论文不是为了"交差""还账"，也不只是为了发表。科技论文的写作是科学技术研究的一种手段，是科学技术研究工作的重要组成部分。最好的做法是，课题研究的开始就是论文写作的开始，因为思考一个比较复杂的问题，借助于写作，效果会更好些。如果把写作贯穿在整个研究工作中，边研究，边写作，则可及时发现研究工作的不足，补充和修正正在进行的研究，使研究成果更加完善；同时也还有这样的可能，即写作灵感的突发将导致研究方案的重大改进，从而最终提高研究成果的水平和价值。

　　科技论文写作水平的高低往往直接影响科技工作的进展。例如，一篇写得好的科研选题报告或建设项目可行性论证报告，可以促进一个有价值的科研项目或建设项目尽快上马；反之，一篇写得不好、表达不规范的论文，也将会妨碍某项科研成果得到公认，妨碍某种新理论、新方法被人们所接受，妨碍某项先进技术得到迅速推广。或者，尽管研究成果具有发表的价值，但由于文稿写作质量太差，有时也不易被期刊编辑部门所接受。因此，作为科技工作者，应当掌握科技论文写作的一般方法，了解编辑出版部门对文稿质量和规格的要求，熟悉有关的国家标准和规定，不断提高自己的写作能力，从而使自己能够得心应手地写出学术价值或实用价值高、科学性强、文字细节和技术细节表达规范性好的科技论文，以此奉献给社会，让它们在促进学术交流和推动科学技术及经济建设的发展中发挥应有的作用。

3.1.1　科技论文的定义及分类

　　科技论文的定义有很多。简单地说，科技论文是对创造性的科研成果进行理论分析和总结的科技写作文体。比较翔实的定义为：科技论文是报道自然科学研究和技术开发创新工作成果的论说文章，它是通过运用概念、判断、推理、证明或反驳等逻辑思维手段来分析表达自然科学理论和技术开发研究成果的。

从论文内容的角度定义，使读者对于什么样的文章才叫作科技论文有一个明确的概念，这个定义也恰恰反映了科技论文区别于其他文体的特点。科技论文是创新性科学技术研究工作成果的科学论述，是某些理论性、实验性或观测性新知识的科学记录，是某些已知原理应用于实际中取得新进展、新成果的科学总结。

科技论文的分类就像它的定义一样，有很多种不同的分法。下面从两个不同的角度对科技论文进行分类，并说明各类论文的概念及写作要求。

1. 从作用上分

科技论文按其发挥的作用可分为 3 类：学术性论文、技术性论文、学位论文。

1) 学术性论文

学术性论文指研究人员提供给学术性期刊发表或向学术会议提交的论文，它以报道学术研究成果为主要内容。学术性论文反映了该学科领域最新的、最前沿的科学水平和发展动向，对科学技术事业的发展起着重要的推动作用。这类论文应具有新的观点、新的分析方法和新的数据或结论，并具有科学性。

2) 技术性论文

技术性论文指工程技术人员为报道工程技术研究成果而提交的论文，这种研究成果主要是应用已有的理论来解决设计、技术、工艺、设备、材料等具体问题而取得的。技术性论文对技术的进步和生产力的提高起着直接的推动作用。这类论文应具有技术的先进性、实用性和科学性。

3) 学位论文

学位论文指学位申请者提交的论文。这类论文根据学位的高低又分为以下 3 种：学士论文、硕士论文、博士论文。

学位论文要经过考核和答辩，因此，无论是论述还是文献综述，或是介绍实验装置、实验方法都要比较详尽，而学术性或技术性论文是写给同专业的人员看的，要力求简洁。除此之外，学位论文与学术性论文和技术性论文之间并无其他严格的区别。就写作方法而论，这种分类并无太大意义，这里仅从分类说明一下它们各自的特点和一般写作要求。

2. 从研究方式与论述内容上分

在科学技术研究工作中，人们的研究内容和方式是不同的，有的以实验为研究手段，通过实验发现新现象，寻找科学规律，或验证某种理论和假说，总之，实验结果的科学记录和总结就是研究工作的成果。有的是先提出假说，进行数学推导或逻辑推理，或者借助数学方法作为研究的手段，用实验结果来检验理论，这类论文以论述或论证为中心，或提出新的理论，或对原有的理论作出新的补充和发展，或作出否定。有的研究对象虽然属于自然科学或工程技术范畴，但论述的方式却类似于社会科学的某些论文，即用可信的调查研究所得的事实或数据来论证新的观点，等等。所以，按照研究的方式和论述的内容可对科技论文作如下分类。

1) 实(试)验研究报告

这类论文不同于一般的实(试)验报告，其写作重点应放在"研究"上。它追求的是可靠的理论依据，先进的实(试)验设计方案，适用的测试手段，合理、准确的数据处理及科学、严密的分析与论证。

2) 理论推导

这类论文主要是对提出的新假说通过数学推导和逻辑推理，得到新的理论，包括定理、定律和法则。其写作要求是数学推导要科学、准确，逻辑推理要严密，并准确地使用定义和概念，力求得到无懈可击的结论。

3) 理论分析

这类论文主要是对新的设想、原理、模型、机构、材料、工艺、样品等进行理论分析，对过去的理论分析加以完善、补充或修正。其论证分析要严谨，数学运算要正确，资料数据要可靠，结论除了要准确，一般还须经实(试)验验证。

4) 设计计算

它一般是指为解决某些工程问题、技术问题而进行的计算机程序设计；某些系统、工程方案、机构、产品的计算机辅助设计和优化设计，以及某些过程的计算机模拟；某些产品(包括整机、部件或零件)或物质(材料、原料等)的设计或调、配制等。对这类论文总的要求是相对要"新"，数学模型的建立和参数的选择要合理，编制的程序要能正常运行，计算结果要合理、准确；设计的产品或调、配制的物质要经实(试)验证实或经生产、使用考核。

5) 专题论述

这类论文是指对某些事业(产业)、某一领域、某一学科、某项工作发表议论(包括立论和驳论)，通过分析论证，对它们的发展战略决策、发展方向和道路，以及方针政策等提出新的独到的见解。

6) 综合论述

这类论文应是在作者博览群书的基础上，综合介绍、分析、评述该学科(专业)领域里国内外的研究新成果、发展新趋势，并表明作者自己的观点，作出发展的科学预测，提出比较中肯的建设性意见和建议。一篇好的综合论述，对于学科发展的探讨，产品、设计、工艺材料改进的研究，科学技术研究的选题，以及研究生学位论文的选题和青年科技人员及教师进修方向的选择等的指导作用都是很大的。对这类论文的基本要求是资料新而全，作者立足点高、眼光远，问题综合恰当、分析在理，意见和建议比较中肯。

3.1.2 科技论文的突出特点

科技论文同一般的科技文章有共同之处，具有准确、鲜明、生动的特点，但作为科技论文，它又有自身的特殊性。

1. 创新性或独创性

科技论文报道的主要研究成果应是前人(或他人)所没有的。没有新的观点、见解、结果和结论，就不能称其为科技论文。对于某一篇论文，其创新程度可能很大，也可能很小，但总要有一些独到之处，总要对丰富科学技术知识宝库和推动科学技术发展起到一定的作用。"首次提出""首次发现"，当然是具有重大价值的研究成果，这毕竟为数不多。在某一个问题上有新意，对某一点有发展，应属于创新的范围。基本上是重复他人的工作，尽管确实是作者自己"研究"所得的"成果"，则不属于创新之列。在实际研究中，有很多课题是在引进、消化、移植国内外已有的先进科学技术，以及应用已有的理论来解决本地区、本行业、本系统的实际问题，只要对丰富理论、促进生产发展、推动技术进步有效果，有作用，报道这类成果的论文也应视为有一定程度的创新。

由于创新性的要求，科技论文的写作不应与教科书(讲义)和实验报告、工作总结等同。科技论文报道的是作者自己的研究成果，因而与他人相重复的研究内容，基础性的知识，某些一般性的、具体的实验过程和操作或数学推导，以及比较浅显的分析等都应删去，或者只做简要的交代和说明，同时应对原始材料有整理、有取舍、有提高，要形成新观点、新认识、新结论。

2. 理论性或学术性

理论性指一篇科技论文应具有一定的学术价值，它有两个方面的含义。

(1) 对实验、观察或用其他方式所得到的结果，要从一定的理论高度进行分析和总结，形成一定的科学见解，包括提出并解决一些有科学价值的问题。

(2) 对自己提出的科学见解或问题，要用事实和理论进行符合逻辑的论证与分析或说明，总之要将实践上升为理论。

3. 科学性和准确性

所谓科学性，就是要正确地说明研究对象所具有的特殊矛盾，并且要尊重事实，尊重科学。具体说来，包括论点正确，论据必要而充分，论证严密，推理符合逻辑，数据可靠，处理合理，计算精确，实验可重复，结论客观等。所谓准确性，是指对客观事物即研究对象的运动规律和性质表述，包括概念、定义、判断、分析和结论要准确，对自己研究成果的估计要确切、恰当，对他人研究成果(尤其是在做比较时)的评价要实事求是，切忌片面性和说过头话。

4. 规范性和可读性

撰写科技论文是为了交流、传播、储存新的科技信息，让他人利用，因此，科技论文必须按一定格式写作，必须具有良好的可读性。在文字表达上，要求语言准确、简明、通顺，条理清楚，层次分明，论述严谨。在技术表达方面，包括名词术语、数字、符号的使用，图表的设计，计量单位的使用，文献的著录等都应符合规范化要求。科技论文规范表达的要求来自科学技术期刊编排的标准化和规范化。科技论文表达规范，不仅能提高论文本身的水平，而且可以反映出作者严谨的治学态度和优良的写作修养。这为论文被期刊选中发表提供了极为有利的条件。诚然，一篇论文能否被期刊采用，主要决定于论文报道的研究成果是否有发表价值，但是，表达规范与否也是不能忽视的因素。尤其是对于稿源丰富的期刊，当在两篇都有发表价值的论文中只能选用一篇时，被选中的肯定是表达比较规范的那一篇，因为它的编辑加工量小，或者不必要经过作者再修改，从而可以保证出版质量，缩短发表周期。因此，为了使确有发表价值的论文能得到及时发表，避免因表达不规范被退稿或推迟发表，作者应努力提高论文的写作质量，使之达到规范表达的要求。

科技论文的规范表达涉及如下主要内容。

(1) 编写格式的标准化。

(2) 文字细节和技术细节表达的标准化或规范化，主要包括名词名称、数字、量和单位、数学式、化学式等的规范表达，以及插图和表格的合理设计。

(3) 科技语言和标点符号的规范运用。

3.1.3 科技论文的结构及编写格式

科技论文一般由引言、方法、结果和讨论等主要部分构成。在引言中回答研究什么问题，问题的位置；在方法中回答怎样研究这个问题；在结果这一部分阐述新的发现；对于新发现的意义可在讨论部分回答。

科技论文的基本格式为：题名(Title)、著者(Authors)、通信地址(Address)、摘要(Abstract)、关键词(Keywords)、引言(Introduction)、方法(Methodology)、结果和讨论(Results and Discussion)、结论(Conclusion)、附录(Appendix)、致谢(Acknowledgement)、参考文献(References)等。

题名(Title)是科技论文的必要组成部分。它要求用最简洁、恰当的词组反映文章的特定内容，把论文的主题明白无误地告诉读者，并且使其具有画龙点睛、启迪读者兴趣的功能。一般情况下，题名中应包括文章的主要关键词。题名像一条标签，切忌用冗长的主、谓、宾语结构的完整语句逐点描述论文的内容，以保证达到"简洁"的要求；而"恰当"的要求应反映在用词的中肯、醒目、好读好记上。当然，也要避免过分笼统或哗众取宠的所谓简洁，缺乏可检索性，以至于名实不符或无法反映出每篇文章应有的主题特色。

著者(Authors)署名是科技论文的必要组成部分。著者是指在论文主题内容的构思、具体研究工作的执行及撰稿执笔等方面的全部或局部上做出主要贡献，能够对论文的主要内容负责答辩的人员，是论文的法定主权人和责任者。合写论文的各著者应按论文工作贡献的多少顺序排列。著者的姓名应给出全名，同时还应给出著者完成研究工作时的单位或著者所在的工作单位或通信地址(Address)，以便读者在需要时可与著者联系。

摘要(Abstract)是以提供文献内容梗概为目的，不加评论和补充解释，简明确切地记述文章重要内容的短文。学位论文等文章具有某种特殊性，为了评审，可写成变异式的摘要，不受字数的限制。摘要的编写应该客观、真实，切忌掺杂编写者的主观见解、解释和评论。

为了便于读者从浩如烟海的书刊中寻找文献，特别是适应计算机自动检索的需要，GB/T 3179—2009规定，现代科技期刊都应在学术论文的摘要后面给出3~8个关键词(Key Words)。

引言(前言、序言、概述)(Introduction)经常作为论文的开端，主要回答"为什么研究(Why)"这个问题。它简明介绍论文的背景、相关领域的前人研究历史与现状(有时也称这部分为文献综述)，以及著者的意图与分析依据，包括论文的追求目标、研究范围和理论、技术方案的选取等。引言应言简意赅，不要等同于摘要，或成为摘要的注释。引言中不应详述同行熟知的，包括教科书上已有陈述的基本理论、实验方法和基本方程的推导；除非是学位论文，为了反映著者的学业等，允许有较详尽的文献综述段落。如果在正文中采用比较专业化的术语或缩写词时，最好先在引言中定义说明。

正文是科技论文的核心组成部分，主要回答"怎么研究(How)"这个问题。正文应充分阐明论文的观点、原理、方法及具体达到预期目标的整个过程，并且突出一个"新"字，以反映论文具有的首创性。根据需要，论文可以分层深入，逐层剖析，按层设分层标题。一般应包括材料、方法、结果和讨论等几个部分。

结论(Conclusion)是整篇文章的最后总结。尽管多数科技论文的著者都采用结论的方式作为结束，并通过它传达自己欲向读者表述的主要意向，但它不是论文的必要组成部分。结论不应是正文中各段小结的简单重复，主要回答"研究出什么(what)"。它应该以正文中的实(试)验或考察中得到的现象、数据和阐述分析作为依据，由此完整、准确、简洁地指出以下内容：

(1) 对研究对象进行考察或实(试)验得到的结果所揭示的原理及其普遍性。
(2) 研究中有无发现例外或本论文尚难以解释和解决的问题。
(3) 与先前已经发表过的(包括他人或著者自己)研究工作的异同。
(4) 本论文在理论上与实践上的意义与价值。
(5) 对进一步深入研究本课题的建议。

致谢(Acknowledgement)一般单独成段，放在文章的最后面，但它不是论文的必要组成部分。它是对曾经给予论文的选题、构思或撰写以指导或建议，对考察或实(试)验过程中做出某种贡献的人员，或给予过技术、信息、物质或经费帮助的单位、团体或个人致以谢意。

文后参考文献(References)是现代科技论文的重要组成部分，但如果撰写论文时未参考文献也可以不写。它是反映文稿的科学依据和著者尊重他人研究成果而向读者提供文中引用有关资料的出处，或为了节约正文篇幅和叙述方便，提供在论文中提及而没有展开的有关内容的详尽文本。

3.2 科技论文写作

科技论文(Research Paper)是在科学研究、科学实验的基础上，对自然科学和专业技术领域里的某些现象或问题进行专题研究、分析和阐述，为揭示这些现象和问题的本质及其规律而撰写成的文章。也就是说，凡是运用概念、判断、推理、论证和反驳等逻辑思维手段，来分析和阐明自然科学原理、定律和各种问题的文章，均属科技论文的范畴。

科技论文是作者用科学思维，将通过科学实践所获得的科研成果进行总结归纳后，按论点和论据所写成的论证性文章。一篇优秀论文既要内容丰富新颖、科学性强，又要富有理论性、实践性和创新性，且文字通顺，层次清楚，逻辑性强。

为了写一篇科技论文，必须进行很多带有评判性的阅读并对获得的材料进行评估。这些经历对大学学习和大学毕业以后的工作都有益处。写作的过程也给了学生学习如何使用图书馆，如何使用文献的机会。这个过程也会使学生熟悉一篇科技论文的结构和写作要素，并学习到一些从前不了解的知识。

3.2.1 科技论文写作步骤

任何两个人的写作过程都不会相同。但是在写作的时候，每一位作者都可以遵从一定的写作步骤。这里给出了这些步骤。要注意这些步骤都不是相互排斥的，有时当处于某一阶段时，很可能又要回到早已完成的阶段。

1. 选择一个能够研究下去的主题

所有的研究论文写作都是从确定一个主题开始的，因此确定主题是写作论文的第一个重要步骤。一个不合适的研究主题有可能导致整个研究任务的失败，并且浪费时间和精力。确定一个主题是一个迂回曲折的过程。

选择主题是一件非常困难的事情。选择的主题是不是太宽？是不是太窄？能不能找到足够的材料来写一篇研究性论文？必须找一个感兴趣的并且能够进行下去的主题。建议按照下述过程选择主题。

(1) 选择一个方向。

选择一个感兴趣的方向，然后到图书馆或者其他能查到所需资料的地方，查找是否有足够多的相关材料，如果找不到就放弃。

选择主题的时候，不要为了方便就自动选择一个早已经熟悉的方向，但也不要放弃某些你已经很熟悉的方向。应该选择一个感到好奇并且认为如果研究下去，能够学习到一些新知识的主题。

(2) 阅读并思考。

阅读尽可能多的资料，并进行深入的思考。也可以通过网络查找一些适合于该主题的材料。在阅读的过程中，考虑该主题是否已经被研究透，是否可以进一步进行研究，从而发现一些新的东西。如果已经被研究透，不能发现新的东西就放弃该主题。

(3) 细化主题。

选择的主题不要太宽，以至于必须写一本书才能完成。一定要把主题限制在某个特殊的方面，以在有限的时间内完成论文。

把选择的主题用问题的形式给出。例如：媒体是否影响到选举？使用主题词来描述主题。在这个例子中，明显的主题词是 media 和 elections，但是也有其他可能。

television   AND   elections
press   AND   politics
press   AND   influence

太宽的主题可能检索到太多的材料，而太窄的主题有可能检索到的资料太少或者检索不到资料。如果主题太宽，可以尝试重新表述问题。对上面提到的例子，可以重新表示为电视覆盖率对2008年美国总统选举有什么影响？

下面给出适用于论文主题的一些标准。

① 主题必须是有意义的和严肃的。一篇研究论文必须能使人思考和学习。论文不是告知听众已有的信息、数据和分析，而是创造新的知识。

② 必须是一个能够操作的主题。不能处理一些没有进行过必要训练的主题。例如，你主修英语，但是却想写一篇有关核物理方面的论文。

③ 选择的主题必须是可以获得足够多材料的主题。

④ 选择的主题必须能够被客观对待，不能有个人喜恶。

⑤ 选择的主题不能太热门。

如果选择的主题符合以上的标准，就可以进入下一阶段，否则必须修改主题直到符合上述标准。

下面看一个如何选择和细化科技论文主题的例子。

General topic: Channel Equalization
Restricted: Channel Equalization for IEEE 802.16

More restricted:　　Channel Equalization for IEEE 802.16 Single-Carrier System
Topic chosen:　　MLSE Equalization Algorithm for IEEE 802.16 Single-Carrier System

2. 收集材料

确定一个研究主题后，就可以开始收集相关材料了。到图书馆标出所有需要的书籍、期刊、杂志，然后对这些材料进行复印。如果有电子版材料，可以马上打印出来。

这里的材料指的是与研究相关的材料。不可能没有任何材料就能把论文写出来，所参考材料的数量和质量反映了研究的深度。应该从决定写论文的时候就开始收集材料。

收集材料的时候要注意：需要多少信息？这取决于需要信息的理由；写论文的目的是什么？论文需要多少页？需要一些深层次的信息还是仅仅是一些背景信息？需要什么类型的信息？什么级别的，学术的还是大众的？

可以找到材料的地方很多，下面列举一些。

(1) Internet：有很多搜索工具，如 Google、Dog Pile、Yahoo 等。当使用 Web 搜索工具时，注意以下事项。

① 仔细阅读搜索工具的使用帮助。例如，Google 的高级搜索可以使搜索结果仅仅限于教育性的，非营利性的，或者政府网站。

② 不要期望能从搜索结果中直接获得相关期刊、杂志、报纸的详细内容。很多材料是受版权保护的，不能免费获得这些材料。

③ 不要期望一种搜索工具能够搜到所有的信息。同样，不要期望两种搜索工具搜索的结果是一样的。

④ 不要认为搜索结果中的材料顺序就显示了材料的价值顺序。每一个搜索工具都有自己的搜索策略。

⑤ 不要随意相信所读取的信息，特别是在 Web 上的信息。

(2) 图书馆的在线目录。

(3) 期刊、杂志。

大部分原始材料来自书籍、杂志、期刊或网络。收集信息的主要方法就是阅读这些原始材料。在阅读的时候，应该在最短的时间内，判断阅读的内容是不是有用的信息。要快速并带有评判性地阅读原始材料。对一篇论文和一本书，不需要都从头到尾进行阅读。查看目录或者索引，来发现哪些章节有可能成为有用的材料，忽略一些不相关的内容。

当发现有用材料时，必须考虑它是否可靠。如果材料来源可疑，则没有任何价值。因此必须知道有哪些人对该材料进行了评价，评价内容是什么。如果是书籍，最好找到该书的最新版本，并且同其他相同主题的书籍进行比较。必须保证材料不是过时的或者带有偏见的。

评价材料来源的标准有如下几条。

① 权威性：看看该来源是出自何处，并且他/它的信用等级如何。从书、期刊、Web 上查找该出处的所有信息。作者是一个自由作者还是一个研究者？他隶属于某个协会还是某个组织？出版社或者期刊是否权威？

② 精确性：考虑材料是否前后一致，是否被其他资源证实或引用。如果是一本书或者

一篇论文，查找它是否被引用过。对 Web 上的材料，一定要从其他地方得到证实。记住，大多数 Web 上的内容是没有经过严格审核的，是需要查证的。

③ 客观性：考虑提供该材料的作者或者组织的最终目的是什么，其目的是告知性的、劝说性的，还是纯粹为了卖产品。

④ 实时性：检查材料来源是不是最新的。要记住书籍从写作到发行，通常至少要一年。因此，即使最新的书籍，通常其内容也是"过时"一两年的。而期刊、杂志往往能提供实时性信息。

⑤ 全面性：考虑收集的材料在深度上和广度上是否适合你的主题。

一旦确定了主题，并且收集到一些必要的材料后，你应该开始做笔记。没有人能够记住他所读过的所有材料，也没有人不做笔记就能写出好的研究论文。做笔记的最好时刻是在阅读的时候。阅读时，信息在你的脑子里是最清晰的。不要说你会在阅读完一份材料后马上回过头来做笔记，因为你记不住所有你想记住的内容，也记不住在哪里再找到它们。

在做笔记时应该注意以下事项。

① 使用自己的字词。用自己的字词总结材料也是为了防止剽窃他人成果。

② 引用时要使用引用标记。这提醒你这是一个引用，并且需要进行解释。

③ 使用较短的句子，避免使用长的句子。

④ 记住所记录内容的出处和页码。

3. 明确你的论点或研究问题

确定主题并阅读了一些材料后，必须为论文明确一个论点或研究问题，也就是你写论文的最终目的是什么。不同性质的论文有不同的确定方式，以下分别叙述分析性论文和辩论性论文两种研究性论文。

(1) 分析性论文：分析就是把一个主题或概念进行分解，并按照自己的想法进行重组。在一篇分析性论文中，你会在该主题上成为一个专家，并按照自己的观点对该主题进行重组和表述。在没有完成论文之前，你对该主题还没有任何结论。你的任务是调查并研究，这需要评判性的思考和阅读，并对材料进行评估。当论文写作结束时，你会在该主题上有自己的想法，并得出一些结论。

(2) 辩论性论文：辩论是用事实或者逻辑来维护一个论点或者驳斥某个论点。同分析性论文相比，辩论性论文就某个主题提出一个论点，并使用证据来支持这个论点，而不是对该主题进行研究，从而提出一个新的论点。

针对辩论性论文，重点是论点陈述；针对分析性论文，重点是一个没有解决的问题，也就是研究问题。

这里没有给出一些抽象的定义，而是给出一个例子来说明二者的不同。

假设你要根据"现代媒体技术对个人的影响"写一篇论文，可以选择写成分析性论文或者辩论性论文，论文要求中也没有给定论点或者研究问题。但是你知道无线电是一种现代媒体，并对个人有影响。经过一些阅读和思考，并细化主题后，你决定写一篇有关"听音乐对学生的影响"的论文。

如果选择写辩论性论文：经过阅读和思考，你决定论文的论点陈述可能是："Contrary to popular, parental, and librarian opinion, 'quiet study time' does not in fact enhance but instead impairs students' productivity. Listening to music while studying is in fact a beneficial activity to add to a study regime for better grades because of the way music motivates students and keeps them alert."

如果选择写分析性论文：你的研究问题可能是"What is the ultimate effect of music-listening while studying on grades?"这篇论文就会对该问题进行分析，并给出一些答案。

4. 写出一个提纲

有了一个比较满意的论点或者研究问题后，下一步就是为论文写出一个提纲。

提纲是论文的写作计划。到这个阶段，知道了论文写作出发点，也就是论文的论点或者研究问题；也知道目的地，即一些总结或者结论。但是如何从出发点到达目的地？提纲不但给出计划想说的内容，也给出了在两段之间进行过渡的方法。

提纲无疑是很重要的。如果到现在还不能写出一个提纲，根本就不能写出一篇论文。如果在写提纲的时候发现文章结构有问题，就比较容易进行纠正。这总比在写第三稿或第四稿的时候进行纠正要容易得多。提纲也告诉了你在什么地方该叙述或论述什么。

假如确定的论文主题是：Performance Analysis of the IEEE 802.11a Protocol at the Physical Layer，写出的提纲如下。

I. Introduction

A. 802.11a MAC and PHY PDUs

B. OFDM PHY Layer

II. Motivation

Cross Layer Interaction

III. Experimental Analysis

A. Model

B. Parameters

C. Metrics

D. Indoor

E. Outdoor

IV. Conclusion

A. WLAN Performance highly dependant on the ability of the PHY Layer to equalize the channel

B. Significant dual effect of TCP Layer

V. Future Work

A. Proposed Multi-rate switching algorithm

B. Cross Layer Interaction

C. Improved PHY Layer

1. MIMO antenna systems for improved bandwidth efficiency at low SNR values

2. Improved channel equalization techniques such as adaptive semi-blind equalization

5. 写初稿

写初稿是写论文过程中耗时最少的阶段。写初稿可以分为以下几个部分。

1) 写引言

引言很重要，它的目的是引起读者的兴趣。引言同时介绍主题。简而言之，引言是论文的第一印象。不论论文是什么风格的，一般会把论点或问题放在段落的末尾，而把一些重要的背景信息放在它们的前面。引言的第一句话可以是一个引用、一个问题、一个简短的叙述、一个有趣的事实、一个定义或者对术语的解释、一句反话或者自相矛盾的话等。

2) 写论文主体

论文主体是论文最重要的部分，没有它们，论点是没有意义的，研究问题仍然是没有解决的问题。

写一篇论文应该像在陡峭的山上行走。在山顶上，用比较概括抽象的语言向读者介绍最全面的景观。然后从山顶下行到山谷，也就是从概括到具体。在这个过程中用具体的内容来论述论点。最后又返回到山顶，读者可以从中看到很多例子。也就是论文应该做到从上到下，再从下到上；从概括到具体，再从具体到概括。如果山谷变成巨大的草原，读者就会对原来的概括陈述感到疑惑。如果山顶变成平原，读者就会感到混乱，就会希望有具体的例子。因此，论文必须在一般性和特殊性两个方面得到平衡。

论文主体段落的数目依赖于论文的长度和主题的复杂度。段落有 3 个要素，分别是统一、一致和充分发展。"统一"就是从一个主题句开始，段内其他每一句话都是该主题句的发展、论证或说明。"一致"就是段内内容的前后一致性。可以有很多方法来获得一致性。

(1) 重复关键词。

(2) 对一些重要的名词使用代名词。

(3) 使用类似于"This policy…,""that event…,""… these examples"等句子。

(4) 段内句子要有逻辑顺序。

(5) 使用一些连接词。"therefore""moreover""however"等词不但是句子的过渡词，更表明了语句之间的关系。"充分发展"就是履行你在主题句中的承诺。如果你想讨论一些商店的不平常条款，那么就列举几种，给你的读者足够的材料进行思考。

把材料整合到论文主体中是一件艰苦的工作。但是如果做得好，论文就会比较出色。

(1) 使用材料来支持你的论点，而不是作为论文的支柱。材料的拼凑永远不是一篇研究论文。

(2) 要经常使用总结(用自己的话来对一段话进行压缩)和解释(用不同的方式来说明同一件事情)，而不是总是使用直接引用。

(3) 不要使用直接引用，除非原作者的话是非常经典和非常适宜的。

(4) 如果使用了直接引用，那么对此解释的长度要大于引用语的长度，即使用自己的话对材料进行总结和解释。要让读者了解为什么要包含这些材料。

(5) 如果多个材料说明了同样一件事情，总结它们所说的，并对此进行注释。这就增加了材料的可信度，也节省了论文的篇幅。

3) 写总结

如同引言，总结也没有什么固定的模式。总结的内容依赖于论文的内容。注意以下几点。

(1) 不要依靠总结来对论文各段落进行总结。

(2) 应该行文流畅，从正文平滑过渡到总结部分。

(3) 总结很重要，但要注意总结应该是简洁的。

(4) 不要仅仅重复引言，试着用另外一种方式叙述主题。

(5) 指出所陈述论点的重要性。

(6) 对分析性论文，可以提到结论的不足。这也表明理解了该主题的复杂性。

(7) 不要用引文来进行总结，也不要用可能是另外一篇论文的论点来总结。

6. 对草稿进行修改

应该反复地、带有评判性地阅读草稿，并进行修改。即使是非常专业的写作者也不能一次就写出完美的论文。应反复阅读草稿，审查是否有错误或不妥之处。一开始，应该把注意力集中在高层次方面上(如论文的各段结构是否合理)，然后是低层次方面上(如句子、词的选择、技巧等)。

在修改的时候，应该注意以下几点。

(1) 论文标题是否能够说明论文主要讨论的内容。

(2) 论点或者研究问题是否明确。

(3) 引言中是否有足够的篇幅对论点和问题进行了说明，来表示它们的重要性。这些说明是太多了还是太少了。在引言的末尾，读者是否能够清楚地了解论文后面部分会有什么内容。

(4) 论文段落是否逻辑清晰。也就是引言的结尾，论文主体的开始及结尾，结论的开始都要清楚。

(5) 论文各节和段的衔接是否流畅。

(6) 主体各段是否都有一个主题句。把各段的主题句和论文的论点/问题都提取出来，看看它们是不是你想在论文中表达的内容。如果不是，必须修改论点/问题或者各段的主题句。

(7) 各段的主题句应该做到与论点/问题相联系，同时与上一段的主题句有某种联系(也许是某种顺序，也许是一种比较和对比)。还要注意能否给读者以足够的信息，让读者猜知该段的主要内容。

(8) 各段是否有一个正式的结尾句。在各段的末尾部分，是否提到了该段与文章主题的某种联系/关系，以提醒读者为什么要写该段。

(9) 各段的顺序是不是有意义(例如，各段的顺序是否符合逻辑)。

(10) 段落是否太短或太长，各段是否可以合并，某些段是否可以拆分，是否需要对内容进行增加或删减。

(11) 举例是否可信、有代表性、有说服力，举例是否太多或者太少。

(12) 材料来源是否可信，自己的观点与专家的观点是否一致。

(13) 是否还有些内容需要给出出处。

(14) 是否有内容脱离主题，或者不是必要的。

(15) 结论是否与引言有所不同，是否给人印象深刻。

在修改的时候，有可能会出现4种操作。

(1) 添加：插入必需的词、句、段。

(2) 删除：去掉脱离主题的，或者重复的内容。

(3) 替代：如果需要，用新的词、新的句子、新的段进行内容更替。

(4) 移动：改变材料的顺序，以使它们符合逻辑。

这些操作在计算机上可以很容易地进行。但是，为了修改进展顺利，最好在"屏幕"和"纸"上交替进行。

7. 用一种可行的风格和格式完成你的论文

论文的风格取决于个人爱好。每个人的风格都有所不同，但必须让论文容易被阅读和理解。语言必须简单、清楚、易懂，尽量避免复杂的句子。华而不实的语言和结构复杂的句子不会凑成好的研究论文。使用引言时，要尽量自然，以使文章顺畅和风格一致。

根据论文的写作目的，可能会有不同的格式要求。具体内容，可以参考本书 3.2.4 节。

最后，必须保证文章中没有标点符号、语法、拼写错误，没有参考文献等格式上的错误。仔细阅读最终版本，如果没有上述错误，论文写作就结束了。

3.2.2 风格

科技论文主要是摆事实、讲道理。出色的研究不一定就能写出出色的论文。出色的论文应该精确、清楚、直截了当，不要使用一些诡辩、夸大的词语，从而使论文让人糊涂。

1. 清晰(Clarity)

论文写作的一个重要品质就是清晰。最重要的任务就是把思想清楚地表达出来，并用一种读者可以理解的方式来表达。

(1) 说你想表达的内容。

写作的内容应该很清楚地表达出你所想表达的内容。如果做不到这一点，你就有可能像下面这些话一样"名垂千古"了。

在一个希腊旅馆：Visitors are expected to complain at the office between the hours of 9 and 11 a.m. daily.

在一个苏黎世旅馆：Because of the impropriety of entertaining guests of the opposite sex in the bedroom, it is suggested that the lobby be used for this purpose.

在一个罗马洗衣店：Ladies, leave your clothes here and spend the afternoon having a good time.

在一个瑞士山间小酒店：Special Today—No Ice Cream.

在一个挪威鸡尾酒会：Ladies are requested not to have children in the bar.

在布达佩斯动物园：Please do not feed the animals. If you have any suitable food, give it to the guard on duty.

在一个巴黎旅馆：Please leave your values at the front desk.

(2) 要用准确的语言来写作。

科技论文最忌讳使用含糊不清的语言。形容词、副词的含义多半是含糊不清的，因为它们涉及作者的印象和判断，而不是事实本身。例如，The efficiency of that algorithm is high. 这句话中的 high 是一个相对的概念，因为效率达到什么程度才算是高效的？并没有一个客观的标准。也许对某一个目的来说，这种算法就是高效、满足要求的。The efficiency of that algorithm is high enough to deal with the coming data from the port. 但是这还不够确切，因为应用该算法的程序是否能够及时处理数据，与运行该程序的主机性能及数据的速率有关。所以应该说明算法的处理速度与数据数目的关系。We have given an algorithm with expected running time $O(n^2)$, and now improve it to be $O(n\log_2 n)$.

这并不是说作者不能在科技论文中对事实做任何定性判断，相反，作者在很多场合需要对事实做出判断，但同时应该给出一些定量的数据。

2. 简洁(Concision)

简洁与清晰密切相关。简洁应该是每一位作者努力的目标。写作是一个过程性、发散性的活动，伴随着一定的紧张和一定程度的混乱。思想在脑子当中打转，必须要使得这些思想能够以一定的顺序、一定的简洁性，还有一定的活力表达出来。

通常，作者都有种想对写作内容进行填充材料的冲动。一定的字数要求是很多人写废话的一个理由。写废话的另外一个理由就是，通过废话可以进行一定的伪装，来掩盖由于作者本身对某些内容的不理解。

对比下面两个例子可以看出，B 句不但比 A 句用词少，而且比 A 句更容易看懂。

(1) A. Experimentations are being done on the communication system. These experimentations strive to make the communication efficiency in that system more efficient, thus minimizing the resource and financing waste in the telecom company.

B. For reducing the waste in resource and financing, experiments are being done to improve the efficiency in the communication system.

(2) A. Some changes are expected to be made in the organization of this department but no one as yet knows what changes are going to take place.

B. No one can anticipate the changes that will be made in the organization of this department.

3.2.3 几个问题

在科技论文中，图、表、符号、单位、缩写语和标点符号会大量出现。本节就这些问题给出一些必要的信息，以便给遇到这类问题的读者提供帮助。

1. 使用表格

表格常用来简化统计数字的表达。如果表格的内容可以用一句话来总结，使用表格没有任何意义。如果使用得当，表格能比文字更有效、清楚地表达信息。一个好的表格应该提供有意义的数据。表中数据应该是明确的，能有效地传递信息。

数据是否有意义取决于数据是否和正在分析、论述的内容密切相关。数据及包含在数据中的关系用于帮助论文得出结论。当然，这个结论应该是重要的结论，是正在分析的内容所不可或缺的部分。

表格中表达的内容是否明确取决于表格中所包含的文字说明是否清晰、明确。表格中包含的信息为数据、标题、脚注、参考文献等。这些内容应该自我包含、自我解释，不需要从正文中获取支持。标题和表格中的文字应该定义确切。参考文献应该使读者相信数据的有效性和可靠性。

有效的表格表示，可让读者从中得出很多重要的结论。读者能否从表格中快速得出结论，能否从中发现数据之间的重要关系，得出多少有意义的结论都取决于表格是否安排得合理有效。Table 1 和 Table 2 是两个表格示例。

Table 1　Network Operators and Licensing

Company	Fixed Line	Cellular	Paging	VoIP	Data	Int'l Gateways	Satellite
China Telecom	△		△	△	△	△	
Unicom	△	△	△	△	△	△	
CMCC		△			△	△	
CNC				△	△	△	
Jitong	△			△	△	△	△
Railcom				△	△		△
ChinaSat							△

Source: Compiled by authors, 2001

Table 2　CT International Long-distance rates

Destination Country	Previous(RMB/minute)	Current(RMB/minute)	Percentage Change (as result of latest reduction)
Australia	4.8	3.6	25%
Canada	4.8	2.4	50%
Italy	4.8	3.6	25%
Japan	4.8	3.6	25%
USA	4.8	2.4	50%

Source: China Telecom, 2000

2. 使用数据图

一张图片胜过千言万语。同样地，一张数据图可以总结成百上千的数字。某些统计信息，如果用表格的形式来表示就不易读，也很难理解。但是如果使用图的形式，则比较容易读懂。数据图用图片的方式而不是数字或者文字来传递信息。

表格表示数据的 3 个标准——有效性、有意义、明确性，同样适应于数据图。用数据图的形式表示数据，选择有意义的数据、清楚地定义数字代表的内容、使用一种有效的方式让读者快速明白数据表达的含义都是至关重要的。

设计好的数据图要比设计好的表格需要更多的科学和艺术才能。要知道和理解自己的数据，但同时也要预测读者会如何理解图表内容。好的数据图会比表格告知读者更多的信息。相反，差的数据图会破坏或隐藏应该告诉读者的信息。

下面介绍几种常见的图表形式。

(1) 饼图。

饼图(Pie Chart)表示变量频率或者百分比上的差异。它把一个圆分成几块面积与变量所占百分比相对应的扇形。饼图应该尽量少用，因为它不如柱形图能够清楚地表示各个数据之间的相互关系，如 Fig.1 所示。

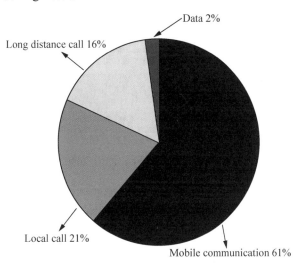

Fig.1　Telecom service revenue of China, 2005

(2) 柱形图。

柱形图(Bar Graph)表示变量在频率或者百分比上的差异。它用相同宽度、不同高度的矩形来表示数据的差异。可以垂直或水平放置矩形，如 Fig.2 所示。

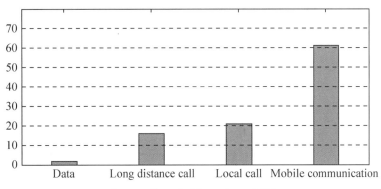

Fig.2　Telecom service revenue of China, 2005

(3) 直方图。

直方图(Histogram)用来表示一定时间间隔上的变量在频率或者百分比上的差异。但是直方图的矩形是连续的，宽度与变量的时间间隔成正比，高度与变量的频率或百分比成正比。直方图与柱形图类似，只是矩形之间是连续的、相互接触的，如 Fig.3 所示。

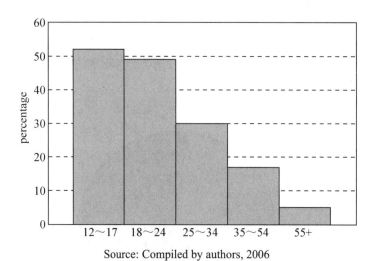

Fig.3　The percentage of downloading color ring back tone in various age groups in America, 2005

(4) 多边形图。

多边形图(The Frequency Polygon)也用于表示一定时间间隔上的变量在频率或者百分比上的差异。注意观察 Fig.4 的特点。

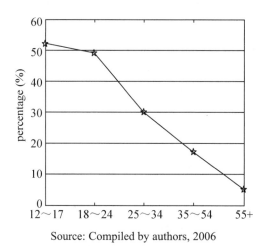

Fig.4　The percentage of downloading color ring back tone in various age groups in America, 2005

(5) 时间序列图。

时间序列图(Time Series Chart)用于表示不同时间点上变量的变化。横坐标表示时间，纵坐标表示变量值。注意观察 Fig.5 的特点。

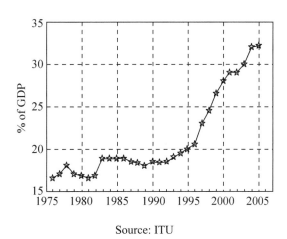

Source: ITU

Fig.5　Telecom service revenues, worldwide

3．标点

标点可以把文章分成符合逻辑的单元，使读者容易读下去。标点包括所有用于分开词的符号、空格、每段第一句的缩排、空白行、大写字母，以及各种标记或停顿符(如逗号、分号、冒号等)。使用标点是传统的，并且随时间演化。最早的写作语言是没有标点的，现在的正式写作中，标点是必不可少的。

标点符号的选择影响着意思的表达。如果使用不同的标点符号组合，有可能使表达的意思完全相反。请阅读下面的例子。

Dear John,

　　I want a man who knows what love is all about. You are generous, kind, thoughtful. People who are not like you admit to being useless and inferior. You have ruined me for other men. I yearn for you. I have no feelings whatsoever when we're apart. I can be forever happy—will you let me be yours?

Gloria

Dear John,

　　I want a man who knows what love is. All about you are generous, kind, thoughtful people, who are not like you. Admit to being useless and inferior. You have ruined me. For other men, I yearn. For you, I have no feelings whatsoever. When we're apart, I can be forever happy. Will you let me be?

Yours,

Gloria

幸运的是，标点符号不会总是造成这么戏剧性的后果。但是适当的标点法仍然是写作的重要部分。

(1) 逗号和句号。

逗号(Comma)用于连接两个独立从句。

Planck's ideas seemed incredible, many scholars simply ignored him.

句号(Period)用在很多场合。最方便的是把两个独立从句分成独立的句子。

Planck's ideas seemed incredible. Many scholars simply ignored him.

此句也可以使用分号。

Planck's ideas seemed incredible; many scholars simply ignored him.

破折号有时也用于两个独立从句的连接，特别是当第二个从句较短时。

Planck's ideas seemed incredible—many scholars simply ignored him.

并列连词也能完成这个任务。

Planck's ideas seemed incredible, and many scholars simply ignored him.

或者用主从句。

Since Planck's ideas seemed incredible, many scholars simply ignored him.

(2) 分号。

分号(Semicolon)可以把两个独立从句连接成一个句子。分号也可以告诉读者，当分号出现的时候，他遇到了一个语义上的完整停顿，但是后面的从句与前面的从句具有紧密的联系。另外，当使用逗号来分割几个从句，有可能造成意义混淆时，也用分号来替代逗号。

Hobbes's *Leviathan* has many memorable passages: his audacious view of human beings as mere mechanical constructions, his evocation of a brutish, savage state of nature, his establishment of a binding, permanent social contract to protect individuals, and his refusal to place any limits on the power of a duly established ruler.

使用分号进行修改。

Hobbes's *Leviathan* has many memorable passages: his audacious view of human beings as mere mechanical constructions; his evocation of a brutish, savage state of nature; his establishment of a binding, permanent social contract to protect individuals; and his refusal to place any limits on the power of a duly established ruler.

(3) 冒号。

冒号(Colon)用于连接两个具有直接逻辑关系的独立从句。

This form of social organization creates habits that are carried into the business world: Some companies are literally families.

也可以使用冒号来连接句子的具有紧密关系的两个部分，而不一定是独立从句。

The data point to only one conclusion: fraud.

(4) 破折号。

破折号(Dash)的使用比较灵活。如果不过分使用，破折号可以使文章生机勃勃。破折号也可以用来连接独立从句。

During Machiavelli's lifetime, Italy as a single political entity did not exist—instead, there was a patchwork of little city-states, petty kingdoms, republics, duchies, and ecclesiastical states, constantly at war with each other.

请注意，连字符 Hyphen(-)和破折号 dash(—)是不同的。连字符连接多个词以组成复合词(shoo-in, a run-of-the-mill transaction)。

错误：In Coriolanus, Sicinius and Brutus are the tribunes of the people-the voice of the people.

正确：In Coriolanus, Sicinius and Brutus are the tribunes of the people—the voice of the people.

(5) 括号。

括号(Parenthes)包括()、[]、{}。注意在括号的外部添加空格，而不是在括号的内部添加。不是 not(this)，而是 not (this)。

(6) 问号和惊叹号。

在论文写作当中，很多场合可以使用问号(Question Mark)和惊叹号(Exclamation Mark)。事实上，尖锐的问题和感叹可以带来活力和能量，引起读者的注意。

How might this anomaly be explained?

Does Beatrice's decision make sense?

4．数词

科技英语写作中常常涉及数字，因此多写成阿拉伯数字的形式。具体写法如下。

(1) 10 及 10 以上的数字写成阿拉伯数字。

(2) 10 以下的数字拼写出来，如 5 写成 five。但是如果数字后面带单位，则仍然写成阿拉伯数字，如 8 inches 等。

(3) 如果 21 到 99 间的数字要拼写出来，十位与个位之间需加连字号。如 22 写成 twenty-two，99 写为 ninety-nine。

(4) 当数字频繁出现时则仍然写成阿拉伯数字。

He used a crew of 3 carpenters, 1 plumber, 6 laborers, 1 foreman, and 1 timekeeper.

(5) 仅作为估计数的数字一般都拼写出来。

The communication system can be used for twenty years.

(6) 一个句子不要以阿拉伯数字开始。遇到这种情况时，应该将数字拼写出来或者采用一些变通的方法。

错误：105 television stations are in this country.

变通为：There are 105 television stations in this country.

(7) 对于整数，3 位以内的没有特殊要求。4 位数时，可以写成 1234 或者 1,234。

超过四位时，每向左增加 3 位加一个逗号，如 54,251,000。

(8) 带小数时，小数点前多带有 0，如 0.0256。对于算法语言产生的结果或者有很多数据时，也可以不带 0，如 .0256。

(9) 数字和文字间有连字号时，一位数字多用文字拼写表达，如 five-wire circuit；多位数字用拼写或阿拉伯数字表示都可以，如 50-channel system 或 fifty-channel system。

5．单位

对外交流的科技写作当中，应该采用国际单位制(简称为 SI 制)。国际单位制分为两大系统，一个为基本单位系统，一个为导出单位系统，见 Table 3。

Table 3 SI Units (国际单位制单位)

In English [en]		Symbol 符号	Names used in People's Republic of China	
Quantity	Name		量	名称
SI Base Units			基本单位	
length	meter	m	长度	米
mass	kilogram	kg	质量	千克(公斤)
time	second	s	时间	秒
electrical current	ampere	A	电流	安[培]
thermodynamic temperature	kelvin	K	热力学温度	开[尔文]
amount of substance	mole	mol	物质的量	摩[尔]
luminous intensity	candela	cd	发光强度	坎[德拉]
Examples of SI derived units in terms of base units			以基本单位表示的导出单位举例	
area	square meter	m^2	面积	平方米
volume, capacity	cubic meter	m^3	体积，容积	立方米
speed, velocity	meter per second	m/s	速度	米每秒
acceleration	meter per second squared	m/s^2	加速度	米每秒平方
density, mass density	kilogram per cubic meter	kg/m^3	密度，质量密度	千克(公斤)每立方米
SI derived units with special names			具有专门名称的导出单位	
plane angle	radian	rad	[平面]角	弧度
solid angle	steradian	sr	立体角	球面度
frequency	hertz	Hz	频率	赫[兹]
force	newton	N	力；重力	牛[顿]
pressure, stress	pascal	Pa	压力，压强；应力	帕[斯卡]
energy, work, quantity of heat	joule	J	能量；功；热量	焦[耳]
power, radiant flux	watt	W	功率；辐[射能]通量	瓦[特]
electric charge, quantity of electricity	coulomb	C	电荷[量]	库[仑]
electric potential difference, electromotive force	volt	V	电位；电压；电动势；(电势)	伏[特]
capacitance	farad	F	电容	法[拉]
electric resistance	ohm	Ω	电阻	欧[姆]
electric conductance	siemens	S	电导	西[门子]
magnetic flux	weber	Wb	磁通[量]	韦[伯]
magnetic flux density	tesla	T	磁通[量]密度，磁感应强度	特[斯拉]
inductance	henry	H	电感	亨[利]
celsius temperature	degree celsius	ºC	摄氏温度	摄氏度
luminous flux	lumen	lm	光通量	流[明]

6. 缩写语

英语中缩写语的使用极为广泛，随着科学技术的飞速发展，科技领域中缩写语的使用日益广泛。除了常见的一些各专业通用的缩写语，不同专业对同一形状的缩写语可能有不同的含义。作者也可以根据自己的需要在文章或者著作中创造一些缩写语。这种创作的缩写语一般只能在它出现的文章或著作中有效，但也不排除日后广为流传的可能性。

缩写语分为 4 种。第一种是由一个词组的各个单词的首字母组成，称为首字母词。第二种为一个词的缩写，即缩写词。第三种是由几个词各取出一部分组成，称作缩拼词。这类词有些已经演变为新词汇，而不按缩写语对待。第四种是由姓名的首字母组成，即姓名首字词。

(1) 首字母词。

当需要将一个词组写成首字母词(Acronym)时，需要在文章或书籍第一次出现时写成它的全称，并把收入 acronym 的单词的首字母大写，以示醒目。一些众所周知的 acronym 可以直接写出而不必写出全称。

BASIC：Beginner's All-Purpose Symbolic Instruction Code；

TOEFL：Test of English as a Foreign Language；

VLSI：Very Large-Scale Integration。

有时将介词的首字母也列入 acronym，如 DoD—Department of Defense。

外来语种取首字母构成 acronym 时，往往不能和英译名相对应。

CCITT(取自法语)：国际电报电话咨询委员会—The International Telegraph and Telephone Consultative Committee。

(2) 缩写词。

缩写词(Abbreviation)可以有很多形式，其构成没有什么规律。

ad.—advertisement 广告　sync—synchronization 同步　info—information 信息

Ltd.—Limited 有限公司　No—number 号码　　　　Xformer—transformer 变压器

(3) 缩拼词。

科技英语中常将两个技术名词缩拼起来构成一个新词，称为缩拼词(contraction)。如：

Heliport—helicopter airport 直升机机场　　telecast—television broadcast 电视广播

Televiewer—television viewer 电视观众　　petrodollar—petrol dollar 石油美元

(4) 姓名的首字母。

在某些场合下，常常使用姓名的首字母(Initials)，如 G. B. S. 是萧伯纳(Grorge Bernard Shaw)姓名的首字母。

缩写语有以下一些注意事项。

(1) 缩写语的含义。同一形式的缩写语可能有多种含义，如 RMS，可以表示 root mean square—均方根，也可以表示 Railway Mail Service—铁道邮政，还可以是自由软件奠基人理查德·马修·斯托曼(Richard Matthew Stallman)的英文首字母缩写(该缩写比他本人的姓名更出名)。又如 OTC，可以是 Office of Technical Cooperation 技术合作处[联合国]，Office of Transport and Communications 交通运输处[美]，Officers' Training Corps 军官训练团，Overseas Telecommunications Commission 海外电信委员会[澳]，Oxytetracycline(药)，土霉素(氧四环素)。

(2) 缩写语的大小写。该问题没有统一的规定，一般来说，作者临时创造的缩写语最好加以说明并采用大写。对于一些已经转化为常规英语词的缩写语则应符合它自身的大小写习惯。

(3) 缩写语的复数形式。许多缩写词有自己的复数形式，有的有一定的规律，有的就没有什么规律。比如 p. 表示 page，但是 pages 用 pp. 表示。有的单复数形式相同，如 foot 或 feet 的缩写都是 ft。

3.2.4 学位论文

学位论文(Thesis，Dissertation)是作者为获得某种学位而撰写的科技论文。thesis 通常指硕士学位论文，而 dissertation 通常指博士学位论文。其中，博士学位论文具有较高的参考价值，它内容丰富，一般侧重于理论。硕士学位论文一般侧重于工程。

学位论文包括 4 个主要部分：摘要(Abstract)、前言(Preliminaries)、正文(Text)以及参考材料(References)。有些 Thesis 或 Dissertation 还包括附录(Appendix)。Table 4 是一篇论文通常包含的主要部分，以及它们出现的先后顺序。

Table 4 论文包含内容

Parts of a Thesis	Status
I) Abstract	Required
II) Preliminaries	
a) Title Page	Required
b) Dedication	Optional
c) Biography	Required
d) Acknowledgements	Optional
e) Table of Contents	Required
f) List of Tables	Required
g) List of Figures	Required
h) List of Symbols or Abbreviations	Optional
i) Preface	Optional
III) Text	Required
IV) Reference Materials	Required
V) Appendices	Optional

1. ABSTRACT (Required)

摘要在学位论文中很重要，它告诉了读者论文讨论的范围以及论文的主题。通常研究者在查找材料的时候，只读一篇论文的摘要部分，来判断该论文是不是与自己的主题相关。因此摘要中必须把重要的发现和方法等叙述清楚。关于如何写摘要？详细内容请参阅 3.3.1 节。

2. TITLE PAGE (Required)

题目页应该包含关键词，来反映研究的独特方面，以便与其他人的工作分开。题目应避免使用诸如"A Study of"等表达形式。

同摘要一样，各种组织、各个学校、各个学科，甚至不同的导师对题目页的格式、字数等具体规范都可能有不同的要求。Table 5 是一个题目页的具体例子。

Table 5　题目页

Performance Analysis of the IEEE 802.11a Protocol at the Physical Layer by KOGER KEITH BALLARD A theses submitted to the Graduate Faculty of North Carolina State University in partial fulfillment of the requirements for the Degree of Master of Science MASTERIALS SCIENCE AND ENGINEERING Raleigh 1993 APPROVED BY:

_____

Chair of Advisory Committee

3. DEDICATION (Optional), BIOGRAPHY (Required), ACKNOW LEDGMENTS (Optional)

这一部分与作者个人有关，可以包含任何作者想同读者分享的内容。没有字数要求和限制。致谢等内容可有可无，但是必须有作者个人信息。

4. TABLE OF CONTENTS (Required)

目录标出论文所有的章节、部分，可以包括论文中所出现的图、表格的目录。注意所有标题应该与其在论文中完全一致。Table 6 是一个目录的具体例子。

Table 6　目录

TABLE OF CONTENTS	
	Page
LIST OF TABLES	v
LIST OF FIGURES	vi
1. INTRODUCTION	1
2. NOISE AND DISTORTION	4
2.1　White Noise	4
2.2　Coloured Noise	5
2.3　Impulsive Noise	8
2.4　Transient Noise Pulses	10

续表

2.5	Thermal Noise	12
2.6	Shot Noise	13
2.7	Electromagnetic Noise	16
2.8	Channel Distortions	18
2.9	Echo and Multi-path Reflections	21
3. PROBABILITY & INFORMATION MODELS		28
3.1	Introduction: Probability and Information Models	28
3.2	Random Signals	30
3.3	Probability Models	31
3.4	Information Models	34
3.5	Stationary and Non-Stationary Random Processes	36
3.6	Statistics (Expected Values) of a Random Process	39
3.7	Some Useful Classes of Random Processes	41
3.8	Transformation of a Random Process	46
4. ADAPTIVE FILTERS		50
4.1	Introduction	50
4.2	State-Space Kalman Filters	51
4.3	Sample Adaptive Filters	60
4.4	Recursive Least Square (RLS) Adaptive Filters	71
4.5	The Steepest-Descent Method	80
4.6	LMS Filter	85
5. LINEAR PREDICTION MODELS		90
5.1	Linear Prediction Coding	90
5.2	Forward, Backward and Lattice Predictors	93
5.3	Short-Term and Long-Term Predictors	95
5.4	MAP Estimation of Predictor Coefficients	97
5.5	Formant-Tracking LP Models	99
5.6	Sub-Band Linear Prediction Model	101
REFERENCES		105
APPENDICES		108
Appendix A. Bessel Functions		108
Appendix B. Confluent Hypergeometric Functions		110

iv

5. LIST OF TABLES, LIST OF FIGURES (Required)

如果在论文中出现表格和图片，需要给出它们的索引。在索引中出现的图表名称应该与论文中相一致，见 Table 7。

第 3 章　科技论文写作的基础知识

Table 7　索引

List of Tables		
		Page
Table 1.1	Network Operators and Licensing	2
Table 2.1	Major Operators by Ownership and Universal Service Obligation	26
Table 3.1	Network Operators: description of network and coverage	47
Table 3.2	CT Domestic Long-distance Telephone Fee	49
Table 3.3	CT International Long-distance rates	50
		V
List of Figures		
		Page
Figure 1.1	Socio-economic, geopolitical and cultural environment	23
Figure 1.2	ICT users worldwide	24
Figure 2.1	Number of economics connected to the Internet	25
Figure 2.2	Telecom service revenue, worldwide	26
Figure 2.3	Comparing developed and developing economics	27
Figure 3.1	Broadband subscribers by region, 2003	31
Figure 3.2	Evolution of the digital divide	32
Figure 3.3	Evolution of the networks index	58
Figure 3.4	Evolution of the divides between economy groups	59
		VI

6. LIST OF SYMBOLS, ABBREVIATIONS OR NOMENCLATURE (Optional)

当出现很多符号、缩写词或命名时，应该给出一个单独的符号表、缩写词表、命名表等。

7. TEXT (Required)

论文正文的组织和格式应该符合一定的规范。一般来说，正文应该包含以下内容。

(1) 一个导言或绪论，有时二者都可以包含。
(2) 一个明确的目标陈述。
(3) 适当的前期研究回顾。
(4) 对研究中所使用的方法进行描述。
(5) 记录研究所获得的结果，并讨论所获得的结果对其他研究的意义。
(6) 研究中所有重大有意义的发现，并进行总结。
(7) 对未来研究的建议。

8. LIST OF REFERENCES, LITERATURE CITED OR BIBLIOGRAPHY (Required)

论文中应该包含适当的材料，也就是论文所参考的原始文献。在人文科学和社会科学论文中，使用脚注(Footnotes)或尾注(Endnotes)，通常称为参考书目(Bibliography)；在自然科学、工程技术类论文中，通常使用参考文献(Cited References)的方式。

原始文献在某种程度上可以使其他研究者能够架构或重现所做的研究。没有原始文献，读者不能确定所提供的信息是否可信。原始文献也可以直接引用其他研究者的研究成果，而不需要对他们的研究工作进行详细的论述。

参考书目或参考文献必须包括直接引用的，或者对论文提供了很多信息的材料；不包括对论文影响很小的材料。注意不要仅仅为了使得这一部分足够长而随意添加原始文献材料。

不同的导师、不同的学校、不同类型的杂志都可能会有不同的参考书目或参考文献格式要求。因此，要根据所提交论文的要求，正确安排参考书目或参考文献的格式。

在研究论文中，通常有 4 种参考格式。

(1) MLA 格式：由 the Modern Language Association 制定，广泛用于英语写作、文学等。

(2) APA 格式：由 the Publication Manual of the American Psychological Association 制定，广泛用于社会科学。

(3) CMS 格式：用于人文科学(不是文学)，使用传统的脚注和尾注。

(4) CBE (Council of Biology Editors，现在称为 the Council of Science Editors)格式：广泛用于医学、物理学、数学等学科。在 CBE 格式中，还分为两种不同的格式。一种称作 Citation-Sequence (CS) system，用于化学、计算机、数学、物理、医学、电子信息等学科；另外一种称作 the Name-Year system，用于生物、地球、考古、农业等学科。

本节只介绍 CBE 格式中的 CS 格式的使用。这种格式需要在文章中使用数字，而不是年代。在文章的末尾要有一个参考文献表(Cited References，或 References)。可以用以下两种方式安排参考文献。

(1) 按照参考文献的字母进行排序，并依次数字标记。

(2) 按照文献在文章中出现的先后顺序进行数字标记。

下面给出了参考文献的一些注意事项。

(1) 在文章正文中使用数字标记。

数字用圆括号(1)或方括号[2]括起，也可以使用上标，如 [3]。不需要也不鼓励使用名称。

It is known (1) that the DNA concentration of a nucleus doubles during Interphase.

A recent study [1] has raised interesting questions related to photosynthesis, some of which have been answered [2].

In particular, a recent study[1] has raised many interesting questions related to photosynthesis, some of which have been answered.[2]

如果在文章中提及了作者的名字，在作者名字后加注数字。

Additional testing by Cooper (3) includes alterations in carbohydrate metabolism and changes in ascorbic acid incorporation into the cell and adjoining membranes.

如果需要，可以添加页码等数字信息。

"The use of photosynthesis in this application is crucial to the environment" (Skelton,[8] p. 732).

The results of the respiration experiment published by Jones (3, Table 6, p. 412) had been predicted earlier by Smith (5, Proposition 8).

(2) 参考文献表中的格式。

参考文献表放在文章的末尾。表的标题是"Cited References"或"References"，居中。表中各条文献使用缩进格式。

① 参考的书籍。首先是数字，然后是作者，书籍的名称、出版地点、出版商、年份和参考的页数范围。

[1] Gehling E. The family and friends' guide to diabetes: Everything you need to know. New York: Wiley, 2000.

[2] Schwartz, M., Information Transmission, Modulation and Noise, Second Edition, New York: McGraw Hill, 1970, pp. 105-160.

[3] L. J. Mordell. Diophantine Equations[M], Academic Press. New York, 1969.

② 期刊。数字，然后是作者、文章的题目、期刊名、年月、卷数，如果需要还可以添加出版期号、参考页码。

[4] Bolli GB, Owens DR. Insulin glargine. Lancet 2000; 356:443-444.

[5] S.L. Ariyavisitakul and G.M. Durant, "A Broadband Wireless Packet TechniqueBased n Coding, Diversity and Equalization", IEEE Communications, Vol. 36, No. 7, July, 1998, pp. 110-115.

[6] H. Sari, G. Karam and I. Jeanclaude, "Transmission Techniques for Digital Terrestrial TV Broadcasting", IEEE Comm. Mag., Vol. 33, No. 2, Feb, 1995, pp. 100-109.

③ 杂志和报纸。在期刊格式的基础上加上日期，如果是报纸，注明是第几版。

[7] Schlosberg S. The symptoms you should never ignore. Shape 2000 Aug:136.

[8] [Anonymous]. FDA approval of drug gives diabetics a new choice. Los Angeles Times Aug 2, 2000; Sect A:4.

④ 网络文章和其他电子出版物。添加访问的日期和现在是否在线。

[9] [Anonymous]. Diabetes insipidus. Amer Acad. Of Family Physicians [online] 2000. Available from: http://www.aafp.org/patientinfo/insipidu.html. Accessed 2000 Aug 8.

[10] Roberts S. The diabetes advisor. Diabetes Forecast [serial online] 2000;53: 41-42. Available from: http://www.diabetes.org/diabetesforecat/00August/default.asp. Accessed Aug 8, 2000.

⑤ 报告。除了作者、报告名称等，还需添加报告号、发布报告的组织、地点和日期。

[11] Bogusch, R. L.,Digital Communication in Fading Channels: Modulation and Coding, Mission Research Corp., Santa Barbara, California, Report no. MRC-R-1043, March 11, 1987.

[12] Holmes-Siedle, A. G. (1980). *Radiation effects in the Joint European Torus experiment: guidelines for preliminary design.* Report No. R857/2 Fulmer Research laboratories, Stoke Poges UK.

(3) 参考文献表的安排。

Table 8 是一个使用 CS 格式的参考文献表的例子。

Table 8　CS 格式参考文献表

REFERENCES
[1] Guthrie DW, Guthrie RA. Nursing management of diabetes mellitus. New York: Springer, 1991.
[2] [Anonymous]. Diabetes insipidus. American Academy of Family Physicians. Available from: http://www.aafp.org/patientinfo/insipidu.html. Accessed Aug 10, 2000.
[3] Clark CM, Fradkin JE, Hiss RG, Lorenz RA, Vinicor F, Warren-Boulton E. Promoting early diagnosis and treatment of type 2 diabetes. JAMA 2000;284:363-5.
[4] Nurses' Clinical Library. Endocrine Disorders. Springhouse, PA: Springhouse, 1984.

9. 附录 APPENDICES (Optional)

附录中包含一些必需的，但不适宜出现在正文中的材料。它可以包含研究中获得的数据、计算机程序、调查数据、详细的程序流程图，以及一些特别的文献。有可能其他学者希望以此为基础进行更进一步的研究。注意，附录部分必须同正文分开，另起一页，并标注"Appendix"或者"Appendices"，居中显示。

3.2.5　科技期刊文章

著名物理学家、化学家法拉第(M. Farady)有一句名言："科学研究有三个阶段，首先是开拓，其次是完成，最后是发表。"很多研究成果都发表在各自的行业期刊上。科技期刊论文既具有一般议论文的特点，由论点、论证、结论构成；又具有与一般议论文不同的特点：科学性和准确性；学术性或理论性；创新性与独创性；规范性与人工语言符号(图表、照片、公式、化学等)的应用。

一篇发表在期刊上的科技论文通常包括以下几项：① 题目(Title)；② 作者姓名；③ 作者单位名称地址；④ 摘要(Abstract)；⑤ 关键词(Keywords)；⑥ 正文(Text)，包括引言、正文论述部分、结论；⑦ 致谢(Acknowledgments)，该项可选，可有可无；⑧ 参考文献(References)等。

期刊论文的写作与上面一节讨论的学位论文的写作有很多相似之处，在此不再对各个部分进行详细的讨论，仅给出一篇科技论文例文，其参考文献为 CS 格式。

Multirate Performance in Multiuser MMSE and
Decorrelating Detectors using Random
Spreading Sequences for AWGN Channels.

Gustavo Fraidenraich, Renato Baldini F. and Celso de Almeida

DECOM - FEEC - UNICAMP

Abstract—This paper presents simplified expressions for the bit error probability for multirate MMSE and decorrelating multiuser detectors. The multiple data rates are achieved by the variations of the processing gain. It is assumed random spreading sequences and AWGN channel.

Keywords—Multiuser, CDMA, multirate, MMSE, decorrelating.

I. INTRODUCTION

The new third generation mobile system will allow multirate schemes. There will be different modulations schemes supporting multiple data rates. The aim of this paper is to unveil simplified expressions for the bit error probability for multirate MMSE and decorrelating multiuser detectors. Those expressions are obtained for the AWGN channel where random spreading sequences are considered.

II. SINGLE BIT RATE PERFORMANCE ON AWGN CHANNELS

It is possible to devise a good approximation for the exact performance expression for synchronous CDMA system, using single bit rate, with N users, processing gain G, perfect power control and BPSK modulation. This approximation can be made by assuming that the multiple access interference is Gaussian distributed with zero mean and variance proportional to the number of users. Thus, the bit error probability can be written as:

$$P_b = Q\left(\sqrt{\frac{1}{\frac{1}{2E_b/N_0} + \frac{N-1}{G}}}\right) \quad (1)$$

where $Q(.)$ is the complementary Gaussian error function and $\frac{E_b}{N_0}$ is the signal-to-noise ratio.

III. MULTI PROCESSING GAIN SYSTEMS

Distinct users using different data rates can be allocated in the same bandwidth B, if the processing gain is variable. Thus, high data rate implies low processing gain for a given user.

It is going to be assumed a multi processing gain system with N users and rates $r_1 > r_2 > ... > r_n$, with no loss of generality. All users have the same energy per bit to noise ratio $\frac{E_b}{N_0}$ and the processing gain is defined as $G_i = B/r_i$, where r_i is the bit rate for the i-th group with N_i users. The system is defined in such way that $\sum_{i=1}^{n} N_i = N$, where n is the number of groups with distinct bit rates. It is also assumed that random spreading sequences are utilized for all users. The performance of user k with rate r_k in a synchronous CDMA system using matched filter detector can be expressed as [1]:

$$P_b = Q\left(\sqrt{\frac{1}{\frac{1}{2E_b/N_0} + \frac{1}{G_j}\left(\sum_{i=1}^{n} \frac{r_i}{r_j} N_i - 1\right)}}\right) \quad (2)$$

IV. BIT ERROR PROBABILITY OF DECORRELATING AND MMSE DETECTORS IN A SINGLE BIT RATE SYSTEM ON AWGN CHANNELS

The result given in (2) can be extended to the multiuser MMSE and decorrelating detectors. In [2, 3, 4], equivalent expressions to (1) were derived as a function of the processing gain and the number of users. The bit error probability in any linear multiuser detector can be evaluated by the expression:

$$P_b = Q\sqrt{\frac{2E_b}{N_0}\bar{\eta}} \tag{3}$$

where $\bar{\eta}$ is the near-far resistance[2]. In the case of the decorrelating detector $\bar{\eta}$ can be expressed by:

$$\bar{\eta} = E\left[\frac{1}{R_{k,k}}\right] \tag{4}$$

where R is the spreading sequences crosscorrelation $N \times N$ matrix and $E[.]$ is the average operator. The result in (4) applied to random spreading sequences can be simplified to:

$$\bar{\eta} = 1 - \frac{N-1}{G} \tag{5}$$

Thus the bit error probability P_b for the decorrelating detector with perfect power control in a synczhronous system on AWGN channel can be expressed by:

$$P_b = Q\left(\sqrt{\frac{2E_b}{N_0}\left(1 - \frac{(N-1)}{G}\right)}\right) \tag{6}$$

For the MMSE detector, a similar procedure as for the decorrelating detector case can be made to achieve P_b which is given by [2], [4]:

$$P_b = Q\left(\sqrt{\frac{2E_b}{N_0} - \frac{1}{4}F\left(2\frac{E_b}{N_0}, \frac{(N-1)}{G}\right)}\right) \tag{7}$$

with:

$$F(x,y) \stackrel{\Delta}{=} \left[\sqrt{x(1+\sqrt{y})^2 + 1} - \sqrt{x(1-\sqrt{y})^2 + 1}\right]^2 \tag{8}$$

V. MULTIUSER PERFORMANCE IN A MULTIRATE SYSTEM ON AWGN CHANNELS

Based on the above assumptions it is possible to devise the bit error probability for the decorrelating detector in a multirate synchronous CDMA system using random spreading sequences with multiprocessing gain on AWGN channel:

$$P_b = Q\left(\sqrt{\frac{2E_b}{N_0}\left(1 - \frac{\left(\sum_{i=1}^{n}\frac{r_i}{r_j}N_i - 1\right)}{G}\right)}\right) \tag{9}$$

For the MMSE detector it can be shown that P_b can be evaluated by:

$$P_b = Q\left(\sqrt{\frac{2E_b}{N_0} - \frac{1}{4}F\left(2\frac{E_b}{N_0}, \frac{\left(\sum_{i=1}^{n}\frac{r_i}{r_j}N_i - 1\right)}{G}\right)}\right) \tag{10}$$

Equations (9) and (10) are tight approximations of the real bit error probabilities for the decorrelating and the MMSE detectors, respectively, in a multirate system.

VI. NUMERICAL RESULTS AND COMPARISONS

Simulations were carried out in order to validate the approximations (9) and (10). The results of the comparisons are shown in Figure 6 and Figure 7. All the simulations were made using $N=10$ users. The system was subdivided into two subgroups, the first with five users and processing gain $G=64$ and the other with five users and $G=128$. The results show that this system is equivalent to a system with 15 users and a processing $G=128$ or to a system with a fictitious 7.5 users and processing gain $G=64$.

Fig.6 shows the comparison between the simulation and the analytic expression (9) for the decorrelating detector. Fig.7 shows the comparison between the simulation and the analytic expression (10) for the MMSE detector. Notice that in both figures the simulations and the analytic expressions match perfectly. Note also that it is possible to define the parameter *equivalent number of users*, which allows to represent a multirate system by its equivalent single rate system. For instance, for the parameters used in this paper the equivalent number of users is 15.

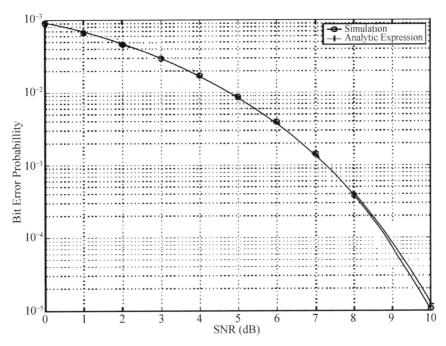

Fig.6   Decorrelating on AWGN channel with 5 users with *G*=64 and 5 users with *G*=128

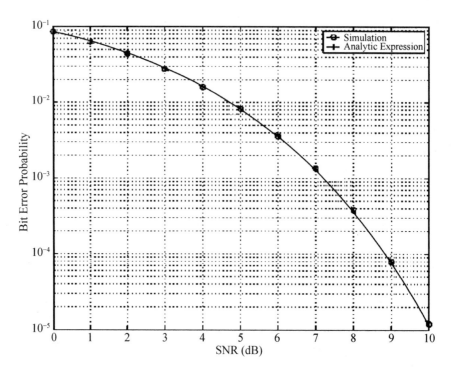

Fig.7　MMSE on AWGN channel with 5 users with G=64 and 5 users with G=128

VII. CONCLUSIONS

Approximated expressions for the bit error probability with random spreading sequences on AWGN channel using the multiuser MMSE and decorrelating detectors in multirate systems were presented. Those analytic expressions have shown to be a very good approximation when compared to those obtained by simulation.

ACKNOWLEDGEMENTS

This work is supported by ERICSSON and FAPESP under the grant number 00/07633-9.

REFERENCES

[1] T. Ottosson, and A. Svensson, "Multi-rate performance in DS/CDMA systems," Tech. Report no. 14, ISSN 0283-1260, Dept. of Information Theory, Chalmers University of Technology, Gothenburg, Sweden, March 1995.

[2] S. Verdu, Multiuser Detection, Cambridge: Cambridge Press, 1998.

[3] Celso de Almeida and Gabriel M. da Silva. On the performance of CDMA Systems with multiuser Decorrelating Detectors for Random Sequences on AWGN channels. Master Thesis, UNICAMP, 2002.

[4] G. Fraidenraich, R. Baldini F. and C. de Almeida-On the Performance for MMSE Detection of Direct Sequence CDMA Signals with Random Spreading in Multipath Rayleigh Fading Channels. Ericsson Report no. 2, Unicamp, Fev. 2002.

[5] J. G. Proakis, Digital Communications, 2nd ed. New York: McGraw-Hill, 1995.

3.3 科技写作实例

3.3.1 摘要

对于会议报告、科技文章、学位论文等，通常要求写一篇摘要(Abstract)。要记住的主要一点是摘要必须短，因为它是对研究的一个概述。事实上，摘要不仅短，而且通常是一个给定的、特别的长度。所以在开始写之前，必须知道摘要应该是多长(比如，硕士论文的摘要通常是200字)，那么写摘要时应接近这个数字，而不应超出这个数字。超出最大字数限定的摘要经常被否定，因为这种摘要不能被数据库检索使用。

1. 什么是摘要

摘要是对"论文的内容不加注释和评论的简短陈述"。其作用主要是为读者阅读、信息人员及计算机检索提供方便。摘要显示了读者如果继续阅读，要寻找的东西和期望得到的东西。一篇好的摘要可能是文章最重要的段落，也可能是这篇文章值得看与否的原因所在。人们通常是通过快速阅读摘要来决定这篇文章是不是自己需要的。摘要不宜太详尽，也不宜太简短，应将论文的研究体系、主要方法、重要发现、主要结论等，简明扼要地加以概括。

摘要有不同的种类，可以使用描述性(Descriptive)文体或信息性(Informative)文体。

(1) 描述性文体：简要叙述(大约120字，一段)原始文档的内容。
① 告诉读者这篇论文所包含的信息是什么。
② 包括了论文中研究的目的、方法和研究领域。
③ 不提供结果、结论或建议等。
④ 把该论文的主题介绍给读者，文中可以找到作者的结论或建议。

(2) 信息性文体：提供了原始文档中更多的信息(200～300字)；总结了主要的论点和主要数据等。
① 从这篇论文中交流特殊的信息。
② 包括了论文中研究的目的、方法和研究领域。
③ 提供该论文的结论、结果或建议等。
④ 篇幅要短，从一个段落到一页或两页不等，长度取决于被摘要的原始研究工作。通常信息性文体摘要占原始工作量的10%或更少。

2. 写摘要时存在的通病

(1) 太长。如果摘要太长，它也许会被否定掉。摘要要进入数据库，因此常常规定它的最大字数。

(2) 太详细。太长的摘要经常是包含了一些无用的细节。摘要不是用来详细地叙说研究工作所用的方法，而是只需说出研究的主要点。

(3) 太短。太短的摘要也不是所需要的。如果字数限制为200字，但仅写了95字，有可能写得不够详尽。应该重新审读这篇摘要，看看哪些地方应该写得更详细。在许多情况下，读者通过看摘要来决定是否读这篇研究论文，而许多作者却对他们的发现成果没有给出充足的信息。

(4) 没有包括重要信息。作者经常是用太多的篇幅来解释有关研究工作采取的手段和方法，而没有表达出研究的最终结果。

3. 摘要与引言的比较

初一看，摘要和引言非常相似，因为二者都包含了研究问题、研究目标；简要回顾了研究方法、主要发现和主要结论。然而，它们有两点重要差别。

(1) 引言应该短，但没有字数限制。写引言的主要目的是通过上下文或背景知识的介绍来阐述研究的主要目的。引言通常是从一般到特殊，介绍研究问题如何被发现。

(2) 摘要有一个最大字数限制，是整篇研究报告的概述。写摘要的主要目的是概括研究工作(尤其是目标和主要发现及结论)，而不是介绍研究领域。

4. 如何写摘要

(1) 带着写摘要的目的去重读整篇文章。
① 重点看论文的主要部分，包括目的、方法、研究领域、结果、结论和建议等。
② 用标题、提纲性标题、内容列表来指导写摘要。
③ 如果你正在写另外一个作者文章的摘要，最好的开始地方在引言和概要部分，因为这些地方通常覆盖了论文的重点。

(2) 在看完这篇论文之后，先写草稿。
① 不要仅仅复制文章中的关键句。
② 不要依赖于文章中的材料组织方式，而是以一种新的组织方式来概括信息。

(3) 修改草稿，改正文中组织的缺陷，一点一点地改进文中信息的自然过渡。剔除不必要的信息，增加忽略的重要信息，消减重复单词的使用。修正语法、拼写和标点符号的错误。

(4) 打印最后的文稿，再看一遍，尽量将摘要写得尽善尽美。

5. 写一篇好摘要的几点建议

(1) 易读，语句组织得好，简明而自成一体。

(2) 摘要中包含许多的关键词，以便用户通过图书馆系统能找到相应的主题。

(3) 不要附加原始文章中不包含的信息。

(4) 以第三人称作主语，因为以第一人称作主语常带有强烈的个人感情色彩。主题句可用主动语态，主语为"作者、本人或本论文的目的……"；也可用被动语态，主语为"本文、本报告……的实质……"。

(5) 众所周知的国家、机构、专用术语尽可能用简称或缩写。

(6) 要采用规范化的名词术语；不使用图、表或化学结构式，以及相邻专业的读者难以清楚理解的缩略语、简称、代号。如果确有必要，在摘要中首次出现时必须加以说明。

(7) 定义特殊的专业术语。要求使用法定计量单位以及正确地书写规范字和标点符号。

(8) 保持主语和动词紧密联系。

(9) 使用现在时态。仅在描述试验和特殊变量时用过去时态。

6. 文章摘要实例之一

PASM: A partitionable SIMD/MIMD System for Image Processing and Pattern Recognition

PASM, a large-scale multimicroprocessor system being designed at Purdue University for image processing and pattern recognition, is described. This system can be dynamically reconfigured to operate as one or more independent SIMD and/or MIMD machines. PASM consists of a parallel computation unit, which contains N processor, N memories, and an interconnection network; Q microcontrollers, each of which controls N/Q parallel secondary storage devices; a distributed memory management system; and a system control unit, to coordinate the other system components. Possible values for N and Q are 1024 and 16, respectively. The control schemes and memory management on PASM are explored. Examples of how PASM can be used to perform image processing tasks are given.

7. 文章摘要实例之二

The Center for Technology in Government worked with the Adirondack Park Agency to develop a prototype system that combines document records and geographic data into a unified workstation or "electronic reference desk." This report presents the finding of the technical staff responsible for developing the prototype system. It covers the gathering of geographic data and the development of the database as well as the data conversion process. Hardware and software configurations are included as well as lessons learned from the process and recommendations for other GIS system developers.

8. 文章摘要实例之三

ABSTRACT

TOM, PHILIP HILL
Low-Complexity Equalization of OFDM in
Doubly Selective Channels
(Under the direction of Worner Akaiwa Aldrich.)

Orthogonal frequency division multiplexing(OFDM)systems may experience significant inter-carrier interference (ICI)when used in time-and frequency-selective, or doubly selective, channels. In such cases, the classical symbol estimation schemes, e.g., minimum mean-squared error (MMSE) and zero-forcing(ZF)estimation, require matrix inversion that is prohibitively complex for large symbol lengths. An analysis of the ICI generation mechanism leads us to propose a novel two-stage equalizer whose complexity (apart from the FFT) is linear in the OFDM symbol length. The first stage applies optimal linear preprocessing to restrict ICI support, and the second stage uses iterative MMSE estimation to estimate finite-alphabet frequency-domain symbols. Simulation results indicate that our equalizer has significant performance and complexity advantages over the classical linear MMSE estimator in doubly selective channels.

9. 文章摘要实例之四

以上 3 例都属于描述性摘要，接下来看一个信息性摘要的例子。

"The Effects of Power, Knowledge and Trust on Income Disclosure in Surveys," by Catherine E. Ross and John R. Reynolds (1996. Social Science Quarterly 77:899-911).

ABSTRACT

Why do some social groups report income less often than others? We propose that powerlessness in the household and in society decrease the likelihood of reporting income because they decrease knowledge and trust. (研究目的)Knowledge of household finances affects the ability to report household income. Trust affects the willingness to report it. (研究主题)We analyze the reporting of exact or approximate income in a national U.S. probability sample of 2,031 respondents interviewed by telephone in 1990. (研究范围)Mistrust reduces the probability of reporting income, whether exactly or approximately. Homemakers and those with little household power report income as often as others if allowed to report approximate rather than exact amounts. The same applies to African Americans, the poorly educated, the unmarried, and people who feel powerless. Older persons and those in larger households report income less often than others and tend to give approximate amounts. (报告结论)The results confirm that knowledge and trust affect the reporting of income in surveys. (总结)

3.3.2 实验报告

实验报告(Laboratory Report)是为了与其他人交流做了什么；解释为什么这么做；描述是怎么做的；表达发现了什么；综述这个实验结果有何含义等内容。

撰写实验报告，一般有一个通用的格式：包括题目(Title)、摘要(Abstract)、引言(Introduction)、方法(Method)、结果(Results)、讨论(Discussion)、参考文献(References)等。

题目(Title)，应该简洁、清楚地给予读者和有关实验者主要关心的内容，即反映出这篇报告的确切含义。

摘要(Abstract)是一段自成一体的短文，又是整篇实验报告主要观点的概述。它包含了被观察问题的简要表述、所使用的设计、被观察的主题、所包含的实验材料及任何重要仪器、得到的重点结果及其分析、最后的主要结论等。摘要字数通常为 100 字左右。一个快速写摘要的原则是从报告的每个部分摘取主题句。

引言(Introduction)，表达研究的原因，这意味着已阅读了整个引言的读者应该能够猜测到实验将要做什么。引言包括以下内容。

(1) 与研究相关的背景材料的回顾(已存在的发现和理论)。
(2) 概括用以研究的准确问题及采用的方法。
(3) 概括研究推测出来的结果等。

方法(Method)必须包含足够的信息，使读者能重复该项实验。它分成以下几个子部分：设计(Design)、实验人员(Subjects)、仪器及材料(Apparatus & Materials)、过程(Procedure)等。

(1) 设计(Design)部分必须表示所用的设计类型。非相关变量包括所选择的条件(以表征实验不同等级)；相关变量包括测量单位的详细内容(如秒、微秒或正确响应数)。还有实验的假设。

(2) 实验人员(Subjects)包括人员数量；他们是如何被选拔出来的；其他重要特征，如平均年龄、年龄范围、男女比例、受教育程度、职业等。

(3) 仪器及材料(Apparatus & Materials)包括仪器清单，如果用到复杂的仪器，如正在运行特殊软件的计算机，应该详细地进行描述。另外，对选用的特殊材料，应该描述选用的一般准则。

(4) 过程(Procedure)描述设计是如何实现的，而且应该确切地描述参加的实验人员及实验所需的仪器和材料；应包含足够的信息使其他人能正确地重复实验。

结果(Results)部分提供给读者一个清晰的、准确的所收集的数据概述及通过任何统计测试过程之后得到的结果；结果部分报告包括实验数据及其分析。它不是对结果进行翻译，而是将结果放在讨论部分。图表都应有标题，而且要被仔细清楚地标号。报告中必须包括一些解释文本以描述什么数据出现在表格中。

讨论(Discussion)，在这部分中可以解释实验的结论及对此进行进一步讨论。很重要的一点是讨论应与引言中提到的论点相关。讨论部分也应给进一步的实验提出一些建议，当然也可以讨论实验中还不是很明朗的一些限制因素。撰写讨论(Discussion)的步骤如下。

(1) 表述所得结论，以摘要的形式列出。

(2) 统计所有的发现。

(3) 挖掘这些发现中隐含的东西。在表述结论时，应该通过概述结论的主要特征展开讨论。例如，实验条件不同，结果是否有明显差别？如果有，则什么条件下产生相应的结果？这些发现是否与实验假设相关联等？接下来就是讨论这些发现的含义。如果已经摒弃了不合理的假设，则有必要确认这是不是非相关变量的操作所导致的；有必要确保不是其他易混淆的变量或实验加工产品而导致的实验结果。如果不能摒弃这不合理的假设，则让读者相信这种近乎合理的解释是因果的缺乏并影响相关与非相关变量之间的关系。

当写参考文献(References)时，应区分原始资料(已看过)和第二手资料(引用但没有看过)。可以通过互联网查找与所写实验报告相关联的进一步信息。

实验报告实例如下。

Title: Laboratory Report on Control System Design for Hang Motion

Abstract: Based on microcontroller mega 16, the control system can control an object to motion, including line motion, circle motion and any assigned motion. The system can also control the object identify route, judge the setover from assigned track and adjust its route automatically. The object is driven by walking beam engineer, the engineer controlled by PWM mode.

Introduction: The motion control system ensures that the requirements are met:

(1) Setting the parameter of coordinates at discretion by keyboard or other means.

(2) The automatic operation to limit in 80cm*100cm and the length of motion track should more than 100cm, the object draws its motion track on the board and all of these are finished in 300s.

(3) The object can be the centre of a circle at discretion and the circle motion of diameter of 50cm completes in 300s.

(4) The object motion is finished in 150s from the origin of the coordinates at lower left to

certain coordinates (the length should be more than 40cm).

This paper mainly tells about the design of the motion control system. The first part is the modules consisting of the control system and the method of implementing of modules. The main body of this paper is the design detail of every module and some test results.

Testing Procedures & Testing Results:

Design Project: the module of project; the choosing and argumentation of modules of project (content omitted).

(1) Unit Circuit Design: control module circuit design; motor driving module circuit design; LCD display module design (content omitted).

(2) System Software Design: seeking mark subroutine design (taking the air line subroutine; taking the circle subroutine; taking willfully assigns the drop procedure from the zero point subroutine; taking the free curve subroutine); system flow chart (content omitted).

(3) System Test: measuring instruments；the target tests(the status of motor driving circuit test; the hanged object walks the straight line determines; the hanged object walks the circle determines; the hanged object walks the zero point as the beginning to the determination end point movement determines); (content omitted).

Discussion and Conclusions:

The error of this system mainly exists in the following several aspects:

(1) The hanged object moves from one to another. Although the distance between two points obtains quite slightly, the actual path between two points has the certain determinism. And when prearranging the track, it has some displacements, thus creates the error.

(2) The line and hanging point with the paint brush central position isn't superposition, the electronic contact of paint brush with leaned board and the pulley center line is not parallel with leaned board, all of these will create the error.

3.3.3 技术指南

技术指南(Technical Manuals)是帮助专业技术人员和消费者适当使用和维护产品的说明。这些产品包括从顾客购买的简单装置到制造厂家、企业和政府部门购买的高级尖端系统。技术指南要提供具体的技术信息，如产品如何使用，机器如何操作，设备如何维修、保养，系统如何安装或设置。所以技术指南可分为产品说明(书)、用户手册、操作指南、管理入门、维修保养手册等。各类指南的内容可能分别包括：产品介绍、应用、功能特点、故障检修、零部件浏览、设计参数、标准符号、注意事项中的一项或几项内容。

技术指南通常被厂家看成是重要的销售工具，消费者可以从中判别哪一类的设备更易操作或维修。技术指南一般由专业从事科技写作的人撰写，但有些单位也可以让该产品的制造工程师和技术人员来写，因为他们对产品的性能、特点、用途、理论等方面都很熟悉。技术指南的作者喜欢使用常用的词汇，语法结构简洁，语言浅显易懂，确切明了，注意表达的科学性和逻辑性，多使用祈使句、简单句、短句和省略句。避免过多使用被动语态和比喻语句。

技术指南实例如下。

DESIGN AND OPERATION OF AUTOMATIC GAIN CONTROL LOOPS FOR RECEIVERS IN MODERN COMMUNICATIONS SYSTEMS

This article is intended to provide insight into the effective operation of variable gain amplifiers (VGA) in automatic gain control (AGC) applications. Fig.8 is a general block diagram for an AGC loop. The input signal passes through the VGA to produce the output level to be stabilized. The detector's output is compared against a setpoint voltage to produce an error signal, which is then integrated to produce a gain control voltage. This is applied to the control input of the VGA. The attenuator shown between the VGA and the detector is used to align the maximum output level of the VGA with the maximum input level of the detector. In the course of this article several key issues will be addressed, including VGA types, loop dynamics, detector types, the operating level of VGA and the operating level of the detector. Then an example application revolving around an AD8367 VGA will be presented for further discussion of the material.

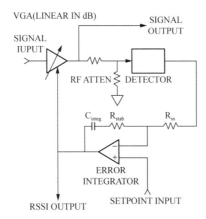

Fig.8 VGA-based AGC loop block diagram

VGA TYPES

There are two major classes of VGA in use today. The first type is the so-called IVGA (input VGA), which can be regarded as a passive variable attenuator followed by a fixed-gain amplifier. The second type is the output VGA (OVGA), which is essentially equivalent to a fixed-gain amplifier followed by a passive attenuator.

An IVGA is the preferred choice for a receive AGC system because the available out-put level at low distortion is relatively independent of the gain setting. This is the desired trait for an AGC system, whose very object is to maintain a constant output in the face of varying input signal amplitude.

The OVGA is generally ill suited to AGC applications because of its reduced output signal handling capability at low gain settings and therefore will not be discussed further here.

When a single IVGA is used in a situation in which the VGA sets the system noise floor, the output SNR is essentially independent of the input signal; it does not improve as is often preferred. Occasionally, it is desirable to cascade two VGAs in order to ameliorate this behavior or simply to obtain more gain control range. Doing so requires proper coordination of the gain control inputs of the two devices.

If the gain control of only the second stage VGA is manipulated in the weak signal regime, the signal level to the first stage VGA's amplifier increases with increasing input level, so the output SNR improves with increasing input level. It is necessary to hand off the gain control from the second stage to the first stage only when overload of the first stage's amplifier is imminent.

Alternatively, the two gain control inputs may simply be driven in parallel, in which case the output S/N (expressed in dB) improves at half the rate at which the input level (also expressed in dB) rises. In cases where the VGAs used have residual ripple in their gain control functions, an additional benefit of this approach can be obtained if the two gain control input signals are intentionally offset by half the period of the ripple. This can provide considerable reduction of the ripple.

One of the benefits of using an IVGA in an AGC loop is that the VGA's gain control voltage bears an accurate logarithmic relationship to the input signal level when the loop is in equilibrium. This means that the gain control voltage may also be used as an excellent received signal strength indicator (RSSI).

LOOP DYNAMICS

Response time is an important issue when designing any AGC loop. There is usually a compromise between having the loop respond to undesired input level fluctuations as rapidly as one would like, and having it undesirably modify amplitude modulation on the signal. Additionally, large and/or abrupt changes in the input level may lead to unacceptable recovery behavior, necessitating further adjustments of the response time. The issue of excessive loop bandwidth deserves a bit more explanation. If the loop responds too quickly, it will introduce undesired gain modulation arising from the loop's efforts to stabilize the output level of a signal containing legitimate amplitude modulation. This is referred to as "gain pumping." In the context of digital modulation, the presence of appreciable gain pumping can result in significant modulation errors and perhaps even noticeable spectral re-growth in extreme cases. A tolerable value of gain pumping would generally be only a fairly small fraction of 1 dB.

DETECTOR TYPES (DETECTOR LAW)

One convenient aspect of an AGC loop is that the detector need not necessarily have a very wide dynamic range over which it obeys any particular law. This is because the detector operates at a constant average level when the AGC loop is in equilibrium; thus, the detector should only need to cope accurately with the level range associated with a modulated signal. However, as mentioned earlier, the detector's response law (that is linear, log, square law, etc.) can play a significant role in determining the loop's dynamic response during large, abrupt changes in signal level. Perhaps more importantly, the detector's response law influences the dependency of the loop's equilibrium level on the input's waveform or crest factor.

Four detector types will be considered here: envelope detector; square-law detector; true-RMS detector; and log detector.

ENVELOPE DETECTOR (RECTIFIER)

The output voltage of the envelope detector is proportional to the magnitude of the instantaneous RF input voltage. Assuming that sufficient low pass filtering is applied at its output to eliminate RF ripple, this detector produces a voltage proportional to the envelope amplitude of the RF signal.

Assuming that the loop's bandwidth is made sufficiently small as to avoid significant gain pumping, the effect of the loop using an envelope detector is to stabilize the average rectified voltage of the signal. The resulting power is therefore dependent on the RF signal's envelope waveform. Such a loop acting on a constant-envelope signal such as GSM will produce an average output power which is different than that for a heavily-amplitude-modulated signal, such as CDMA or 64QAM.

The output of the envelope detector can not go negative no matter how weak the input signal, but may reach extreme positive values in response to very strong signals. Starting with the AGC loop in equilibrium, a sudden large increase in input amplitude causes a very large initial increase in detector output, which very rapidly drives the loop towards lower gain. On the other hand, an abrupt reduction of the input signal level (no matter by how many dB) cannot reduce the detector output below zero, and the loop's best response is to slew towards equilibrium at a fairly low rate until the detector output begins to change by a significant fraction of the reference voltage, at which point the recovery trends towards an exponential decay. In the slew rate limited region, the gain of the signal path is varying at a constant number of dB per second.

Fig.9 shows the behavior of such a loop for a large input level step (note that curves for all four detector types are superimposed on this plot). These results were obtained from simulations in which the VGA has representative limits on the gain range and on the maximum output level. The detectors contrived for these simulations have no particular limits, on the grounds that in most practical situations the designer will scale the circuit so that the detector does not limit appreciably before the VGA does.

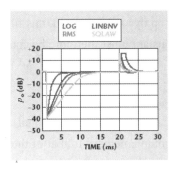

Fig.9 Simulated response of AGC loop to large amplitude steps for various detectors

SQUARE-LAW DETECTOR

This type of detector has an instantaneous output which is proportional to the square of the instantaneous RF input voltage, which is equivalent to say that its output is proportional to input power. This behavior, when incorporated into an AGC loop of sensible bandwidth, makes the loop's equilibrium average output power independent of the input waveform. As with the envelope detector, the output can never go negative, resulting in the loop having a similar tendency towards slew rate limited behavior when reacting to abrupt decreases in input amplitude. The response to large abrupt increases in input amplitude can be even more striking, however, because the square-law detector characteristic exaggerates the effect of the input increase. The extent to which this happens depends on the clipping level of either the VGA or the detector, whichever appears at a lower level.

TRUE-RMS DETECTOR

This detector comprises a square-law detector followed by a low pass filter followed by a square-root function. The low pass filter performs the "mean" operation associated with the root-mean-square (RMS) function, and it should have a sufficiently long time constant to smooth the output variations of the squaring detector that would otherwise arise from the legitimate modulation of the signal.

Because of the square-root element in this detector, the average output is proportional to the signal voltage, not power, so the loop's response to small abrupt decreases or increases of signal level should essentially be the same as that for an envelope detector, provided that the added filter pole within the RMS detector is correctly compensated for elsewhere in the loop. The fact that the added pole is located in a region of the signal path that is square law brings forth the possibility of the large-step response being different from that of the simple envelope detector, which can indeed be seen in the figure. Note that the RMS detector has a slightly slower recovery from a large downward amplitude step than does the standard envelope detector, but a slightly faster recovery (and a bit of overshoot) from a step up in input amplitude. In common with the square-law detector, the true-RMS detector will make the AGC loop's equilibrium point independent of the RF signal waveform.

It should be noted that the presence of the long-time-constant low pass filter in this detector may have a marked influence on loop dynamics; indeed, this filter may even provide the dominant pole in some designs. This time constant must therefore be coordinated with the remainder of the loop design.

LOG DETECTOR

This type of detector produces an output proportional to the logarithm of the RF input voltage. Because this behavior is complementary to that of the linear-in-dB VGA in the loop, the resulting loop dynamics are those of a linear system, assuming that signal level fluctuations during transients remain within the measurement range of the log detector. Subject to that assumption, the AGC loop's response to abrupt large changes in input level will not be slew-rate limited, and will often be faster to recover from amplitude decreases.

As with the envelope detector, the equilibrium point of an AGC loop using the log detector will depend on the RF input waveform.

COMPARISON OF RESPONSES WITH DIFFERENT DETECTORS

The AGC loops whose simulation results are shown were designed so that the small-signal response speeds are identical. The results show that the loop's large-step transient response is markedly dependent on the type of detector. At one extreme, the log detector gives the fastest response to large abrupt decreases in input level because the logarithmic curve has a very steep slope for low inputs, which exaggerates the loop's response. However, the log detector has a shallow slope for high input levels, resulting in a diminished response rate to sudden increases in signal level. At the other extreme, the square-law detector's small slope near zero input level gives it a very sluggish response to large decreases in input amplitude. Conversely, the square-law detector exaggerates the response to large signals, giving the fastest response to increasing signals. The envelope and RMS detectors, having intermediate characteristics, give response speeds in between.

OPERATING LEVEL OF DETECTOR

Ideally the operating level of the detector should be set as high as possible in order to minimize the error due to residual DC offsets. However, other considerations often rule. For signals with amplitude modulation, the peak input to the detector when the loop is in equilibrium must be no higher than what the detector will support, and so the average must be lower. Even for constant-envelope signals, the average level must be reasonably lower than the maximum, so that there is room for the detector level to increase if the system input level increases; otherwise, there could be little or no error signal to drive the loop back towards equilibrium. Note that there will generally be unequal amounts of room for the detector output to swing up or down from the design equilibrium level, which will make the apparent attack and decay speeds of the loop differ.

DESIGN EXAMPLE OF A WORKING AGC LOOP

Let's now put the above considerations to work in a practical design. The design assumptions and goals are as follows:

- Signal modulation: W-CDMA (15 users); symbol rate = 3.84 Msymbols/s
- IF frequency: 380MHz
- VGA: AD8367
- Detector: AD8361 (true RMS, for waveform independence)
- Power supply: 5V DC

From these, reasonable constraints will be established for operating levels to maximize the adjacent channel power ratio (ACPR) and AGC loop bandwidth (to avoid excessive gain pumping).

Previous bench measurements on the AD8367 had revealed that the best ACPR at 380MHz occurs with an output level of about 112mVrms, which gives about –12dBm into 200.

Detector Operating Level

The peak-to-average power ratio for the chosen signal is about 18 dB. When operating from a 5V supply, the maximum output level of the AD8361 is about 4.8V (from the AD8361 datasheet). The squarer in the detector will be assumed to go into clipping at the same input level that results in maximum output, for a CW signal. Thus, assuming that the peaks of the modulated signal should not drive the detector's squarer into clipping when the loop is in equilibrium, the average output level of the detector must be such that it is at least 18dB below 4.8V; $4.8 \times 10 - 18/20 = 604$mV. Since the conversion gain of the detector is 7.5V/Vrms, the loop-equilibrium level at the detector's input should be 604mV/7.5 = 80mVrms.

This level can be obtained from the desired output level of the VGA by adding a series resistor of 90., which combines with the 225. input resistance of the AD8361 to form a voltage divider that achieves the desired result. Note that this loads the output of the VGA with 315, which means that the lowest additional parallel load impedance on the VGA would be 547. in order to satisfy its design minimum load impedance of 200. However, in this case more than half of the VGA's power output is going to be feeding the detector. This could be remedied by driving the VGA end of the 90. resistor with an emitter follower, raising the input impedance of the overall detector by the beta of the transistor used in the follower. This would free up almost all the output current capability of the VGA for use by the useful load.

Estimation of Target AGC Loop Bandwidth

Here a judgment call must be made, based on an empirical measurement, to establish the maximum loop bandwidth that will avoid intolerable gain pumping. For purposes of this design example, it is assumed that up to 0.5dB p-p gain variation is acceptable. An estimate of the desired loop bandwidth will be made by passing a W-CDMA signal through a spectrum analyzer with very wide resolution bandwidth, zero span and linear detector, and observe what video bandwidth results in 0.5dB p-p output variation. The result turns out to be 200Hz, which means the initial design of the AGC loop will have a 200Hz bandwidth.

The simulation and measured results will be used to see how this choice works out.

RMS Detector Filter

The RMS detector's "mean value" filter comprises an internal filter resistance combined with an external shunt capacitance. The effective value of the filter resistance varies with drive level, from about 2000. at very low drive level down to about 500. at maximum drive level. For this example a value of 1800. will be used, which was determined empirically for the operating level established earlier.

In general，an AD8361 would be taken into the lab with a W-CDMA signal source in order to ascertain a suitable filter capacitor value. However, the previous measurement for loop bandwidth gives a clue that allows a reasonable estimate of the required value to be made. A loop bandwidth of 200Hz resulted in a 0.5dB p-p (about6 percent) variation of detector output. It so happens that this is just about the maximum amount of variation of RMS filter level that still gives good RMS accuracy. So, the bandwidth of this filter will simply be made equal to 200Hz, which requires a filter capacitor of about 0.44 µFagainst the 1.8k. filter resistance.

Loop Dynamics Design

A first order loop will be developed, with a small-signal bandwidth of 200Hz. Note that the RMS detector's filter already contributes one pole at 200Hz, so the remainder of the loop will clearly need to take this into account. This will be achieved by choosing Rcomp to create a zero at 200Hz in conjunction with Cinteg (see Appendix A). The response speed of all the other elements in the loop is so much faster than that of the desired loop that all other poles can be safely ignored.

The loop bandwidth designed will apply only for small deviations from the AGC loop's equilibrium level. Large transients will behave differently because of the nonlinear character of the loop, and simulation and/or breadboarding will be relied upon to investigate the large signal behavior.

The next items on the agenda are the determinations of the incremental gains of the VGA and of the detector from the loop dynamics viewpoint. For the VGA, this means the slope of Vout versus control voltage, not the RF gain.

VGA Gain

Vin and Vout will represent RMS values of the VGA's RF input and output, respectively, and Vg will represent the gain control voltage. From examination of the AD8367 performance data in the datasheet for 240MHz, combined with a bit of extrapolation and rounding, 0dB of gain is found to occur at a control voltage of 0.1V and the control slope is 50dB/V. By formulating and then differentiating Vout with respect to Vg at the equilibrium output of 112 mVrms, the incremental slope is evaluated to be 0.6447Vrms/V.

Next the Detector Slope

The nominal conversion gain of the AD8361 is 7.5. However, a 90 series resistor was added at the input of the detector; this has the effect of reducing the detector's effective gain to 5.357, which is the value that will be used in the loop analysis.

Avoidance of Excessive Recovery Delay

If the loop is left sitting with a very low (or zero) input signal level for a time, the output voltage of the integrator will continue to rise until it reaches saturation of the op-amp as the loop tries to find more gain. When a significant signal does suddenly arrive at the system input, one has to wait for the integrator's output to ramp back down to 1V before the loop can begin reducing the gain. To reduce this "overload delay" a 4.3:1 attenuator is inserted between the integrator and the control input of the VGA so that the positive limit (nearly 5V) of the integrator's output is about equal to the maximum effective control input (1V) to the VGA.

Calculation of Component Values

In the loop, a net gain (excluding the integrator for the moment) of 0.644 (VGA incremental slope) • 5.357 (effective detector slope)/4.3 (for the Vagc atten) = 0.803, is obtained. For a loop bandwidth of 200Hz, the loop gain should be unity at that frequency. If the rest of the loop has a gain of 0.803, the integrator must have a gain of 1.0/0.803 = 1.245, which requires that the reactance of Cinteg at 200Hz be 1.245 times the value of Rin. Mathematically, $1/(2\pi \cdot 200 \cdot Cinteg) = 1.245 \cdot Rin$; $Rin \cdot Cinteg = 639.2\mu s$.

Now another constraint must be also noted, which is that the AD8361 cannot source very much current, and can sink even less. Therefore, 50 k. is chosen for Rin in order to minimize total loading on the AD8361's output, which leads to a value of 12.78 nF for Cinteg. Finally, in order to compensate for the 200Hz pole in the RMS detector, Rcomp is chosen as 62.3 k. to provide a loop zero at 200Hz with Cinteg. A 10 k. pulldown is also added on the AD8361's output to improve its effective sinking capacity.

Lab Tests

A prototype circuit was constructed according to the schematic in Appendix A. Fig.10 and Fig.11 show the prototype loop's response to small and large (30dB) input level steps, respectively. Fig.12 shows the measured gain pumping obtained by capturing the signal at the gain-control input of the VGA with an oscilloscope and scaling into 0 ~ 0.2dB.

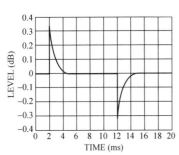
Fig.10 The prototype circuit response to small amplitude stepsis symmetrical and shows exponential recovery

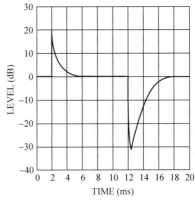
Fig.11 The prototype circuit response to large amplitude steps is asymmetrical and exhibits slow-rate-limited recovery

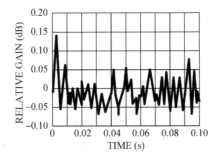
Fig.12 The prototype circuit has about 0.2dB p-p gain pumping

CONCLUSION

Numerous basic and finer points of AGC design have been discussed, and a detailed example of a practical design was worked out. Practical considerations and difficulties encountered along the way were emphasized, as opposed to reiterating textbook loop design equations. Finally, a working circuit was constructed and measurement results presented.

3.3.4 科技广告

科技广告(Technical Advertising)涉及的范围很广，在写作时可用劝诱技巧。广告的感召力必须有逻辑性，即正确地陈述事实、统计数字和实例。应该积极考虑读者的感情，不要偏离主题，避免含混不清的措辞，不要提出无关紧要或虚假的要求。但是，如果读者对广告有怀疑，则需要采用诱导的方法，用有力具体的证据来说服读者。所以，科技广告的遣词造句既有科技性，又有促销宣传之意。

科技广告实例之一。

The gratis catalogue of NI measuring and automatic products in 2005

The brand new catalogue of NI measuring and automatic products in 2005 will display a serious of important information, including figures comparing and structural frame and products features. This annual catalogue will simply outline all kinds of NI products line. This includes:

NI LabVIEW^{TM} graphics development environment

- Visual Basic and C/C++ programming tools
- Data collecting and signals modulating devices
- Decisional real-time controlling
- Standard hardware platform of measuring and automation—PXI
- Industrial controlling and distributed I/O
- Machine view and dynamical controlling
- GPIB and other instruments controlling of bus

Please visit ××××.com/china. If inputting info code (cnkm2c), you will freely take this catalogue.

NI in shanghai：the 6th floor at the building of business, ×××× Qv Yang Road(20××××)

Tel：(021)6555××××　　FAX: (021)6555××××

Email:china.info@××××.com

科技广告实例之二。

Total Solution for Industrial Device Networking

Famous manufacturer of Serial and Network Communication in Asian—Moxa Technologies provides total solution for industrial device networking, including Multiport Serial Board, Serial Device Server, Industrial Ethernet Switch. Moxa Technologies is leader in the field of industrial communication.

NPort multiport serial device networking server

- RS-232/422/485 having the capability of networking

- Extending COM/tty/ports controlling through Ethernet/Internet
- Providing 1/2/4/8/16 serial number and RS-232/422/485 interface compounding products
- Protecting from surge and magnetic; designing DIN Rail and 19th frame

Industrial Ethernet Switcher
- Eight 10/100 Mbps networking port, selecting Single Mode or Multi Mode (optical mode)
- Supporting Redundant Ethernet Ring
- Working temperature: 0~60℃
- Remotely managing through IE; having the capability of E-mail warning and IP restoring

For detailed information, please visit www.××××.com.cn.

附录 A　常用通信与电子信息词汇及注解

A

3GPP (Third Generation Partnership Project)			第三代伙伴计划
AAON (ATM Active Optical Network)			ATM 有源光网络
Abis-interface			GSM BSC 与 BTS 之间的接口
abrasion	[əˈbreɪʒn]	n.	磨损
acoustical	[əˈkuːstɪkl]	adj.	听觉的，声学的
acoustics	[əˈkuːstɪks]	n.	声学
active component			有源元件
active satellite			有源卫星
active	[ˈæktɪv]	adj.	有源的
Ad hoc network			自组织网络
adaptive control			自适应控制
Adaptive Signal Control Technology			自适应信号控制技术
ADC (Analogue-to-Digital Converter)			模/数转换器
additive printed circuit-board process			印制电路板添加工艺
ADM (Add-Drop Multiplexer)			分插复用器
ADSL (Asymmetric Digital Subscriber Line)			非对称数字用户线
aggregation	[ˌæɡrɪˈɡeɪʃn]	n.	聚合
agile	[ˈædʒaɪl]	adj.	敏捷的
A-interface			GSM BSS 与核心网之间的接口
AIPN (All IP Network)			全 IP 网络
algorithm	[ˈælɡərɪðəm]	n.	算法
amplifier	[ˈæmplɪfaɪə(r)]	n.	[电工]扩音器，放大器
amplitude	[ˈæmplɪtjuːd]	n.	振幅
AMPS (Advanced Mobile Phone Service)			高级移动电话业务(北美)
analog signal			模拟信号
analog	[ˈænəlɔːɡ]	adj.	模拟的
analytics	[ˌænəˈlɪtɪks]	n.	解析学
ANN (Artificial Neural Network)			人工神经网络
anode	[ˈænəʊd]	n.	阳极
ANSI (American National Standard Institute)			美国国家标准协会

antenna	[æn'tenə]	n.	天线
antimony	['æntɪməni]	n.	锑
aperiodic	[ˌeɪpɪərɪ'ɒdɪk]	adj.	不定期的，[物]非周期的
AoA (Angle of Arrival)			到达角
APON (ATM Passive Optical Network)			ATM 无源光网络
approximation	[əˌprɒksɪ'meɪʃn]	n.	近似值
arc	[ɑːk]	n.	电弧
argon-ion laser			氩离子激光器
argument	['ɑːgjumənt]	n.	自变量
arithmetic	[ə'rɪθmətɪk]	n.	算术
ARPA (Advanced Research Project Agency)			(美国)高级研究计划局
ARPANET (Advanced Research Project Agency Network)			(美国)高级研究计划局通信网
arsenic	['ɑːsnɪk]	n.	砷
artificial intelligence			人工智能(abbr. AI)
ASCII (American Standard Code for Information Interchange)			美国信息交换标准码
ASICs (application-specific integrated circuits)			专用集成电路
aspect ratio			纵横比，屏幕高宽比
ASR (Automatic Speech Recognition)			自动语音识别
asynchronous transmission			异步传输
AT&T (American Telephone and Telegraph)			美国电报电话(公司)
ATM (Asynchronous Transfer Mode)			异步传输模式
attenuation	[əˌtenjuˈeɪʃn]	n.	衰减，衰耗
audio recording		n.	唱片
auditory	['ɔːdətri]	adj.	耳的，听觉的
autocorrelation	[ɔːtəʊkɒrɪ'leɪʃən]	n.	自相关
autonomous	[ɔː'tɑːnəməs]	adj.	自动的
auxiliary pilot			辅助导频
auxiliary storage (secondary storage)			辅助存储器
avalanche	['ævəlɑːnʃ]	n. & v.	雪崩
avalanche-type			雪崩型

B

backbone	['bækbəʊn]	n.	支柱
bandpass filter			带通滤波器
bandwidth	['bændwɪdθ]	n.	带宽
baud rate			波特率
Bernoulli distribution			贝努利分布
bias	['baɪəs]	n.	偏差，偏置

binary	[ˈbaɪnəri]	adj.	二进位的，二元的
binomial distribution			二项分布
bipolar	[ˌbaɪˈpəʊlə(r)]	adj.	有两极的，双极的
B-ISDN (Broad band Integrated Service Digital Network)			宽带综合业务数字网
block out			阻断，封闭
BPL (Broadband Over Power Line)			电力线宽带
bps (bits per second)			每秒钟传输的比特
bridge tap			桥式分接头
broadband	[ˈbrɔːdbænd]	n.	宽带
buffer	[ˈbʌfə(r)]	n.	缓冲器
bus network			总线型网络

C

CAI (Computer Aided Instruction)			计算机辅助教学
calculus	[ˈkælkjələs]	n.	微积分
capacitor	[kəˈpæsɪtə(r)]	n.	电容器
capacity	[kəˈpæsəti]	n.	容量
carbon	[ˈkɑːbən]	n.	[化]碳(元素符号 C)
carbon-dioxide laser			二氧化碳激光器
carrier	[ˈkæriə(r)]	n.	载波
carrier-frequency			载波频率
case-specific		adj.	特定案例的
cathode	[ˈkæθəʊd]	n.	阴极
CATV (cable television)			有线电视
causal system			因果系统
CCIR (International Radio Communications)			
CCITT (Consultative Committee in Telegraphy and Telephony)			国际电报电话咨询委员会
CD (Compact Disc)			光盘
CDMA One			码分多路接入
CDMA (Code Division Multiple Access)			码分多址
CDMA2000			基于 ANSI-41 标准的码分复用接入
cellular	[ˈseljələ(r)]	adj.	蜂窝状的，格形的，多孔的
centigrade	[ˈsentɪɡreɪd]	adj.	分为百度的，百分度的，摄氏温度的
channel	[ˈtʃænl]	n.	信道，频道
channelized receiver			信道化接收机
chaotic	[keɪˈɒtɪk]	adj.	混乱的，无秩序的，混沌的
charge carrier			载流子

charge	[tʃɑːdʒ]	n.	电荷
chart	[tʃɑːt]	n.	图表(曲线图，略图)
chatterbot	[ˈtʃætəbɒt]	n.	聊天机器人
chip capacitor			片式电容器
chrominance	[ˈkrəʊmɪnəns]	n.	色度
CIM (Computer Integrated Manufacturing)			计算机集成制造
circuitry	[ˈsɜːkɪtri]	n.	电路，线路
closed loop gain			闭环增益
CMC (Computer Mediated Communications)			计算机中介通信
CMOS (Complementary Metal Oxide Semiconductor)			互补金属氧化物半导体
CO (Central Office)			中心交换局
CoA (Care of Address)			转交地址
coating	[ˈkəʊtɪŋ]	n.	涂层，层
coax	[kəʊks]	n.	同轴电缆
coaxial	[kəʊˈæksɪəl]	adj.	同轴的，共轴的
code book			码本
coefficient	[ˌkəʊɪˈfɪʃ(ə)nt]	n.	系数
collision	[kəˈlɪʒ(ə)n]	n.	碰撞，冲突
communication networks and protocol			通信网络与协议
communication session			通信会话
commutative	[kəˈmjuːtətɪv]	adj.	可交换的
compact	[kəmˈpækt]	adj.	紧密的
compatibility	[kəmˌpætəˈbɪləti]	n.	兼容性
compatible	[kəmˈpætəbl]	adj.	兼容的
complicated	[ˈkɒmplɪkeɪtɪd]	adj.	复杂的
computability	[kəmˌpjuːtəbɪləti]	n.	可计算性
concentrator	[ˈkɒnsənˌtreɪtə(r)]	n.	集中器，集线器
conductor	[kənˈdʌktə(r)]	n.	导体
configuration	[kənˌfɪgəˈreɪʃn]	n.	组态，构造
configure	[kənˈfɪgə(r)]	vt.	配置，设定
congestion	[kənˈdʒestʃən]	n.	拥塞
consciousness	[ˈkɒnʃəsnəs]	n.	意识
constant	[ˈkɒnstənt]	n.	常数
Consultative Committee			国际无线通信咨询委员会
consumption	[kənˈsʌmpʃn]	n.	消耗
contour	[ˈkɒntʊə(r)]	n.	轮廓
contrast enhancement			对比度增强
converge	[kənˈvɜːdʒ]	v.	收敛(n. convergence)
conveyance	[kənˈveɪəns]	n.	运送

convolution	[ˌkɒnvəˈluːʃn]	n.	卷积
coordinate	[kəʊˈɔːdɪneɪt]	n.	坐标(用复数)
correlation	[ˌkɒrəˈleɪʃn]	n.	相互关系，相关(性)
cosine	[ˈkəʊsaɪn]	n.	余弦
covalent bond			共价键
CR (Cognitive Radio)			认知无线电
CRC (Cycling Redundancy Check)			循环冗余校验
criterion	[kraɪˈtɪəriən]	n.	标准，规范
critical dimension			临界尺寸
critical value			临界值
cross talk			串音
cross-border			跨国的
crosscorrelation	[ˈkrɒskɒrɪˈleɪʃən]	n.	互相关
cumulative	[ˈkjuːmjələtɪv]	adj.	累积的
current	[ˈkʌrənt]	n.	电流
cursor	[ˈkɜːsə(r)]	n.	指针
cut-off frequency			截止频率
combinational logic circuit			组合逻辑电路
CVO (Commercial Vehicle Operations)			商用车量营运系统
cyber-physical			信息物理的
cyborg	[ˈsaɪbɔːg]	n.	赛博格(音译)，改造人

D

data fusion and mining			数据融合与数据挖掘
data independence			数据独立
data integrity			数据完整性，数据一致性
data management			数据管理
data security			数据安全性
database transaction			数据库事务
database	[ˈdeɪtəbeɪs]	n.	[计]数据库，资料库
DBMS (Database Management System)			数据库管理信息系统
DCS (Digital Communication System)			数字通信系统
DCT (Discrete Cosine Transform)			离散余弦变换
decimal part			小数部分
decision support systems			决策支持系统
depletion layer			耗尽层
deployment	[dɪˈplɔɪmənt]	n.	部署
derivative	[dɪˈrɪvətɪv]	n.	导数

detector	[dɪˈtektə(r)]	n.	探测器
dialing pulse			拨号脉冲
dielectric	[ˌdaɪɪˈlektrɪk]	n.& adj.	电介质，绝缘体；电介质的，绝缘的
differentiable	[ˌdɪfəˈrenʃɪəbl]	adj.	可微分的
differential input amplifier			差分放大器
differentiation	[ˌdɪfəˌrenʃɪˈeɪʃn]	n.	微分
diffraction	[dəˈfrækʃən]	n.	衍射
diode	[ˈdaɪəʊd]	n.	二极管
dioxide	[daɪˈɒksaɪd]	n.	二氧化物
discipline	[ˈdɪsəplɪn]	n.	学科
discrete device			分离元件
discrete	[dɪˈskriːt]	adj.	离散的
diskettes (floppy disk)			软盘
disproportionate	[ˌdɪsprəˈpɔːʃənət]	adj.	不成比例的，不相称的
dissipation	[ˌdɪsɪˈpeɪʃn]	n.	损耗
distortion analyzer			失真分析仪
distortion	[dɪˈstɔːʃn]	n.	扭曲，变形，失真
distributed	[dɪsˈtrɪbjuːtɪd]	adj.	分布式的
distributive	[dɪˈstrɪbjətɪv]	adj.	分配的
disturbance	[dɪˈstɜːbəns]	n.	打扰，干扰，骚乱，搅动
dominant	[ˈdɒmɪnənt]	adj.	占优势的，支配的
downlink	[ˈdaʊnlɪŋk]	n.	下行线，向下链路
DSL (Digital Subscriber Line)			数字用户线
DSLAM (Digital SUBSCRIBER Line Access Multiplexer)			数字用户线接入多路复用器
duality	[djuːˈæləti]	n.	二元性，对偶性
duration	[djuˈreɪʃn]	n.	持续时间

E

earth orbit			地球轨道
eavesdropping	[ˈiːvzˌdrɒpɪŋ]	n.	窃听
edge	[edʒ]	n.	边缘
EDI (Electronic Data Interchange)			电子数据交换
EIA (Electronic Industries Association)			电子工业协会
electrical conductivity			导电率
electrocardiogram	[ɪˌlektrəʊˈkɑːdiəʊɡræm]	n.	心电图(ECG)
electromagnetic wave			电磁波
electromagnetic	[ɪˌlektrəʊmæɡˈnetɪk]	adj.	电磁的
electromechanical	[ɪˌlektrəʊmɪˈkænɪkəl]	adj.	电动机械的，机电的

electron-hole pair			电子空穴对
electronics	[ɪˌlekˈtrɒnɪks]	n.	电子学
emulation	[ˌemjuˈleɪʃn]	n.	仿真
encapsulation	[ɪnˌkæpsjuˈleɪʃn]	n.	包装,封装
end-to-end			端对端的
energy-efficient			高能效的
entity	[ˈentəti]	n.	实体,存在,本质
entropy	[ˈentrəpi]	n.	熵,平均信息量
envelope	[ˈenvələup]	n.	包络
equalizer	[ˈiːkwəlaɪzər]	n.	均衡器
equation	[ɪˈkweɪʒn]	n.	方程(式);等式
equivalent	[ɪˈkwɪvələnt]	adj.	等效的
ETC (Electronic Toll Collection)			电子收费系统
Ethernet	[ˈiːθənet]	n.	以太网
ETSI (Europe Telecommunication Standard Institution)			欧洲电信标准学会
evaluation	[ɪˌvæljuˈeɪʃn]	n.	赋值,值的计算
expected value			期望值
expert system			专家系统
exponential	[ˌekspəˈnenʃl]	adj.	指数的,幂数的
externality	[ˌekstɜːrˈnæləti]	n.	外部效应
extraterrestrial	[ˌekstrətəˈrestriəl]	adj.	地球外的,地球大气圈外的

F

fabricate	[ˈfæbrɪkeɪt]	v.	制造,装配
facsimile	[fækˈsɪməli]	n.	摹写,传真
fading	[ˈfeɪdɪŋ]	n.	衰落,消失,衰减
fall within			属于
family	[ˈfæməli]	n.	族,一群相似的事物
fault tolerance			容错
FCC (Federal Communications Commission)			(美国)通信委员会
FDD (Frequency Division Duplex)			频分复用
FDDI (Fiber Distributed Data Interface)			光纤分配数字接口
FDM (Frequency Division Multiplexing)			频分多路复用
FEC (Forward Error Correction)			前向纠错
feedback	[ˈfiːdbæk]	n.	[电子、生理]回授,反馈,反应
feedforward	[fiːdˈfɔːwəd]	n.	前馈
FET (Field Effect Transistors)			场效应管
fiber optic			光纤

fiber-optic communication			光纤通信
fidelity	[fɪˈdeləti]	n.	逼真度，保真度
field	[fiːld]	n.	磁场，字段，领域
FIR (Finite Impulse Response)			有限冲击响应
filter	[ˈfɪltə(r)]	n.	滤波器，过滤器，滤光器，筛选
		vt.	过滤，渗透，用过滤法除去
flexibility	[ˌfleksəˈbɪləti]	n.	灵活性
fluctuation	[ˌflʌktʃuˈeɪʃn]	n.	波动，起伏
fly-by-light			光控飞行
fly-by-wire			线控飞行
footprint	[ˈfʊtprɪnt]	n.	(尤指计算机)占用的空间
form factor			波形因数；形状因数
formula	[ˈfɔːmjələ]	n.	公式，规则
forum	[ˈfɔːrəm]	n.	论坛
Fourier series			傅里叶级数
FPGA (Field Programmable Gate Array)			可编程门阵列
fractal	[ˈfræktl]	n.	(计)分形，分数维
frame	[freɪm]	n.	(图像)帧
frame rate			帧频率
frequency divider			分频器
frequency translation			频率转换
front-end			前置，前级
full-duplex transmission			全双工传输
fuzzy logic control			模糊逻辑控制
fuzzy	[ˈfʌzi]	adj.	模糊的，失真的

G

gate	[geɪt]	n.	逻辑门
gateway	[ˈgeɪtweɪ]	n.	网关
generator	[ˈdʒenəreɪtə(r)]	n.	发电机，发生器，产生器
genetic algorithm and evolutionary computation			遗传算法与进化计算
geoinformation		n.	空间信息
gigahertz	[ˈgɪgəhɜːts]	n.	千兆赫
GIS (Ground Instrumentation System)			地面测量系统
goal-oriented			目标导向性的
GPRS (General Packet Radio Service)			通用分组无线业务
graceful	[ˈgreɪsfl]	adj.	平滑的

granular	[ˈɡrænjələ(r)]	adj.	颗粒状的
gray level			(图像的)灰度级
ground station			地面站
ground	[ɡraʊnd]	vt.	使接地
		n.	接地，地线
GSM BSC (GSM Base Station Controller)			GSM 基站控制器
GSM BSS (GSM Base Station Subsystem)			GSM 基站子系统
GSM BTS (Base Transceiver Station)			GSM 基站发送接收器
GSM (Global System for Mobile Communications)			全球移动通信系统
GSM-MAP (GSM-Mobile Application Part)			GSM 移动应用部分

H

half-duplex transmission			半双工传输
half-wave rectified			半波整流
Hamming window			汉明窗
handover	[ˈhændəʊvə(r)]	n.	移交，越区切换
handset	[ˈhændset]	n.	手持(移动)设备
hard disks			硬盘
harmonic distortion			谐波失真
harmonic	[hɑːˈmɒnɪk]	n.	谐波，谐函数
HDSL (High Bit-Rate Digital Subscriber Line)			高比特速率数字用户线
HDTV (High-Definition TV)			高清晰度电视
helium-neon laser			氦氖激光器
hexagonal	[hekˈsæɡənəl]	adj.	六角形的，六边形的
HF (High-frequency)			高频
HFC (Hybrid Fiber Coaxial Network)			混合光纤同轴网络
hierarchical architecture			分层架构
hierarchy	[ˈhaɪərɑːki]	n.	层次，层级，分层
histogram	[ˈhɪstəɡræm]	n.	直方图
hole	[həʊl]	n.	空穴
hologram	[ˈhɒləɡræm]	n.	全息摄影，全息图
homogeneity	[ˌhəʊməʊdʒəˈniːəti]	n.	齐次性
hypermedia	[ˌhaɪpəˈmiːdiə]	n.	超媒体
hyper-scale			超大规模的
hypertext	[ˈhaɪpətekst]		超文本

I

IC (Integrated Circuit)			集成电路
ideal operation amplifier			理想运放(abbr.ideal op amp)
IDLC (Integrated Digital Loop Carrier)			综合数字环路载波
IDSL (ISDN Digital Subscriber Line)			ISDN 数字用户线
IEEE (Institute of Electrical and Electronics Engineers)			电气与电子工程师协会
IIAF (Industrial Internet of Things Analytics Framework)			工业物联网分析框架
IIC (Industrial Internet Consortium)			工业互联网联盟
IIR (Infinite Impulse Response)			无限冲击响应
IIRA (Industrial Internet Reference Architecture)			工业互联网参考体系结构
IJCI (International Journal of Computational Intelligence)			国际计算智能期刊
image	[ˈɪmɪdʒ]	n.	图像，镜像
impedance	[ɪmˈpiːdns]	n.	阻抗
impurity	[ɪmˈpjʊərəti]	n.	杂质，混杂物
in essence			本质上
incident light			入射光
independent identically distributed			独立同分布(缩写 i.i.d.)
inductive	[ɪnˈdʌktɪv]	adj.	感应的，电感的，归纳的
Industrial Internet			工业互联网
inference	[ˈɪnfərəns]	n.	推论，推理，推断
infinitesimal	[ˌɪnfɪnɪˈtesɪməl]	adj.	无穷小的，极小的，无限小的
		n.	极小量，极微量，无限小
inflection	[ɪnˈflekʃn]	n.	变形
infrared	[ˌɪnfrəˈred]	adj.	红外线的
		n.	红外线
instantaneous amplitude			瞬时振幅
insulator	[ˈɪnsjuleɪtə(r)]	n.	绝缘体
integration	[ˌɪntɪˈgreɪʃn]	n.	积分
intellectual property			知识产权
intelligent network			智能网
INTELSAT (international telecommunication satellite)			国际通信卫星
intended recipient			预定接收机
intensity	[ɪnˈtensəti]	n.	亮度，强度
interconnect	[ˌɪntəkəˈnekt]	vt.	互相连接，互连
interdisciplinary	[ˌɪntədɪsəˈplɪnəri]	adj.	跨学科的
interface	[ˈɪntəfeɪs]	n.	分界面，接口
interference	[ˌɪntəˈfɪərəns]	n.	干扰

interlace	[ˌɪntəˈleɪs]	vi.	隔行扫描
interleaving	[ˌɪntəˈliːvɪŋ]	n.	交叉，交错
intermodulation distortion			互调失真
interoperability	[ˌɪntərˌɒpərəˈbɪləti]	n.	互用性，互操作性
inverse	[ɪnˈvɜːs]	n.	(矩阵的)逆
inverting input			反相输入端
ion	[ˈaɪən]	n.	离子
ionosphere	[aɪˈɒnəsfɪə(r)]	n.	电离层
IoT (Internet of Things)			物联网
IPSec (Internet Protocol Security)			因特网安全协议
IR emitter			红外发射器
IR sensor			红外传感器
irrevocably	[ɪˈrevəkəbli]	adv.	无法恢复地
ISDN (Integrated Services Digital Network)			综合业务数字网
ISO (International Standards Organization)			国际标准化组织
isolate	[ˈaɪsəleɪt]	v.	隔离，绝缘
ITS (Intelligent Transportation Systems)			智能交通系统
ITU (International Telecommunication Union)			国际电信联盟
Iu-interface			WCDMA与核心网之间的接口

J

jamming	[ˈdʒæmɪŋ]	n.	干扰台，人为干扰
JPEG (Joint Photographic Experts Group)			联合图像专家组(静止图像数据压缩标准)

K

kilohertz	[ˈkɪləhɜːts]	n.	千赫
knowledge base			知识库
knowledge representation			知识表示

L

Large-Scale Integrated (LSI) circuit			大规模集成电路
laser diode			激光二极管
laser emitter			激光发射器
latency	[ˈleɪtənsi]	n.	反应时间，等待时间

Leased-line			租用线
LED (Light Emitting Diode)			发光二极管
legacy device			传统设备
lens	[lenz]	n.	透镜
level	[ˈlev(ə)l]	n.	电平
light beam system			光束系统
Light-dependent resistor (LDR)			光敏电阻
limit	[ˈlɪmɪt]	n.	极限
limiter	[ˈlɪmɪtə(r)]	n.	限幅器
linear	[ˈlɪniə(r)]	adj.	线性的,线状的(nonlinear 非线性的)
linearity	[ˌlɪniˈærəti]	n.	线性度
line-of-sight			视线,瞄准线
linguistics	[lɪŋˈgwɪstɪks]	n.	语言学
LNA (Low-noise Amplifier)			低噪放大器
LO (Local Oscillator)			本地振荡器
logarithmic	[ˌlɒgəˈrɪðmɪk]	adj.	对数的
logical relationships			逻辑关系
long haul			长途电话,长途运输
low-pass filter			低通滤波器
LPC (Linear Predictive Coding)			线性预测编码
LPR (License Plate Recognition)			车牌识别
LSB (Least Significant Bit)			最低有效位
lumped element			集总元件

M

MA (Moving Average)			移动平均
magnitude	[ˈmæɡnɪtjuːd]	n.	量级
mainstay	[ˈmeɪnsteɪ]	n.	支柱
mainstream	[ˈmeɪnstriːm]	n.	主流
MAN (Metropolitan Area Network)		n.	城域网,城市网络
manmade	[ˈmænˈmeɪd]	adj.	人造的
map	[mæp]	v.	映射
marketability	[ˌmɑːkɪtəˈbɪləti]	n.	市场性
M-ary			M 进制
matrix	[ˈmeɪtrɪks]	n.	矩阵
mean square error criteria			均方误差准则
mean	[miːn]	n.	平均数
mechanism	[ˈmekənɪzəm]	n.	机理,机制

megabit	[ˈmegəbɪt]	n.	百万位，兆位，兆比特
membrane	[ˈmembreɪn]	n.	膜，隔膜
mercury	[ˈmɜːkjəri]	n.	水银，汞
meteorology	[ˌmiːtiəˈrɒlədʒi]	n.	气象学，气象状态
metropolitan	[ˌmetrəˈpɒlɪtən]	adj.	大都市的
microelectronic	[ˌmaɪkrəʊɪˌlekˈtrɒnɪk]	adj.	微电子的
microprocessor	[ˌmaɪkrəʊˈprəʊsesə(r)]	n.	[计]微处理器
microwave	[ˈmaɪkrəweɪv]	n.	微波
military services			军事服务
millionfold	[ˈmɪljənfəʊld]	adj.	百万倍的
		adv.	百万倍地
minicomputer	[ˈmɪnɪkəmˌpjuːtə]	n.	小型计算机
misaligned	[ˌmɪsəˈlaɪnd]	adj.	方向偏离的
mixer	[ˈmɪksə(r)]	n.	混频器
mobile	[ˈməʊbaɪl]	adj.	可移动的，机动的，装在车上的
modem pool			调制解调器(存储)池
modulating signal			调制信号
modulation strategy			调制方式
modulation	[ˌmɒdjəˈleɪʃn]	n.	调制
mold	[məʊld]	n.	模型
monochromatic	[ˌmɒnəkrəˈmætɪk]	adj.	单色的，单频的，黑白的
monochrome	[ˈmɒnəkrəʊm]	n.&adj.	单色；单色的
MOS (metal oxide semiconductor)			金属氧化物半导体
MPEG (Moving Picture Expert Group)			活动图像专家组(活动图像数据压缩标准)
MSB (Most Significant Bit)			最高有效位
multi-access			多路存取，多路进入
multiframe	[ˌmʌltɪˈfreɪm]	n.	多帧
multi-path fading			多径衰落
multi-path			多路，多途径；多路的，多途径的
multiplexing	[ˈmʌltɪˌpleksɪŋ]	n.	多路技术

N

nanometer	[ˈnænəʊmiːtə(r)]	n.	毫微米，纳米
narrowband	[ˈnærəʊbænd]	n.	窄带
negative	[ˈneɡətɪv]	adj.	负的
neural network			神经网络
neuroscience	[ˈnjʊərəʊsaɪəns]	n.	神经科学

neutron	[ˈnjuːtrɒn]	n.	中子
NF (Noise Figure)			噪声系数
NMT (Nordic Mobile Telephone)			北欧移动电话
NN (Neural Networks)			神经网络
NNI (Network Node Interface)			网络结点接口
nonlinear	[nɒnˈlɪnɪə]	adj.	非线性的
nonsynchronous	[ˌnɒnˈsɪŋkrənəs]	adj.	异步的
normal distribution			正态分布
NTSC (National Television Systems Committee)			全国电视系统委员会制式
nucleus	[ˈnjuːklɪəs]	n.	原子核
numeral	[ˈnjuːmərəl]	n.	数字

O

ODE (Ordinary Differential Equation)			常微分方程
OFDM (Orthogonal Frequency Division Multiplexing)			正交频分多址
offset	[ˈɒfset]	n.	偏移量，抵消
OLT (Optic Line Terminal)			光纤线路终端
one order of magnitude			一个数量级
one-dimensional			一维的
ONU (Optical Network Unit)			光网络单元
operational amplifier			运放
operator	[ˈɒpəreɪtə(r)]	n.	算子
optic core			纤芯
optical computer			光计算机
optical disks			光盘
optical	[ˈɒptɪk(ə)l]	adj.	眼的，视力的，光学的
optically	[ˈɒptɪkli]	adv.	光学地，光地
optimum	[ˈɒptɪməm]	n.	最佳条件，最适宜的
optocoupler	[ˌɒptə(ʊ)ˈkʌplə]	n.	光电耦合器
optoelectronic	[ˌɒptəʊɪlekˈtrɒnɪks]	adj.	光电子的
orientation	[ˌɔːriənˈteɪʃn]	n.	定位，定向
orthogonal diversity			正交分集
orthogonal	[ɔːˈθɒɡən(ə)l]	adj.	正交的
orthogonality	[ɔːθɒɡəˈnælɪti]	n.	正交性，正交状态
oscillator	[ˈɒsɪleɪtə(r)]	n.	振荡器
oscilloscope	[əˈsɪləskəʊp]	n.	示波器
OSI (open-system-interconnection)			开放系统互连
OT (Operational Technology)			操作技术

outage	[ˈaʊtɪdʒ]	n.	停止，运行中断
out-of-band signaling			带外信令
overhead	[ˌəʊvəˈhed]	n.	开销
overlapping	[ˌəʊvəˈlæpɪŋ]	n.	重叠
oxygen	[ˈɒksɪdʒən]	n.	[化]氧气, 氧元素
ozone	[ˈəʊzəʊn]	n.	海边的清新空气, [化]臭氧

P

PAL (Phase Alternating Line)			逐行倒相制式
PAPR (Peak-to-Average Power Ratio)			峰值平均功率比
parallel	[ˈpærəlel]	adj.	平行的，并行的
parameter	[pəˈræmɪtə(r)]	n.	参(变)数，参量
parasitic	[ˌpærəˈsɪtɪk]	adj.	寄生的
passband	[ˈpɑːsˌbænd]	n.	通频带，传输频带
passive component			无源元件
passive satellite			无源卫星
passive	[ˈpæsɪv]	adj.	无源的，被动的
pattern recognition			模式识别
payload	[ˈpeɪləʊd]	n.	有效载荷
PBX (Private Branch Exchange)			用户小交换机或专用交换机
PCI (Peripheral Component Interconnect)			外设部件互联
PCM (pulse code modulation)			脉冲编码调制
PDC (Personal Digital Cellular)			个人数字蜂窝(日本)
PDH (Plesiochronous Digital Hierarchy)			准同步数字序列
peripheral devices			外设
permissible	[pəˈmɪsəb(ə)l]	adj.	可允许的
phase detector			鉴相器
phase shift		n.	相移
phasor	[ˈfeɪzə(r)]	n.	向量
phonetics	[fəˈnetɪks]	n.	语音学，发音学
photoconductive	[ˌfəʊtəʊkənˈdʌktɪv]	adj.	光电导的，光敏的
photodiode	[ˌfəʊtəʊˈdaɪəʊd]	n.	光敏二极管，光电二极管
photoluminescence	[ˌfəʊtəˌluːməˈnesns]	n.	光致发光
photon	[ˈfəʊtɒn]	n.	光子
phototransistor	[ˌfəʊtəʊtrænˈzɪstə(r)]	n.	光电晶体管
photovoltaic cell			光伏电池

photovoltaic	[ˌfəʊtəʊˌvɒlˈteɪɪk]	n.	光伏的
physical property			物理性质
pictorial	[pɪkˈtɔːrɪəl]	adj.	图像的
PIN-type			PIN 型
pixel	[ˈpɪksl]	n.	像素
playback	[ˈpleɪbæk]	n.	播放(录音带，唱片)
Plesiochronous			准同步的
PLL (Phase-Locked Loop)			锁相环
POH (Path Overhead)			通道开销
Poisson distribution			泊松分布
polarity	[pəˈlærəti]	n.	极性
population	[ˌpɒpjuˈleɪʃən]	n.	总体
positive	[ˈpɒzətɪv]	adj.	[数]正的
potential difference			电位差
potential	[pəˈtenʃl]	n.	电势，电位
preamplifier	[priːˈæmplɪfaɪə]	n.	前置放大器
precarious	[prɪˈkeərɪəs]	adj.	不稳定的
precisely	[prɪˈsaɪsli]	adj.	精确地
printed circuit boards			印刷电路板
prior	[ˈpraɪə(r)]	adj.	优先的
probability density function			概率密度函数(abbr. pdf)
product	[ˈprɒdʌkt]	n.	乘积
profile	[ˈprəʊfaɪl]	n.	剖面，侧面，外形，轮廓
progressive scanning			逐行扫描
propagation	[ˌprɒpəˈgeɪʃn]	n.	(声波、电磁辐射等)传播
proportion	[prəˈpɔːʃn]	n.	比例，比率，部分
protocol	[ˈprəʊtəkɒl]	n.	协议
proton	[ˈprəʊtɒn]	n.	[核]质子
proxy	[ˈprɒksi]	n.	代理
pseudo-random			伪随机的
psycho-acoustic			心理(精神)听觉的，传音的

Q

QAM (Quadrature Amplitude Modulation)			正交幅度调制
QoS (Quality of Service)			服务质量
QPSK (Quadrature Phase Shift Key)			正交相移键控
quantization	[ˌkwɒntɪˈzeɪʃən]	n.	量化

R

RAB (Radio Access Bearer)			无线接入承载器
Radar (Radio detective and ranging)			雷达，电波探测器
radiation	[ˌreɪdiˈeɪʃn]	n.	辐射
radio-relay transmission			无线电中继传输
radius	[ˈreɪdiəs]	n.	半径范围，半径，径向射线
RAN (Radio Access Network)			无线接入网络
random	[ˈrændəm]	adj.	随机的
RBS (Radio Base Station)			无线基站
reconfigurability		n.	可重构性
record	[ˈrekɔːd]	n.	记录
recursive	[rɪˈkɜːsɪv]	adj.	递归的
refraction	[rɪˈfrækʃn]	n.	折射
register	[ˈredʒɪstə(r)]	n.	寄存器
relay	[ˈriːleɪ]	n.	中继
remote monitoring			远程监控
repeater	[rɪˈpiːtə(r)]	n.	转发器，中继器
resistor	[rɪˈzɪstə(r)]	n.	电阻器
resolution	[ˌrezəˈluːʃn]	n.	分辨率
resonance	[ˈrezənəns]	n.	谐振，共振
resonator	[ˈrezəneɪtə(r)]	n.	共鸣器
reverse biased junction			反向偏置结
ring network			环形网
RMS (Root Mean Square)			均方根
RNC (Radio Network Controller)			无线网络控制器
roaming	[ˈrəʊmɪŋ]	n.	漫游
robotics	[rəʊˈbɒtɪks]	n.	机器人技术
robust	[rəʊˈbʌst]	adj.	稳定的，(robustness 鲁棒性，稳定性)
round	[raʊnd]	vt.	四舍五入
route	[ruːt]	n.	路由
		v.	发送
router			路由器
routing	[ˈruːtɪŋ]	n.	路由选择
ruggedness	[ˈrʌgɪdnəs]	n.	结实，强度，紧固
rule of thumb			单凭经验的方法
run length encoding			行程编码

S

sampling	[ˈsɑːmplɪŋ]	n.	取样
satellite communication			卫星通信
satellite network			卫星网络
scalability	[ˌskeɪləˈbɪləti]	n.	可量测性
scenario	[səˈnɑːriəʊ]	n.	脚本
SDN (Software Defined Networking)			软件定义网络
SDR (Software Defined Radio)			软件定义无线电
SDSL (Symmetric Digital Subscriber Line)			对称数字用户线
SECAM (Sequential Color Avec Memoire)			顺序与存储彩色电视系统
sector	[ˈsektə(r)]	n.	扇区
segmentation	[ˌsegmenˈteɪʃn]	n.	分割
selenium	[səˈliːniəm]	n.	硒
self-configuration			自配置
self-healing			自我修复的
self-monitoring			自我监控的
semiconductor	[ˌsemikənˈdʌktə(r)]	n.	半导体
sequence	[ˈsiːkwəns]	n.	序列
sequential logic circuit			时序逻辑电路
sequential	[sɪˈkwenʃ(ə)l]	adj.	顺序的，串行的
series	[ˈsɪəriːz]	n.	串联
serrated	[səˈreɪtɪd]	adj.	锯齿状的，有锯齿的
shift-invariance			时不变特性
signal-to-noise			信噪比
silicon germanium			硅锗
silicon	[ˈsɪlɪkən]	n.	硅，硅元素
silver	[ˈsɪlvə(r)]	n.	银
simplex transmission			单工传输
simultaneous	[ˌsɪm(ə)lˈteɪniəs]	adj.	同时的，同时发生的
sinusoidal	[ˌsaɪnəˈsɔɪdəl]		正弦波的，正弦曲线的
skeletal	[ˈskelət(ə)l]	adj.	骨骼的，骸骨的
solar cell			太阳能电池
solar panel			太阳能板
solvent	[ˈsɒlvənt]	n.	溶质，溶解
Sonar (Sound detective and ranging)			声呐，声波定位仪
SONET (Synchronous Optical Network)			同步光网络

sophisticated	[səˈfɪstɪkeɪtɪd]	adj.	复杂的，高级的，现代化的
spatial diversity			空间分集
SPC (Stored Program Control)			存储程序控制
speaker	[ˈspiːkə(r)]	n.	扬声器
specification	[ˌspesɪfɪˈkeɪʃ(ə)n]	n.	详述，规格，说明书，规范
spectrum analysis			谱分析
spectrum	[ˈspektrəm]	n.	光谱，频谱
spiral inductor			螺旋电感器
splice	[splaɪs]	n.	接头
SSL (Security Socket Layer)			安全套接层
stabilize	[ˈsteɪbəlaɪz]	v.	稳定
standard normal distribution			标准正态分布(均值为 0，方差为 1)
state-of-the-art facility			现代化设备
statistical	[stəˈtɪstɪk(ə)l]	adj.	统计的，统计学的
statistics	[stəˈtɪstɪks]	n.	统计，统计学，统计数字
stereophonic	[ˌsterɪə(ʊ)ˈfɒnɪk]	adj.	立体声的
stimulate	[ˈstɪmjuleɪt]	v.	刺激，激励
stochastic	[stɒˈkæstɪk]	adj.	随机的
strand	[strænd]	n.	多芯电缆绞合线
SU (Speech Understanding)			语音理解
sub-layer			子层
subscriber	[səbˈskraɪbə(r)]	n.	用户
subset	[ˈsʌbset]	n.	子集
subsystem	[səbˈsɪstəm]	n.	次要系统，子系统
successive	[səkˈsesɪv]	adj.	连续的
SUI (Sum of Unit Impulse)			单位冲击求和
superposition	[ˌsuːpəpəˈzɪʃn]	n.	重叠，叠加
surveillance	[sɜːˈveɪləns]	n.	监视，监督
switchboard	[ˈswɪtʃbɔːd]	n.	(电话)交换台
symmetrical	[sɪˈmetrɪk(ə)l]	adj.	对称的，均匀的
synchronous transmission			同步传输
synergy	[ˈsɪnədʒi]	n.	协同作用
synthesis	[ˈsɪnθəsɪs]	n.	综合，合成
synthesize	[ˈsɪnθəsaɪz]	v.	综合，合成
synthesizer	[ˈsɪnθəsaɪzə(r)]	n.	合成器
synthetic	[sɪnˈθetɪk]	adj.	合成的，人造的，综合的
system identification			系统辨识

T

TACS (Total Access Communication System)			全球接入通信系统(英国)
take over			接管
TDM (Time Division Multiplexing)			时分多路复用
telecommunication	[ˌtelikəˌmjuːnɪˈkeɪʃ(ə)n]	n.	电信，长途通信，无线电通信，电信学
telemedicine	[ˈtelɪˌmedɪsɪn]	n.	远程医疗
telephony	[təˈlefəni]	n.	电话学，电话
teleprocessing	[ˌtelɪˈprəʊsesɪŋ]	n.	远程信息处理
telex	[ˈteleks]	n.	电报，电传打字机
template	[ˈtempleɪt]	n.	模板(=templet)
tensile	[ˈtensaɪl]	adj.	张力的，拉力的
terminal	[ˈtɜːmɪn(ə)l]	n.	终端，终端设备
terminology	[ˌtɜːmɪˈnɒlədʒi]	n.	术语
texture	[ˈtekstʃə(r)]	n.	(木材、岩石等的)纹理
thermal noise			热噪声
threshold	[ˈθreʃhəʊld]	n.	界限，临界值
time slot			时隙
token	[ˈtəʊkən]	n.	令牌
tonal	[ˈtəʊnl]	adj.	音调的
topology	[təˈpɒlədʒi]	n.	拓扑，布局，拓扑学
track	[træk]	n.	磁道
trade-off			权衡，折中
traffic load			通信负载，话务量
traffic throughput			通话能力
transceiver	[trænˈsiːvə(r)]	n.	无线电收发机，收发器
transducer	[trænzˈdjuːsə(r)]	n.	传感器，变频器
transient	[ˈtrænziənt]	adj.	短暂的，瞬时的
transistor	[trænˈzɪstə(r)]	n.	[电子]晶体管
transmit-power			发射功率
trigonometric	[ˌtrɪgənəˈmetrɪk]	adj.	三角学的，三角法的
truncation	[trʌnˈkeɪʃn]	n.	截断
trunk line			中继线，干线
tuned amplifier			调谐放大器
two-dimensional			二维的

U

ubiquitous	[juːˈbɪkwɪtəs]	adj.	无处不在的
UHF (Ultra High frequency)			超高频
ultrasound	[ˈʌltrəsaʊnd]	n.	超声波
ultraviolet	[ˌʌltrəˈvaɪələt]	adj.	紫外线的，紫外的
		n.	紫外线辐射
underlie	[ˌʌndəˈlaɪ]	vt.	支撑，构成(理论、政策、行为等的)基础，位于……之下
underlying	[ˌʌndəˈlaɪɪŋ]	adj.	根本的
UNI (User-Network Interface)			用户网络接口
UNICODE			统一的字符编码标准，采用双字节对字符进行编码
uniform distribution			均匀分布
uniform	[ˈjuːnɪfɔːm]	adj.	均匀的
upgrade	[ˈʌpɡreɪd]	n.	升级
uplink	[ˈʌplɪŋk]	n.	[电信]向上传输，上行线，卫星上行链路

V

valence	[ˈvæləns]	n.	[化](化合)价，原子价
variable	[ˈveəriəbl]	n.	变量
variance	[ˈveəriəns]	n.	方差
varicap	[væriˈkæp]	n.	变容二极管 (=variable-capacitance diode)
VCO (Voltage Controlled Oscillator)			压控振荡器
VDSL (Very High Bit-Rate Digital Subscriber Line)			甚高比特率数字用户线
vector quantification			矢量量化
vector	[ˈvektə(r)]	n.	矢量，向量
verification	[ˌverɪfɪˈkeɪʃn]	n.	确认，查证
versatile	[ˈvɜːsətaɪl]	adj.	通用的，万能的
vertical	[ˈvɜːtɪk(ə)l]	adj.	垂直的
VHF (Very High frequency)			甚高频
via	[ˈvaɪə]	prep.	经由，取道
vibratory	[ˈvaɪbrətəri]	adj.	振动的，振动性的
videophone	[ˈvɪdiəʊfəʊn]	n.	电视电话

videotex video			可视图文电视
visualization	[ˌvɪʒuəlaɪˈzeɪʃn]	n.	显像
VLC (Variable length coding)			可变长编码
vocal	[ˈvəʊkl]	adj.	嗓音的，发声的，歌唱的
VOD (Video on Demand)			视频点播
VOIP (Voice over IP)			IP 语音
voltage	[ˈvəʊltɪdʒ]	n.	电压
volume	[ˈvɒljuːm]	n.	体积；量，大量；音量
VPN (Virtual Private Network)			虚拟专用网
vulnerable	[ˈvʌlnərəbl]	adj.	易受攻击的，易受……的攻击

W

waveform	[ˈweɪvfɔːm]	n.	波形
wave-guide			波导
wavelength	[ˈweɪvleŋθ]	n.	波长
wavelet	[ˈweɪvlət]	n.	小波，微波
WDM (Wavelength Division Multiplexing)			波分复用
wearables	[ˈweərəbl]	n.	穿戴设备
weight	[weɪt]	n.	加权
wire line			金属线路，有线线路
WLAN (Wireless Local Area Network)			无线局域网
WPAN (Wireless Personal Area Network)			无线个域网

X

xDSL (A,H,I,S,V-DSL)		数字用户线

附录B 科技论文写作常用句型

科技论文一般由摘要(Abstract)、正文(Text)、结论(Conclusion)、致谢(Acknowledgement)、参考文献(References)等组成。以下将按照这几个组成部分分别总结一下常用的句型。

一、摘要

1. 摘要的第一句常常是直接介绍文章的主要内容，通常有以下几种写法。

This paper describes…(本文描述了……)
This paper presents…(本文提出了……)
This paper discusses…(本文讨论了……)
This paper analyses…(本文分析了……)
This paper reports on…(本文报告了……)
This paper investigates…(本文调查了……)
This paper examines…(本文检验了……)
This paper deals with…(本文论述了……)
This paper researches into…(本文探讨了……)
This paper gives…(本文给出了……)
This paper points out…(本文指出了……)
This paper reviews…(本文总结了……)
This paper makes a study of…(本文研究了……)
This paper makes investigations on…(本文研究了……)

在以上各句中，也可用 The author 做主语，但一般不用 I 或 We 做主语。

在科技论文中一般使用被动语态来强调所论述的客观性，因此，以上句子也可以采用被动语态的形式：

Information (regarding… or concerning…) is described.
Information (regarding… or concerning…) is presented.
Information (regarding… or concerning…) is discussed.
Information (regarding… or concerning…) is analyzed.
Information (regarding… or concerning…) is reported.
Information (regarding… or concerning…) is investigated.
Information (regarding… or concerning…) is examined.
Information (regarding… or concerning…) is dealt with.
Information (regarding… or concerning…) is given.
Information (regarding… or concerning…) is pointed out.

除此以外，还可以用以下的句型作为开始。

In this paper a new method of …is introduced. 本文介绍了一种新的……方法。

In this paper a new approach of …is recommended。本文推荐了一种新的……方法。

2．第一句之后，是简述过程及论据，可以用以下几种方式。

An example of …is analyzed in detail.

An example of ...is described in detail.

An example of ...is discussed in detail.

An example of ...is examined in detail.

An example of ...is studied in detail.

3．如果在论文中有图、表的话，可以用以下方式表达。

Data are displayed in graphs and tables. 数据显示在图、表中。

4．对于论文的主要结论，可以用以下方式。

Findings are presented.

Results are reported.

Findings are analyzed

Results are examined.

Findings are discussed.

5．另外，摘要中还有以下常用的表达方式。

A series of experiments were made/carried out on …
对……进行了一系列实验。

Special mention is given here to (sth.).
这里专门提到……

Examples of …demonstrate that…
……的例子表明……

Statistics confirm…
统计数字肯定了……

6．摘要的末尾一般是用来表示论文所做工作的进一步意义及进一步研究方向，因此可以用以下方式表达。

These results also indicate that…　　这些结果也指出……
These data also indicate that….　　　这些数据也指出……
These findings also indicate that…　　这些发现也指出……
These experiments also indicate that…　这些实验也指出……
The findings imply that…　　　　　这些发现暗示……
Based on these conclusions…is discussed. 根据这些结论，讨论了……
The findings suggest that further research into … is called for.
这些发现提示要对……作进一步研究。
The results suggest that further research into…would be worthwhile.
这些发现提示对……进一步研究是值得的。

二、正文

1. 科技英语常用一般现在时态表示客观真理或客观规律。

High-speed digital design <u>studies</u> how passive circuit elements affect signal propagation(ringing and reflections), interaction between signals (crosstalk), and interactions with the natural world (electromagnetic interference).

高速数字设计研究无源电路元件如何影响信号的传播(环绕和反射)，信号间的互相作用(交调失真)，以及信号与自然界的互相作用(电磁干扰)。

2. 科技英语常用被动语态强调所论述的客观事物。

Revolutionary changes <u>have already been made</u> in a broad range of fields: communications, medical imaging, radar & sonar and high fidelity music.

在通信、医学图像、雷达和声呐以及高质量音乐等很多领域发生了革命性的改变。

3. 普遍使用名词词组及名词化结构，强调客观存在的事实而非某一行为，常用表示动作或状态的抽象名词。

Television is the <u>transmission and reception</u> of images of moving objects by radio waves.

电视是通过无线电波对运动物体的图像传送和接收。

4. 科技英语中常会提出一些假设、推理或判断，内容与事实相反，或不大可能实现，为了同客观实际相区别，常使用虚拟语气。

<u>If there were</u> no attraction between the proton and the electron, the electron <u>would fly away</u> from the proton in a straight line.

如果质子和电子之间没有引力，电子会沿直线飞离质子。

5. 常使用添加强调词、或采用强调句型 It is(was)+…+that(which, who, whom)，及改变句子成分的结构位置来强调某些成分。

Beta is approximately constant for an individual transistor, although it <u>does</u> vary with temperature and slightly with the collector current. (加强调动词 does)

对于某个单独的晶体管来说，β 几乎是恒定不变的，尽管它确实会随着温度及集电极电流有微弱的变化。

<u>It was Bell himself who</u> invented one of the earliest light-wave communications devices in 1880. (It 引导强调句型)

是贝尔自己在 1880 年发明了最早的光通信设备。

6. 在正文中常用图表来帮助说明论据、事实等。最常有附图(Figure)和表(Table)，另外还有简图(Diagram)，曲线图或流程图(Graph)，视图(View)，剖面图(Profile)，图案(Pattern)等。在文中提到时常用的表达法如下。

As (is) shown in Fig.4.　　如图 4 所示。
As (is) shown in Tab.1.　　如表 1 所示。

7. "由于……"的表达，可以用以下短语表示。

Because of …
On account of …
As a result of …

Due to …

Owing to …

In view of …

例：An object has dynamic energy because of its motion.

物体由于运动而具有动能。

也可用从句的形式表示"由于……这样……"的因果关系。

because +从句

as+从句

since+从句

now that+从句

in that+从句

例：Now that they have electronic computers, mathematicians are solving problems they would not have dared tackle a few years ago.

由于有了计算机，数学家正在解决若干年前还不敢着手去解决的问题。

8．可以用"cause" "bring about" "give rise to" "produce (sth.)"来表示"引起……""产生……"。

In the past 50 years new technologies have brought about many changes in everyday life.

近50年来，新技术在日常生活中引起了很多变化。

9．可以用"attribute sth. to sth." 或 "ascribe sth. to sth."来表示"归因于……""归功于……"。

The invention of television has been ascribed to a number of scientists.

电视的发明归功于许多科学家。

10．可以用"result from sth." 或 "originate in/from sth." 来表示"起源于……"。

Most scientific progress originates in careful consideration of work that has already been done.

大多数科学进步均起源于对已经完成的工作的认真思考。

11．可用"result in sth." 或 "lead to sth." 表示"导致"。

Such observations lead to the discovery that there can be rapid corrosion when a metal is non-homogeneous.

这样的观察使人们发现，当金属是非均质金属时，就可能很快生锈。

12．可用"so/such … that +从句"或 "so that+从句"或 "with the result that+从句"表示"以至于……"。

In the magnet, the atoms are lined up in such a way that their electrons are circling in the same direction.

在磁铁中，原子的排列方式使得它们的电子按相同的环绕方向在轨道上运行。

13．可用"too…to…"表示"太……以致不能……"。

Atoms are too small to be seen even through the most powerful microscope.

原子太小，以至于用放大倍数最大的显微镜也看不到。

14．可用 "enough to do sth." 表示"足以……"。

These solar batteries supply enough electricity to drive a car.

这些太阳能电池组提供的电力足以驱动一辆汽车。

15．常用"therefore, hence, thus, consequently, as a result, for this reason"表示"因此……"。

Copper losses are proportional to the load being supplied by the transformer and <u>for this reason</u> are sometimes called the load losses.

铜损耗与变压器提供的负荷成比例，因此有时称为负荷耗损。

16．用"be responsible for"表示"是……的原因"。

Electromagnetism <u>is responsible for</u> most of sensory experiences.

电磁对大多数的感知有影响。

17．用"intend to do sth."或"mean to do sth."或"aim to do sth.",或"be going to do sth."或"plan to do sth."或"arrange to do sth."表示"打算做某事"。

Anyone who <u>means to advance science</u> must have a capacity for original thought.

无论是谁，如果想推动科学向前发展，都必须具备创造性思考的能力。

18．用"to do …"或"in order to do…",或"so as to do …"或"in order that+从句"或"so that +从句"或"with view to sth."或"for the purpose of sth."或"for sth's sake"或"for the sake of sth"表示"为了……"。

The resistance must be reduced <u>so that</u> we can have a stronger current.

为了得到更强的电流必须减小电阻。

Bearings are lubricated <u>for the purpose of</u> reducing the friction.

为了减少摩擦要润滑轴承。

He argues <u>for the sake of</u> arguing.

他为辩论而辩论。

19．用"lest+从句"或"for fear that+从句"或"in case+从句"表示"以免……"。

Isotopes of long half-lives must be handled with great care <u>in case they cause radiation damage</u>.

处置半衰期长的同位素必须十分小心，以免引起辐射伤害。

20．用"be intended for sth."或"be meant for sth."表示"供……之用"。

This book <u>is intended for</u> beginners.

这本书供初学者使用。

21．用"The purpose/aim/objective of …is sth./to do …"表示"……的目的是……"。

<u>One aim of</u> cybernetics <u>is</u> the investigation, design and construction of robots of various types.

控制论的一个目的是研究、设计和制造各种类型的机器人。

22．可用"depend on/upon sth."或"rely on/upon sth."或"be dependent on/upon sth."表示"依靠……"。

Sweden is <u>dependent on</u> her hydro-electric resources for power.

瑞典依靠其水力资源作为动力。

23．可用"dependent on sth."或"be dependent on sth."表示"取决于……"。

The value of a metal <u>depends on</u> whether it is rare or abundant.

金属的价值取决于它是稀有的还是丰富的。

24．可用"be based on sth."表示"以……为基础"。

His conclusion was based on experimental data.
他的结论是以实验数据为基础的。

25．可用"according to sth."或"in accordance with sth."或"depending on sth."表示"根据……"。

According to the reaction principle, there is also an equal force in the other direction.
根据反作用原理，在另一个方向也有相等的力。

26．可用"in accord with sth."或"in agreement with sth."或"in conformity with sth."或"agree with sth."或"accord with sth."或"correspond to/with sth."表示"与……一致"。

The actual production figures are in agreement/accord with the estimated figures.
实际的生产量和估计的数字一致。

The current impulses of the incoming signal correspond to the microphone electric impulses.
输入信号的电脉冲与麦克风的电脉冲相对应。

27．可用"compare …and/with …"表示"把……和……相比较"。

Compare vacuum tubes and/with transistors, and you will know the advantages of the latter.
把电子管和晶体管比较一下，就可以知道后者的优点了。

28．可用"compare…to…"表示"把……比作……"。

The tiny currents in the receiving antenna are very small and may be compared to the weak signal coming in over a long distance telephone line.
接收天线中的电流很小，可以和长途电话线路中传来的微弱信号相比。

29．可用"whereas"或"while"表示"而，然而"。

Radio waves go thorough clouds and fog quite well, whereas light waves do not.
无线电波可以很容易地穿过云雾，而光波却不能。

30．可用"the same as sth."或"identical with sth."表示"与……相同"。

This machine is roughly the same as the other one in design.
这台机器的设计与另一台大致相同。

31．可用"similar to sth."或"analogous to sth."表示"与……相似"。

The curved reflector used for radar waves is similar in shape to the reflector of the flashlight.
雷达波用的曲面反射镜的形状与手电筒的反射镜相似。

32．可以用"differ from … in sth."或"be different from …in sth."表示"不同于……"。

Different kinds of radiation energy, such as light, X-rays and radio waves, seem to be quite different from one another.
各种不同的辐射能，如光、X射线、无线电波，看起来彼此很不相同。

33．可以用"differentiate …from sth."或"distinguish … from sth."或"tell …from sth."表示"区分……和……"。

We can tell low from high frequency light waves by the sensation of color they produce.
根据光波所产生的色感，我们能辨别低频光波和高频光波。

34．可以用"by /in contrast"或"by comparison"表示"相比之下"。

The image-oriented remote sensing technology is older. By comparison, the technology of numerically oriented systems is still in its infancy.
图像遥感技术历史较长。相比之下，数字遥感系统还处于萌芽状态。

35．可以用"形容词或副词比较级+than…"表示"比……(大，小，快等)"，可以用"less+形容词或副词原级＋than"表示"不如……"。

Digital computers are much more widely used than analog computer.
数字计算机的使用远比模拟计算机广泛。

Analog computers are much less widely used than digital computers.
模拟计算机的使用远不如数字计算机广泛。

36．可以用"最高级+in+单数名词"或"最高级＋of/among+复数名词"表示"……中最……"。

The speed of light is the greatest speed in the universe.
光速是宇宙间最大的速度。

Uranium is the most complicated of the natural atoms.
铀是天然原子中最为复杂的。

37．可以用"better than sth."或"superior to sth."表示"优于……"。

Radio telescopes are better than ordinary telescopes in that they can operate in all weather conditions.
无线电望远镜比普通望远镜好，因为它可以在一切气象条件下使用。

38．可以用"have the advantage of sth."或"have the advantage that+从句"表示"……的优点为……"。

Such a system has the advantage of eliminating the tremendous pollution of the environment.
这种体系的优点是消除了对环境的严重污染。

39．可以用"either…or…"表示"不是…就是…"，可以用"neither…nor…"表法"不是……也不是……"。

The electronic switches in a computer have two states: they are either off or on.
计算机里的电子开关有两种状态：不是开就是关。

40．可用"if+从句"或"in case +从句"或"in case of sth."或"in the event of sth."表示"如果……"。

In the event of neutron capture, the mass number of the nucleus will be raised, and it will thus become unstable and radioactive.
如果中子被俘获，原子核的质量数便提高，结果就会变得不稳定而且有放射性。

41．用"on condition (that)+从句"表示"条件是……"。

The operation can proceed indefinitely on condition that the controls are pre-set correctly.
此操作可以无限地进行，条件是预先设定好操纵装置。

42．可以用"unless+从句"表示"除非……，如果不……"。

Harmful radiation will result unless the isotopes are shielded properly.
如果同位素不加以适当屏蔽，就会产生有害的辐射。

43．可以用"make…do"或"have…do"或"let…do"或"enable … to do"或"allow… to do"或"permit … to do"或"cause … to do"表示"使……做某事"。

In the broadcasting station, the radio waves are made to correspond to each sound in turn.
广播电台使无线电波依次对每一个声音做出相应变化。

44．可以用"make …+过去分词"或"have …+过去分词"或"get…+过去分词"表示"使……被别人做"。

You should get everything prepared before you begin the experiment.
你必须在开始实验以前把一切准备好。

45．可以用"change…into sth."或"turn…into sth."或"transform…into sth."或"convert…into sth."表示"把……变成……"。

Electric lamps of various kinds change electric energy into light.
各种电灯把电能变为光。

46．可以用"vary with sth."或"vary according to sth."表示"随……而变"。

The internal energy of a gas varies with a rise in temperature.
气体的内能随温度升高而变化。

47．可以用"vary as sth."或"be proportional to sth."表示"与……成比例"。

The insulation resistance of a cable is inversely proportional to its length.
电缆的绝缘电阻与它的长度成反比。

48．可以用"The+比较级…，the+比较级…"表示"……越……，……就越……"。

The heavier the electric current, the stronger is the electromagnetism.
电流越大，电磁力就越强。

49．可以用"consist of sth."或"be made up of sth."或"be composed of sth."或"comprise sth."表示"(整体)由……组成"。

The tranceiver consists of a transmitter and a receiver.
收发信机是由发信机和收信机组成的。

50．可以用"form sth."或"constitute sth."或"make up sth."或"comprise sth."表示"(部分)组成(整体)"。

The sequence of procedures makes up the so-called scientific method.
这一系列程序就构成所谓的科学方法。

51．可以用"send out sth."或"emit sth."或"give off sth."表示"发出"。

The command computer sends out a series of impulses which the receiving computer then absorbs and makes use of.
下达指令的计算机发出一系列电脉冲，接收指令的计算机便加以吸收和利用。

52．可以用"supply A to B"或"supply B with A"或"provide A for B"或"provide B with A"表示"把A供给B"。

Power plants provide electricity for industry.
发电厂为工业提供电力。

53．可以用"join…to sth."或"link … to sth."或"attach … to sth."或"connect … to sth."或"couple…to sth."表示"连接"。

The machine is linked to the motor by a driving belt or chain.
机器用传动皮带或链条与发动机相连。

54．可以用"have…to do with sth."或"be related to sth."或"be associated with sth."或"be connected with sth."或"be concerned with sth."表示"与……有关"。

In the past, the field of robotics has tended to be associated with fiction.
过去，机器人技术领域一直倾向于和幻想相联系。

55．可用"equip …with sth."或"be equipped with sth."表示"装备"。

If an airplane flying at night is equipped with radar, the pilot can see on the radar viewing screen a mountain peak miles away.
如果夜间飞行的飞机上装有雷达，飞行员就能在雷达荧光屏上看到几英里以外的山峰。

56．可以有用"dismantle sth."或"take …to pieces"表示"拆除"。

We had to take the whole engine to pieces to discover the cause of the trouble.
我们不得不把整个发动机拆开，看看故障的原因是什么。

57．可以用"prevent… from sth."或"keep …from sth."或"stop …from sth."来表示"防止……发生"。

Insulators are used to prevent electrical charges from going where they are not wanted.
绝缘体用来阻止电荷流到不需要电荷的地方。

58．可以用"keep…from sth."或"protect…from sth."来表示"保护……使免受……"。

In space, astronauts have to be protected from harmful radiations.
在太空中，宇航员要保护自己不受有害辐射的伤害。

59．可以用"utilize sth."或"exploit sth."或"make use of sth."或"take advantage of sth."表示"利用……"。

Scientists have worked out ways to take advantage of the rise and fall of the tides to generate electric current.
科学家们想出了利用潮汐的涨落来发电的方法。

60．可以用"make the best use of sth."或"make full use of sth."表示"充分利用"。

Such properties of semiconductors have been made full use of in microelectronics.
在微电子学中，半导体的这些特性得到了充分利用。

61．可以用"contract"或"shrink"或"constrict"表示"缩小"。

With the development of the transistor, electronic devices shrank tremendously.
随着晶体管的发展，电子器件的体积大为减小。

62．可以用"the function of …is to do"或"the duty of …is to do sth."来表示"……的用途为……"。

The function of a governor is to control the running speed under all conditions of load.
调速器的作用是在各种负荷条件下控制发动机的转速。

63．可以有"a way of sth."或"a means to do …"或"an approach to sth."或"a method of sth."表示"……的方法"。

A common method of feeding information into the computer is with the use of magnetic tape.
向计算机输入信息的一个常用方法是利用磁带。

64．可以用"by way of sth."或"with the help of sth."或"with the aid of sth."表示"借助于……，通过……"。

These robots have sent back to the earth, by ways of radio, such important information on space as temperature, radiation, and so on.

这些机器人通过无线电将宇宙中的温度、辐射等重要资料发回地球。

三、结论

1. 关于"结论"可有以下表达方式。

The following conclusions can be drawn from...	由……可得如下结论……
It can be concluded that...	可以得出结论……
We may conclude that...	我们得出如下结论……
We come to the conclusion that...	我们得出如下结论……

It is generally accepted (believed, held, acknowledged) that...一般认为……(用于表示肯定的结论)

We think (consider, believe, feel) that...我们认为……(用于表示留有商量余地的结论)

2. 关于"建议"可有以下表达方式。

It is advantageous to (do)... 做……是有益的

It should be realized (emphasized, stressed, noted, pointed out) that...应该意识到的(强调的，注意的，指出的)是……

It is suggested (proposed, recommended, desired) that...建议……

It would be better that...是比较好的

It would be helpful if... 如果……将会是有帮助的

It would be advisable when...建议……

四、致谢

在论文结束后，作者通常会以简短的谢词对曾给予支持与帮助或关心的人表示感谢，可用如下方式。

I am thankful (grateful, deeply indebted) to sb. for sth.

I would like to thank sb. for sth.

Thanks are due to sb. for sth.

The author wishes to express his sincere appreciation to sb. for sth.

The author wishes to acknowledge sb.

The author wishes to express his gratitude for sth.

参 考 文 献

巴尔胡达罗夫, 1985. 语言与翻译[M]. 蔡毅, 虞杰, 段京华, 编译. 北京: 中国对外翻译出版公司.
巴伐, 2003. 兰登书屋英语研究报告高手[M]. 长春: 长春出版社.
曹国英, 2000. 科技英语文献的翻译研究[J]. 中国科技翻译, 13(1): 8-11.
陈枫艳, 2006. 计算机专业英语[M]. 北京: 科学出版社.
陈申, 2001. 语言文化教学策略研究[M]. 北京: 北京语言文化大学出版社.
单献心, 2002. 科技英语翻译应重视的问题[J]. 浙江科技学院学报, 14(3): 46-50.
邓炎昌, 刘润清, 1989. 语言与文化: 英汉语言文化对比[M]. 北京: 外语教学与研究出版社.
丁往道, 吴冰, 钟美荪, 等, 1994. 英语写作手册[M]. 修订本. 北京: 外语教学与研究出版社.
高丽, 2004. 电子信息专业英语课程中翻译技巧的教法研究[J]. 淮南职业技术学院学报, (2): 103-105.
高秀丽, 2001. 科技英语中倍数的表达与翻译[J]. 黑龙江科技学院学报, 11(2): 62-65.
高永照, 程勇, 1998. 科技英语的文体写作与翻译[M]. 北京: 学苑出版社.
郭海平, 2004. 科技英语词汇的构词特点及翻译[J]. 武汉工业学院学报, 23(2): 115-117.
郭沫若, 1959. 雄鸡集[M]. 北京: 北京出版社.
胡文仲, 2012. 跨文化交际学概论[M]. 北京: 外语教学与研究出版社.
黄湘, 2001. 科技英语汉译的词义引申[J]. 中国科技翻译, 14(2): 29-31.
贾晓云, 2003. 科技英语的句法特点及其翻译方法[J]. 太原理工大学学报(社会科学版), 21(2): 67-69.
卡特福德, 1991. 翻译的语言学理论[M]. 穆雷, 译. 北京: 旅游教育出版社.
兰根, 2004. 美国大学英语写作[M]. 北京: 外语教学与研究出版社.
李白萍, 2003. 电子信息类专业英语[M]. 西安: 西安电子科技大学出版社.
李丙午, 燕静敏, 2002. 科技英语的名词化结构及其翻译[J]. 中国科技翻译, 15(1): 5-7.
李霞, 王娟, 2009. 电子与通信专业英语[M]. 2版. 北京: 电子工业出版社.
刘红梅, 2004. 科技英语语篇翻译的语域制约性[J]. 佛山科学技术学院学报(社会科学报), 22(2): 28-32.
刘兰云, 杜耀文, 2000. 科技英语抽象名词的特点及翻译[J]. 中国科技翻译, 13(4): 17-18.
陆国强, 1983. 现代英语词汇学[M]. 上海: 上海外语教育出版社.
吕俊, 1997. 我国翻译理论研究与20世纪西方文论学习[J]. 外国语(上海外国语大学学板) (6): 51-55.
米勒, 2002. 数据与网络通信[M]. 影印版. 北京: 科学出版社.
倪传斌, 2003. 科技英语共轭结构的特点及汉译方法[J]. 中国科技翻译, 16(4): 18-20.
牛灵安, 2004. 科技英语翻译词义的确定[J]. 中国科技翻译, 17(1): 14-16.
牛晓红, 2004. 科技英语翻译探析[J]. 山东煤炭科技, (3): 51-52.
纽马克, 2001. 翻译问题探讨[M]. 影印本. 上海: 上海我语教育出版社.
潘福燕, 2005. 英语科技文体的语词特点及翻译[J]. 中国科技翻译, 18(4): 56-58.
钱旭中, 1994. 英语科技文献的特点及其翻译[J]. 中国科技翻译, 7(2): 21-24.
秦荻辉, 2001. 实用科技英语写作技巧[M]. 上海: 上海外语教育出版社.
任芬梅, 2001. 科技英语的特点及其翻译[J]. 焦作工学院学报(社会科学版), 2(3): 46-47.
任开兴, 2002. 部分否定句型的多义及翻译[J]. 中国科技翻译, 15(1): 38-41.
宋德富, 司爱侠, 2013. 计算机专业英语教程[M]. 4版. 北京: 高等教育出版社.
孙永强, 2004. 科技英语被动语态隐性因果关系及其转换[J]. 中国科技翻译, 17(4): 4-7.

谭力红, 2004. 科技英语的词汇特点及翻译中的选词[J]. 河北职业技术学院学报, 4(2): 22-24.

陶友兰, 查国生, 2002. 研究生英语翻译[M]. 上海: 复旦大学出版社.

特南鲍姆, 1997. 计算机网络: 第3版[M]: 英文版. 北京: 清华大学出版社.

王德春, 孙汝健, 姚远, 1995. 社会心理语言学[M]. 上海: 上海外语教育出版社.

威尔斯, 1989. 翻译学: 问题与方法[M]. 祝珏, 周智漠, 节译. 北京: 中国对外翻译出版公司.

吴娜达, 李辉, 2004. 英汉信息通信技术缩略语词典[M]. 北京: 人民邮电出版社.

辛书伟, 王波, 2003. 英语科技文写作[M]. 天津: 天津大学出版社.

胥懋云, 2000. 二十一世纪大学英语教学改革[M]. 北京: 外语教学与研究出版社.

于建平, 2000. 科技英语长句的分析及翻译[J]. 中国科技翻译, 13(3): 14-16.

张筱华, 石方文, 2001. 通信英语[M]. 北京: 北京邮电大学出版社.

赵晴, 2003. 科技英语术语翻译中常见错误分析[J]. 鞍山科技大学学报, 26(6): 478-480.

周洪洁, 2002. 科技英语的语域特征与科技翻译的标准[J]. 重庆大学学报(社会科学版), 8(5): 85-87.

周秋琴, 2000. 也谈科技文体与科技翻译[J]. 中国科技翻译, 13(1): 42-45.

周振锋, 2003. 科技英语文体中动词形态的用法及翻译[J]. 周口师范学院学报, 20(5): 122-124.

朱俊松, 2002. 科技英语中隐含因果关系句的表达及其翻译[J]. 华东船舶工业学院学报(社会科学版), 2(2): 60-62.

朱小玲, 2005. 科技英语的翻译技巧[J]. 甘肃科技, 21(3): 188-189+191.

CELLO M, DEGANO C, MARCHESE M, et al. , 2016. Smart transportation systems (STSs) in critical conditions[M]. Smart cities and homes: 291-322.

CHEN Z R, YANG C, QIAN J H, HAN D D, MA Y G, 2023. Recursive traffic percolation on urban transportation systems[J].Chaos,33(3):033132.

ERTEL W, 2017. Introduction to Artificial Intelligence[M]. London: Springer.

ESPUÑA A GRAELLS M, PUIGJANER L, 2017. 27th European symposium on computer aided process engineering[M]. Cambridge, MA: Elsevier.

FELITA C, SURYANEGARA M, 2013. 5G key technologies: identifying innovation opportunity[C]. //2013 International Conperence on QiR, June 25-28, 2013, Yogyakarta. IEEE: 235-238.

Hall S H, Hall G W, 2000. High-speed digital system design: A handbook of Interconnect theory and design practices[M]. Wiley-IEEE Press.

HASSANIEN A E, DARWISH A, 2020. Swarm intelligence for resource management in internet of things[M]. London: Academic Press: 131-145.

JUMA M, SHAALAN K, 2020. Cyber-physical systems in smart city: Challenges and future trends for strategic research[C]. //Proceedings of the International Conference on Advanced Intelligent Systems and Informatics 2019. Cham: Springer: 85-865.

NIDA E A, TABER C R, 2004. The theory and practice of translation[M]. Shanghai: Foreign Language Educational Press.

OESTGES C, QUITIN F, 2021. Inclusive radio communications for 5G and beyond[M]. London: Academic Press: 253-293.

RAJ P, DAVID P E, 2020. The digital twin paradigm for smarter systems and environments: The industry use cases[M]. London: Academic Press.

RANAIEFAR F, REGAN A C, 2011. Freight-transportation externalities[M]. //FARAHANI R, REIAPOUR S, KARDAR L. Logistics operations and management. Cambridge, MA: Elsevier.

SHARMA D K, KAUSHIK A K, GOEL A, et al. , 2020. Internet of things and blockchain: Integration, need, challenges, applications, and future scope[M]. KRISHNAN S, BALAS V E, GOLDEN J, et al. Handbook of research on blockchain technology. London: Academic Press.

WOODARD M, WISELY M, SARVESTANI S S, 2016. A survey of data cleansing techniques for cyber-physical critical infrastructure systems. [M]. // HURSON AR, GOUDARII M. Advances in Computers, 102: 63-110.

XIONG G, ZHU F H, DONG X S, et al. , 2016. A kind of novel ITS based on space-air-ground collected big data[J]. IEEE intelligent transportation systems magazine, 8(1)10-22.

XU X L, LIU M, XIONG J B, et al. , 2019. Key technology and application of millimeter wave communications for 5G: A Survey[J]. Cluster Computing, 22(5): 12997-13009.